M Fencing

A Comprehensive Manual for the Foil, Épée, and the Sabre

by

Clovis Deladrier

MR. CLOVIS DELADRIER

Graduate of The Normal School of Physical Education of the
Belgian government.
Maître d'Armes of the First Infantry Regiment and the 12th
Artillery Regiment of the Belgian Army, 1906-1926.
Head Fencing Master, United States Naval Academy, Annapolis
Maryland, 1927-1947.
President, National Fencing Coaches Association, N.C.A.A.

i

Dedication

This book is affectionately dedicated to my son, André Deladrier, in the hope that it may be of some benefit to him in his chosen profession, that of maître d'armes.

Acknowledgements

This book has been made possible chiefly through the industry of Mr. Robert Lewis of Baltimore, several times three-weapon champion of the State of Maryland and neighboring states. Mr. Lewis' intelligent cooperation and labor have brought to completion a manuscript many times abandoned in despair. For his assistance in organizing my material, his pitiless criticism of my theories, his friendly patience in preparing my manuscript, I owe him an immense debt of gratitude.

Nor may I pass by Dr. John R. Huffman, national three-weapon champion and Olympic sabreman, for his valuable suggestions and his criticisms of my material; and Mr. Walter Gaylor, formerly of Annapolis, for his early assistance in the organization of this book.

Preface

After a comprehensive study of the literature of fencing now extant, I have come to the conclusion that there is need for this book. By this statement I do not mean to imply that this work will be better than all other existing works treating of the art of fencing, but that the goal to which this book is dedicated has not hitherto been reached. That goal is this: to combine in one readable volume a study, as complete as is consistent with the needs of all but the most advanced fencers and the limitations of space, of the fundamentals, principles and finer points of the three weapons now used in modern fencing—the foil, the épée and the sabre.

This intention does not slight the merits of other contemporary works, most of which do not have the same purpose. For example, Aldo Nadi's "On Fencing" is a fine psychological study of foil fencing from a personal point of view; but it does not treat of the épée and the sabre. Joseph Vince's manual, adequate as far as it goes, is intended only to impart the barest fundamentals of the three weapons. The works of Rondelle and Barbasetti, on the other hand, are too lengthy to be comprehended in one manageable volume and suffer in readability. Other works—for example, those of Breckenridge and Nobbs—are intended almost exclusively to discuss the conduct of the bout.

The book that to my knowledge most closely approaches the scope of this one is "The Theory and Practice of Fencing," by my friend Julio Martinez Castello, coach of New York University. This work, however, while well-written and thorough, emphasizes the study of the foil over that of the épée and the sabre, proceeding from the theory that the foil is the basis of all three weapons.

While this is the accepted contemporary view, I feel that much time can be saved—and this is of paramount importance in the training of university varsity teams—by treating each of the three weapons as a distinct entity and by training fencers in the exclusive use of one weapon. I do not believe it necessary, for example, that an épée fencer be first trained in the use of the foil. On the contrary, such training, while useful in the development of timing, distance, coordination, etc., will generally delay the development of the proper épée "reaction," which is distinctly different from that of the foil. It has therefore been my practice, in the years I have devoted to the training of varsity fencing teams at the United States Naval Academy, to develop in my pupils the general qualities necessary for all fencing, in addition to the special qualities pertaining individually to the foil, the épée and the sabre, by the exclusive study of one weapon. To anyone who doubts the efficacy of such a method, I suggest that an examination be made of the record of the Naval Academy varsity fencing teams for the past twenty years.

In pursuance of the above policy, I have in this work devoted an approximately equal amount of space to each of the three weapons, going so far as to repeat each time fundamental definitions, even when they are the same for all weapons. Thus, the advance and retreat, the lunge, the redouble, etc., are explained three times. While this extreme of pedagogic logic cannot be defended against the contention that it is wasteful of space, I feel that its practical benefits far outweigh its disadvantages. A fencer who practices only one of the three weapons will not be under the necessity of searching the entire book for pertinent information; nor, in so doing, will he be in danger of applying principles correct for one weapon to the practice of another.

On the other hand, certain advice applicable to all three weapons has been gathered in the Appendix to the entire book.

Most works on fencing offer the reader a brief history of the art. This is omitted here, since I prefer to devote the space to my text and since the subject has been adequately treated in many other works—notably in Barbasetti's "The Art of the Foil"—and I can add nothing new to the field.

It is pertinent here, however, to discuss briefly the results of millennia of combat with the sword, insofar as the development of different schools of fencing is concerned. Today there are three schools of fencing in general usage. These are the French, the Italian and the Spanish.

The French school emphasizes delicacy of movement and accuracy of point, achieved with a minimum of force. The almost straight grip (see Fig. 1, Book I) allows the greatest freedom of movement of the fingers. This school advocates the use of the opposition rather than the beat. Footwork is light and catlike. Guards and parries are very close, and to this end the arm in the guard position is generally more bent than in the other schools.

The Italian school uses the cross-bar on its handle, permitting a firmer grip of the weapon. In addition, the pommel is usually strapped to the wrist. While this restricts somewhat the freedom of the fingers, it allows greater firmness of action. The movements of the Italian school are forceful. The beat is emphasized rather than the opposition. Guards and parries are wider, the arm in the guard position is three-quarters extended, footwork is heavier. Where the French school uses finesse, the Italian school uses force.

The Spanish school, not so widespread as the French and the Italian, is a compromise of the two. It uses the French grip reinforced by two prongs or projections. It uses less force than the Italian school, but more than the French; it uses less finesse than the French school, but more than the Italian. Guards, parries, the extension of the arm, etc., fall midway between the two.

Each school has its advocates and exponents, and it must in all fairness be stated that each school is quite effective, when skillfully practiced by an advanced fencer. This book is not intended to extol the advantages of one school over another. Although my early training took place in Belgium and consisted of the exclusive study of the French school of fencing, with several modifications of the school according to Belgian practices, I have found certain features of the other schools so useful that I have adapted them to my fencing and coaching. In other words, while basically French, my fencing is an amalgamation of what I believe to be the most effective features of all three schools.

I believe that my experience along this line has been shared by most American fencing coaches of today. It is seldom now that a pure school of fencing is taught in this country. That is why this book, which follows the modern eclectic trend, is called "Modern Fencing."

Fencing may be advocated as a perfect exercise and sport for men and women of all ages. While rare physical qualities are required of a fencing champion, anybody at all can learn to fence well enough to derive enjoyment and benefit therefrom. Unlike most other sports, fencing may be practiced without harm at any age, even the most advanced. It is quite usual for a salle d'armes to be frequented by graybeards as well as young men.

Does this mean that fencing is a "sissy" sport? Far from it. Go watch a national championship tournament. Note the lithe figures on the strip, now motionless and wary, now exploding in a sudden burst of energy and speed, so fast that the eye cannot follow it. See them retire from the strip after the bout, drenched with sweat under their canvas clothing. Watch the finalists, those able men who have passed through a grueling weeding-out process, as they fight the deciding bouts. Under the sparkle of their brilliant maneuvers, a practiced eye will become aware of signs of fatigue, certain slight indications to prove that ordinary stamina and condition are not enough, that only a real athlete can hope to come through on top. The truth is that there are many levels of fencing, just as there are of tennis, swimming or basketball. The pudgy little girls who bounce a tennis ball across a net are not to be compared with the Tildens and the Budges; the boy who laboriously covers a few yards of water with the dog-paddle has little in common with the Weissmullers; and so on. It stands to reason that a great deal is required of a champion fencer, who has, in effect, bested thousands of claimants to his eminence.

Fencing will develop grace of carriage, coordination of eye, brain and muscle, speed of reaction, wind; it will improve muscular tone; it will give you the feeling of security consequent upon belief in your own ability to cope with any situation; it will improve your assurance of demeanor; it will train you in a gentlemanly code of behavior. And it will be a source of health and enjoyment the rest of your life.

I wish to explain here that this book is presented from the point of view that the reader is a beginner. I believe, however, that the advanced fencer will also find in it much of value to him. Such a fencer is at liberty to skip the fundamental definitions and pass to more advanced ground. In view of the confusion of fencing definitions now to be noted in this country-for example, the confounding of "remise" and "redouble," or "stop-thrust" and "time-attack"—feel that even an advanced fencer may benefit by brushing up on his fundamental fencing tenets.

Each book of this volume contains eighteen lessons pertinent to the weapon therein discussed. These lessons are intended primarily for use among fencing clubs and groups lacking the services of a professional coach, who would of course have his own system of teaching. Within such clubs it is usually the custom for the more advanced fencers to train the beginners; such non-professional coaches will find the lessons laid out here to be of value. Where no coach is available, two students may alternately assume the role of instructor and pupil.

To facilitate understanding of the detailed explanations that follow, the reader must understand that all positions presuppose a right-handed fencer, unless specifically stated otherwise, and the use of a French foil.

In order to describe graphically the position of the hand in various guards and movements, I have drawn an analogy between the thumb and the hour-hand of a clock. Thus, a hand with the thumb at 12 o'clock is one with the thumbnail turned to the ceiling; at 6 o'clock it is turned to the floor; at 3 o'clock, horizontally to the right; and so on.

It is my belief that a conscientious study of this book, with thorough practice of the movements explained in the text and applied in the lessons, will guide a beginner to the point where he will begin to win bouts in his own class and to derive health and enjoyment from this noblest of all sports.

TABLE OF CONTENTS

Book I: The Foil

CHAPTER I
Preliminary Phases

The Foil

The foil consists of a quadrangular blade terminated at the point by a flat tip, and a mounting at the other end consisting of three pieces, the guard, the grip and the pommel. The guard is the round shield protecting the hand and wrist. The grip is that part of the hilt that is held in the hand. The pommel is the threaded nut which terminates the hilt. The stronger half of the blade, from the guard to the middle, is known as the "forte"; the weaker half, from the middle to the point, as the "foible."

For competitions, the rules prescribe that the overall length of the foil must be less than 43.3 inches, and its weight less than 17.6 ounces.

The balance of the foil should be such that when correctly held in the hand and when all the fingers arc released but the index finger, which acts as a pivot, the tip of the foil will drop slowly.

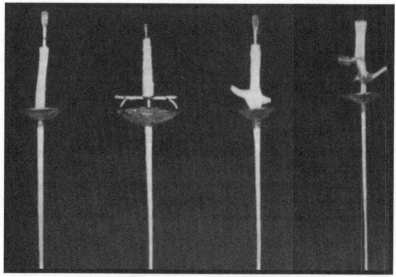

Fig. 1 - Various types of foils

French   Italian   Spanish   Belgian

The make-up of a good foil is as follows:

1.   A No. 5 blade of medium weight.

2.   An ordinary slender-core grip 6 inches in length, with a 2-inch pommel; or a grip 6 ½ inches long and a 1 ½ inch pommel.

3.   A reinforced aluminum guard 3 ½ to 4 ½ inches in diameter.

4.   An ordinary light foil cushion.

5.   The foil should be mounted in such a way that the pommel, grip and the forte are in a straight prolongation without any deviation. The foible may be bent slightly downwards, so that the blade will bend upwards when a touch is scored.

The instruction in this book is predicated upon the use of this type of French foil, considered by the author to be the best. The Italian and Spanish schools of fencing use a different grip, and more recently the pistol-grip has appeared. Good results may be obtained with any of them, but it is perhaps advisable to begin with the French foil as described above, in order to develop the fingers. It will be easy later to change to another type of grip; it is not so easy to change to the French type from one giving more support to the fingers.

A General Discussion Of Foil Fencing

There are certain conventions governing the practice of foil fencing. Some of these conventions have the force of rules, and have been codified, notably in the book "Fencing Rules," published by the Amateur Fencers' League of America (A.F.L.A.) in New York; others may be considered as etiquette, but are to be followed none the less minutely. It will be attempted here to give an overall picture of the most important basic rules regarding the conduct of a foil bout.

Unlike the target in a real duel, the foil target is limited to certain parts of the body. The arms, legs and head are excluded. The target therefore extends from the top of the collar to the groin line (in front) and from the top of the collar to a horizontal line passing across the tops of the hip bones and joining on the sides the groin lines (in back). For women, the foil target is the same as for men, except the lower limit is a horizontal line passing across the tops of the hip bones, front and back. A touch on a normally invalid part of the body counts if this part of the body was substituted for the valid target, through deliberate intent or through an abnormal position, such as ducking, crouching or the like.

Foil bouts are decided in five touches. (Women's bouts are decided in four.) Touches are scored with the point only, and to count must arrive cleanly with the point on the target. A graze with the point, a slap with the flat of the blade, and the like, do not count as touches and do not stop the play. If the point arrives cleanly outside the valid target, it is considered a foul and is counted neither for nor against either fencer; it does, however, stop the play and invalidates any valid touch made after the foul within the same phrase.

If a thrust is directed toward a valid part of the target and is parried, but falls as a result of the parry on an invalid surface, it is not considered a foul and does not stop the play.

When both contestants have been touched in a phrase, not simultaneously, the first touch counts. When the touches land simultaneously, the right of way must be determined. If a foul has the right of way, the whole action is thrown out. If no right of way can be determined for simultaneous touches, the action is considered a double touch and is thrown out, even if one of the touches is a foul.

It can be seen, therefore, that right of way in the foil, like the sabre and unlike the épée, is of extreme importance. This right of way passes back and forth quickly from one contestant to the

4

other, according to the action each one takes. The original right of way within any phrase lies with the fencer initiating the original attack. If that attack is parried, the right of way passes to the defender, who now has the right to return the attack (riposte). The original attacker does not have the right to counter-riposte until he has parried the defender's riposte; and so on.

If the defender has his point in line, that is, his arm extended and his point directed at a legitimate part of the target, the attacker must first deviate the defender's threatening point by an opposition, a beat, press, bind, or the like, so as to avoid falling on the defender's point. If this attempt to deviate a threatening point fails, then the right of way passes to the defender.

The bout is fought on a strip of rubber, cork, or other suitable material giving good purchase to the feet. For championship events, the strip must be 40 feet long and between 5 feet 10⅞ inches and 6 feet 6¾ inches wide. For any other authorized competition, the strip must not be less than 30 feet long and 3 feet in width. The jury is composed of a director or referee and four judges. The director stands midway between the two contestants, about four yards from the strip; the judges form a quadrangle about the contestants, one at each side of each contestant, at least a yard from him and behind him. The two judges flanking Fencer A will watch Fencer B, and the two flanking Fencer B will watch Fencer A.

The two contestants assume their places at the two ends of the strip. They are in the position preparatory to coming on guard. At the director's command to fall on guard, both execute the salute and fall on guard a short distance from the center of the strip. The director, after asking the contestants if they are ready, gives the command "Fence!" The two contestants are now free to conduct their combat in any manner consistent with the rules of fencing. After any decisive phrase the director will call "Halt!" and call for a vote of the jury. Each of the four judges of the jury has one vote; he may vote only on the materiality of any action, that is, whether any attack actually arrived and whether on valid or foul territory. The director has 1½ votes; he is the only one of the jury who may vote on validity, that is, on time and right of way. To the vote of the jury the director will add his own and render the decision.

After the decision, the director will place the two contestants on guard again, and the play will continue in the same manner until one of the two has scored five touches, except that the contestants will change sides when one has scored three touches. Upon the announcement of the last decision, the two contestants salute each other, remove their masks and shake hands.

This in brief is a picture of the conventions of foil fencing and the conduct of a bout. A detailed discussion of the technique of the foil follows.

Fig. 2 - Holding the foil: sixte and quarte

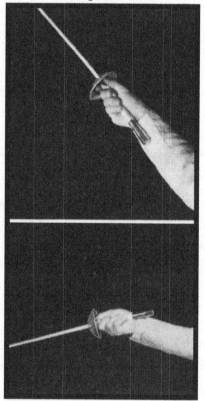

Holding The Foil

Grasp the grip in such a way that the curves on it coincide with the curves of the palm. Place the ball of the thumb flatly on the wider upper surface of the grip near the guard, and then encircle the grip with the other fingers in such a way that the first phalanx (the small bone nearest the tip) of each finger will be on the left side. The grip is maintained, but should be pressed strongly only at the moment of executing a parry or a beat. If the grip is held too tightly, free finger-play will be impossible. The pommel

Fig. 3 - Holding the foil: low sixte and low quarte

will fall across the center of the base of the hand should be kept pressed against the wrist.

Fig. 4 - Holding the foil: tierce

Finger-, Wrist-, And Arm Play

In the attacks the action of the thumb and index finger predominates in directing the point of the foil; the last three fingers are used to maintain the direction of the blade. Take care that an excessive relaxation of the last three fingers does not cause the point to deviate from its line. In any attack in the low line, in the cutover, and in the circling cut, however, relax the last three fingers more.

In the lateral parries of quarte and sixte, pass the forearm horizontally from the right to the left or vice versa, depending on the parry chosen, to give a parry sufficient to protect the body by closing the line to your adversary's blade. In the lateral parries, the action of the fingers and wrist is almost negligible.

The circular parries, or counter-parries, are executed almost exclusively by the fingers. They alternately squeeze and relax the grip, causing the point to describe a clockwise or counterclockwise circle, depending on the parry chosen. The pommel is maintained as close as possible to the wrist.

In the half-circular parries from the high to the low line, hold the blade firmly with the thumb and index finger and relax

7

the last three fingers slightly, so that the point will drop without a corresponding lowering of your hand. The pommel here will have to deviate from your forearm.

The wrist comes into play in the cut-over, the circling cut, the bind, the double bind, in the tierce parry, and in the half-circular parries.

Keep your right elbow inside, that is, in toward the left side of your body and about five inches from the body. If you do not keep your elbow inside, your line of sixte will be open. If you cannot keep your elbow inside, then keep your arm three-fourths extended.

Position Preparatory To Coming On Guard

The guard position is the best one to assume for both offensive and defensive play. It is from this position that attacks will be launched and parries taken.

To take up the position preparatory to coming on guard, place the feet at right angles, the right toe pointing toward your adversary, the heels together; keep the legs straight. Extend the right arm fully, obliquely downward and pointing slightly to the right. The foil is in line with your arm. The thumb is at 1 o'clock. The point of the blade is a few inches above the strip. The head is facing right and the body is turned well to the left. The left arm is extended fully and obliquely downward so that the hand is about fifteen inches from the left thigh, the palm turned upward.

The Guard Position

Coming on guard is clone in three counts, which are to be practiced until they flow into each other.

- **Count 1:** Being in the preparatory position, raise the foil, keeping the arm extended, and stopping the hand at the height of the eyes and a little to the right. The thumb is still at 1 o'clock. The foil is still in prolongation with the arm.

Fig. 5 - Position preparatory to coming on guard

Fig. 6 - The guard position

- **Count 2:** Bend the right arm back halfway and at the same time lower it so that the hand is at the height of the right breast. The thumb is still at 1 o'clock; the right elbow is turned in and about five inches from the front of the body. The point of the foil is at the height of the eyes. At the same time, move the left arm in an arc upward to the rear, without moving the shoulder, until the hand is at the height of the top of your head; the hand is arched.

- **Count 3:** Bend at the knees, separating them; the right foot moves forward a distance approximately two shoe-lengths from the left heel. The right leg from the knee down is perpendicular to the ground. A perpendicular dropped from the left knee should fall just slightly inside the big toe of the left foot. The two heels are in line, at right angles to each other. The body is erect on its haunches and presents as narrow a target for your adversary's blade as your physical makeup will allow.

Reassembling

Reassembling is the movement by which the fencer assumes, from the guard position, the position preparatory to coming on guard. To reassemble to the rear, (1) extend the right arm a little to the right and drop the left as in Count 1 of coming

9

on guard; (2) at the same time, straighten out your knees and move your right foot backward to its original place in the position preparatory to coming on guard; (3) drop your right arm to its place in the preparatory position. To reassemble forward, follow the same movements except for (2), which consists of moving the left foot forward to the preparatory position.

Reassemble whenever the instructor gives a brief rest period during a lesson; at the end of your lesson, followed by a salute; and at the end of a bout, followed by a salute.

The Salute

Being in either the preparatory position or Count 1 of coming on guard, to salute, bend the arm, moving the hand (the thumb at 3 o'clock) level with the chin and about five inches from it. The foil will be vertical, in a prolongation of the forearm. Then lower the blade forward in an arc, slowly, while completely extending the arm, stopping it in the position taken in the position preparatory to coming on guard.

From either this position or the preparatory position, to salute to the left, raise the right hand back to the level of the left breast, nails up, with the tip of the foil falling outside the left limit of the body at the height of the eyes. Turn the head to follow the blade. From here, to salute to the right, turn the nails clown, and move the right hand horizontally across the body to the right breast. The tip of the foil will then fall outside the right limit of the body, at the height of the eyes. Turn the head to follow the blade.

The Advance

The advance is used to approach an adversary out of reach of the blade. To advance, move the right foot forward and follow up with the left to the correct guard distance, without otherwise disturbing the position. Take small, quick, light steps so that you maintain perfect balance at all times. Advance with caution, watching your opponent's movement all the time. Be ready

10

instantly to parry any surprise attack made against your advance. Coordinate your arm movements with your leg movements; all movements of the arm must be completed with the completion of the advance.

The Retreat

The retreat is used to get out of reach of the adversary's blade. To retreat, move the left foot to the rear and follow immediately with the right until the proper guard distance has been attained; the position is otherwise undisturbed. Balance must be maintained at all times. The step used in the retreat is generally longer than that taken in the advance.

Foot-Signals

To execute the foot-signal, tap the strip lightly with the right heel and follow immediately with a heavier stamp of the entire right sole. The weight of the body is shifted slightly on the left leg. Do not otherwise disturb the guard position.

Use foot-signals to check your balance while on guard, or to attract the attention of the judges to the fact that you have a request to make.

Distance

In foil combat, the proper distance is such that with a full lunge your point will reach your opponent's body. Be careful that in the excitement of a bout you do not forget to maintain this distance.

Before a competition, test out your judgment of distance by taking a few full lunges against an opponent.

In practice, train yourself to maintain this distance at all times by following the advances and retreats of your partner with corresponding movements, until the maintenance of the proper distance becomes automatic to you.

Fig. 7 - Extension of the arm

Extension Of The Arm

Extend the arm horizontally without jerking, without exaggeration and without moving the shoulder. The thumb starts at 1 o'clock and moves according to the opposition taken. Hold the foil firmly in a prolongation of the arm and on the same level with your shoulder. The point will fall slightly below the height of the hand. The body is resting firmly on its haunches. The arm should be extended without muscular contraction; there should be no stiffness.

Coming Back On Guard After Extension Of The Arm

To come back on guard, bend the arm without jerking and without moving the shoulder, and take up the correct guard position.

The Thrust

The thrust is the carrying of the point of the foil to the target. It is made with opposition, that is, by simultaneously closing the line in which the attack terminates. Opposition is

12

taken by moving the hand slightly to the right or left during the execution of the thrust, depending upon whether the thrust is given to the outside or inside line.

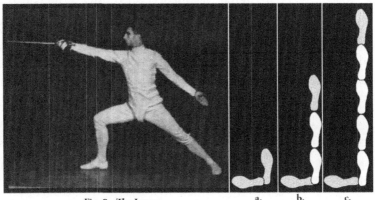

Fig. 8 - The Lunge

a.   b.   c.
Fig. 9 - Position of the feet:
a. Position preparatory to
   coming on guard
b. On guard
c. On the lunge

The Lunge

The lunge is the extension given to the guard position in an attempt to touch the opponent. To lunge, first extend the right arm as indicated in (The Thrust) above. Then snap open the left leg until it is fully extended, keeping the sole of the left foot flat against the strip. At the same time, move the right foot forward, closely skimming the strip, such a distance that when the right sole is flat on the strip, the right leg from the knee down will be perpendicular to the floor. The two heels are in line, at right angles to each other. At the same time, sweep the left arm down sharply in an arc, stopping the hand about fifteen inches from the left thigh, the palm up and fingers extended. The body rests firmly on its haunches, inclined slightly forward in a natural manner. The left shoulder is pulled back as much as possible, and the hips are in line coincidental with the line of the lunge.

Keep your chin in and your eyes fixed on your opponent's guard.

13

Recovery Of The Guard Position After The Lunge

The recovery of the guard position after the lunge is, like the lunge, a combination of distinct movements of arms, body and legs that must be mastered to split-second timing to be effective. In the lunge position the weight of the body is slightly forward. The first movement of the recovery is the bending of the left leg and the flexing upwards of the left arm; these simultaneous movements start the body weight backwards. Immediately after, the right foot pushes against the strip, thus completing the shifting of the weight to the rear, and the right foot skims backwards over the strip to its original guard position. At the same time as the movement of the right foot—and not before—the right arm bends back to the guard position.

It is also possible to recover the guard position forward after a lunge. Such a recovery will gain for you any distance lost by the opponent during his retreat. The occasional use of this movement will disconcert your opponent. In the forward recovery, the weight of the body is held forward on the right leg, which does not move, while the left leg is brought forward to the proper guard distance.

The Lines

The lines are those parts of the body where definite parries are made and to which attacks and ripostes are directed. The target is divided, with reference to the hand and in both a vertical and horizontal sense, into four lines, making four quadrangles. Vertically, the part of the target to the left of the hand will be the inside line, and the part to the right of the hand will be the outside line. Horizontally, the part above the hand will be the high line, and the part below the hand will be the low line. In the next chapter it will be seen that each of these quadrangles—outside high, outside low, inside high and inside low—has its appropriate parries.

14

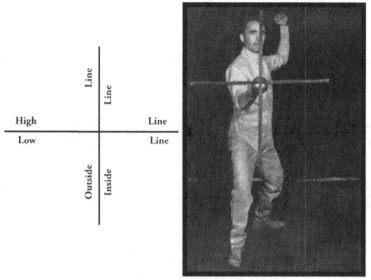

High | Line
Low | Line

Line | Line

Outside | Inside

Fig. 10 - The lines

The Point In Line

When the arm is extended and the point of the foil threatens a valid portion of the target, the point is said to be "in line." (See Fig. 7)

The difference between the feint and "point in line" lies in the fact that while both are extensions of the arm, the latter requires that the point be directed toward the target, while in the former it need not do so.

The expression "point in line," however, is used in teaching foil by the majority of instructors whether the arm is extended or not, simply in order to remind the pupil that the point of the foil, whether the blade is in an engagement or a parry or attack, must always stay in the lines established for those movements.

The action "point in line" is a defensive threat which confers the right of way upon the fencer executing it. In order to obtain the right of way for an attack against a "point in line," the attacker must first divert the extended blade.

15

Engagement

Engagement consists of contacting the adversary's blade three or four inches below its point with the foible of your own foil, the body being in the guard position, for the purpose of protecting yourself on that side. Engagement can be executed in any of the four lines and in either of two different positions of the hand. There are, therefore, eight possible engagements, but the most important are the engagement of quarte (inside, high line) and the engagement of sixte (outside, high line). The other engagements are either impractical or almost never employed.

The Engagement In Quarte

While assuming the guard position, contact the adversary's blade on the inside of his blade and move the hand horizontally at the level of the breast to the left limit of the body. The right elbow is in front of the body and about five inches from it. The thumb is at 1 o'clock. The point of the foil is level with the eyes and only a few inches to the left of center. The pommel is held as close to the forearm as possible. Keep your opponent's blade outside the limit of your body. In this position, your inside line is kept closed.

The Engagement In Sixte

While assuming the guard position, contact the adversary's blade on the outside of his blade and move the hand horizontally at the level of the breast to the right limit of the body. The thumb is at 1 o'clock. The right elbow is still inside, in front of the body and about five inches from it. The point of the foil is level with the eyes and only a few inches to the right of center. The pommel is held as close to the forearm as possible. Keep your opponent's blade outside the limit of your body. In this position, your outside line is kept closed.

Bear in mind that in the foil bout you should be constantly in either the position of quarte or of sixte. One of these two lines must be always closed.

16

Fig. 11 - The engagement in quarte   Fig. 12 - The engagement in sixte

Change Of Engagement

The change of engagement is a change of guard and consists in passing the point of your foil under your adversary's blade in order to close the opposite line. To execute the change of engagement, lower the point of your foil, pass it under your opponent's blade as closely as possible without touching it, and raise your point to the same height it was on the other side. This is all done by finger-play. Then move the hand horizontally to the opposite limit of the body, contacting your opponent's blade and closing the new line.

Double Change Of Engagement

The double change of engagement consists of two immediately successive changes of the line. It is executed from an engagement position by finger-play and without disturbing the position of the hand. It may be done in place or in motion. The single and double change of engagement are executed for the

17

purpose of provoking the adversary to leave himself momentarily unprotected in coping with them. The double change of engagement is especially valuable when made in motion, because it tends to upset the opponent's plan of attack.

When done in conjunction with an advance or retreat, both the single and double change of engagement must be completed with the completion of the footwork.

CHAPTER II
The Parries

The parry is the act of deflecting from the body the attack made by the adversary. It is executed by bringing the forte of your blade into contact with the foible of your opponent's blade. The arm is bent as in the guard position, which allows you to take your parries close to your body and gives you more time to deflect a thrusting blade. During the parry keep the pommel as close as possible to the forearm.

Parries may be lateral, half-circular or circular. Lateral parries are also called simple parries and deflect the adversary's blade in the same line as that in which the attack terminated. In the half-circular parry, the blade passes from the high line to the low line or vice versa, and the opponent's blade is maintained on the same side of your own blade. A circular or counter-parry deflects, by means of a full circle, the adversary's blade into the opposite line from that in which the attack ended.

All parries may be executed by opposition or by beat. In the parry by opposition, the opponent's blade is contacted without shock and maintained by means of pressure outside the line in which his attack ends. In the parry by beat, the opponent's blade is deflected from the target by means of a sharp tap given by contraction of the fingers and wrist, which opens up the opponent's line strongly and thus prepares the way for an immediate riposte.

There are two simple parries for each line, since the hand can be placed in two positions in each line, with the nails up or with the nails down. There are eight parries, then, each of which in turn has its own counter-parry. These eight parries are:

1. For the inside high line: prime and quarte
2. For the inside low line: quinte and low quarte (septime)
3. For the outside high line: tierce and sixte

4.   For the outside low line: seconde   and   low   sixte (octave)

Prime, quinte, tierce and seconde (and their counter-parries) are made in pronation, that is, with the nails down; quarte, low quarte, sixte and low sixte (and their counter-parries) are made in supination, that is, with the nails up.

The most useful parries in foil are those made in supination, and of these the most useful are quarte and sixte. The parries made in pronation find occasional use in special circumstances, but in general are not so effective as the others, both in the parry and as a position from which to launch a riposte when a parry and riposte are made with the nails up, the hand may be kept higher and the point lower, thus permitting opposition in the high line, the most dangerous line. When made in pronation, the riposte requires that the point be raised higher than the hand, leaving the high line vulnerable.

Tierce is the exception; the nails are down, but the hand in tierce position makes it possible to draw the arm well back, elbow outside the limit of the body, and thus to cope better with an adversary who deliberately provokes in-fighting or one who tries to avoid a riposte by ducking from the lunge position. The hand and the point, in their movement in the parries, must stay in line. The hand, regardless of whether it is describing a lateral or a circular motion, must be at the limit of the body to the left or right, so that one line will always remain closed. In this manner, the target will never be exposed by the placing of the hand between two lines. The distance that both the hand and the point will move in the lateral parries will be approximately the same. It is an error to believe that the point must be kept as a fixed pivot in going from one lateral parry to another. It can move and still remain inside the limits of the body.

It is difficult to establish the exact horizontal distance the hand must cover in the lateral parries, as that distance will vary with the position of the body and the hand. A fencer with his body turned well sideways in a good guard position will present the minimum target, and will not have to move his hand horizontally more than a few inches. A person with his arm too much bent, or with his elbow outside, will be forced to make his parries wider; his hand will have to travel a greater horizontal distance. Ordinarily, a fencer properly on guard will not need to move his hand horizontally more than from five to seven inches in taking his parries.

The position of the pommel should be the object of special attention. In the lateral parries in the high line, it will be kept as close as possible to the forearm, with a very slight difference between quarte and sixte.

Quarte Parry

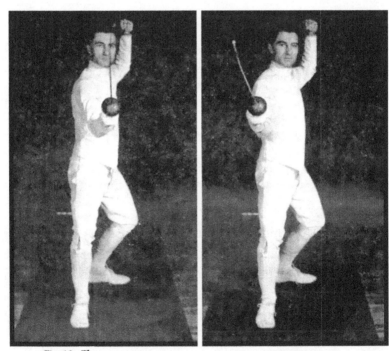

Fig. 13 - The quarte parry   Fig. 14 - The sixte parry

From the sixte position, to take a quarte parry on an attack to your inside line, use the elbow as a fixed pivot, and, without bending the wrist, shift the forearm horizontally at the height of the breast to the left limit of the body. The thumb is still at 1 o'clock. Your point is level with your eyes and a few inches to the left of center. Keep the pommel as close as possible to your forearm. Finger-play in this lateral parry, except for a momentary contraction at the time of contact, is negligible.

Being in this position of quarte, to execute counter-quarte when your opponent disengages, pass your point under his blade by describing a full counter-clockwise circle of the smallest possible circumference. This is done mainly by finger-play, with only slight assistance by the wrist. At the completion of the circle, give a beat to maintain the opposition. Keep the pommel as close as possible to the forearm.

Sixte Parry

From the quarte position, to take sixte parry on an attack to your outside line, move the hand horizontally to the right limit of the body in the same manner as described for the quarte parry.

From the sixte position, to execute a counter-sixte parry on a disengage, follow the directions given for the counter-quarte parry, with the exception that here the circle will be clockwise.

In the simple quarte and sixte parries, the sufficiency of the parry is assured by the speed of the movement itself. A great deal of force is not necessary.

Keep in mind also that the more your arm is bent in the guard position, the more you will have to keep your elbow inside to keep the line closed. Those fencers who experience difficulty in keeping their elbow inside should make their sixte parry with a twist of the wrist to the right, with the palm up, to prevent being touched through the parry.

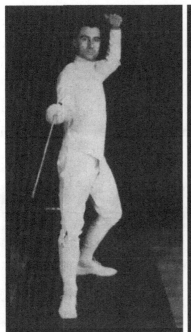 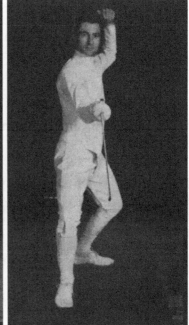

<table>
<tr><td>Fig. 15 - Low sixte parry</td><td>Fig. 16 - Low quarte parry</td></tr>
</table>

Low Sixte (Half-Circular Or Octave Parry)

From the sixte position, to take a low sixte parry when your adversary disengages to the low line, turn the hand and wrist clown and out so as to describe a counterclockwise half-circle. Do not move the elbow. The nails will still be up when the half-circle is completed and the point of the blade is in line with your opponent's waistline, either give a beat or maintain the opposition so that the outside low line is closed. Be careful that the point, after describing the half-circle, does not go outside the right limit of the body.

Counter low sixte is executed by passing the point over the opponent's blade and describing a counterclockwise circle of the smallest possible circumference.

Low Quarte (Half-Circular Or Septime) Parry

From the quarte position, to execute a low quarte parry on a disengage to the low line, do as for low sixte, except that here the half-circle will be clockwise.

Counter low quarte is executed by passing the point over the opponent's blade and describing a clockwise circle of the smallest possible circumference.

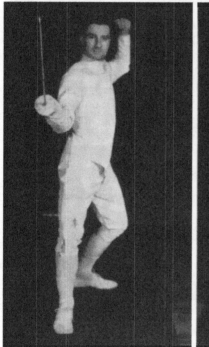

Fig. 17 - Tierce parry   Fig. 18 - Prime parry

Tierce Parry

From the quarte position, to execute tierce parry when the opponent disengages to the high line, move the hand horizontally to the right at breast-level, turning the hand counterclockwise at the same time, until the thumb is at 9 o'clock. The nails are down. The point of the foil is at eye-level and just outside the right limit of the body. The pommel will fall just under and to the right of the wrist.

The tierce parry is not so important as a parry, but rather as a position for the hand for the riposte from a very short distance. In such a case, it is very difficult to riposte from sixte or quarte, because as the arm draws back to clear the opponent's body the elbow comes into contact with the side of the body, and the riposte is likely to be a slap. With the hand in tierce position, however, the elbow may be placed outside the body if necessary, enabling the arm to draw back farther and thus avoiding the interference of the body.

From the tierce position, to execute a counter-tierce parry on your opponent's disengage to the inside high line, describe a full circle under the blade with the point, clockwise, the hand remaining in the tierce position. At the end of the circular motion, give a beat or take opposition. Counter-tierce is not very practical.

Prime Parry

From the position of sixte, on a disengage to the inside high line, move the hand laterally to a position about 6 or 7 inches in front of your chin, at the same time turning the hand and dropping the point so that the palm is forward, the nails forward and the thumb at six o'clock. The arm is bent and the forearm is horizontal; your point now is directed toward your adversary's belt-line.

Seconde Parry

From the position of sixte, on a disengage to the outside low line, drop the hand, turning the palm downward, so that the thumb is at 9 o'clock, the palm and nails down, the forearm horizontal and the point directed toward your adversary's belt-line, slightly lower than your hand.

Fig. 19 - Seconde parry   Fig. 20 - Quinte parry

Quinte Parry

From the position of quarte, on a disengage to the inside low line, drop the hand to the level of the belt, turning the palm downward, so that the thumb is at 9 o'clock, the nails down, the arm almost completely extended and the point just crossing the left limit of the body just above belt-level.

Compound Parries

Compound parries are any series of immediately successive lateral parries, half-circular parries and circular parries, or combination thereof, taken to protect yourself against a compound attack. The final parry may be given by opposition or by a beat; the ones up to the final parry should be taken by opposition.

You should keep your arm bent while taking a series of parries until the last one is completed; this will make your riposte more effective.

Beginners will find that retreating from an attack instead of taking a parry will tend to make them lose confidence in their parries.

Deceiving A Parry

To deceive a parry, simple or counter, is to avoid the opponent's parry of your thrust by disengaging into another line before he finds your blade. This deception should be executed by the fingers only. It is for such light, almost imperceptible movements of the fingers that the French foil-grip is eminently suited.

This movement, taken as an exercise by two fencers, can prove to be of much benefit. The students will face each other in guard position, one with his arm bent, the other with his arm extended. The exercise can be taken in three stages.

1.   One student will take simple parries, calling them off in advance to his partner, who will deceive them.

2.   He will do the same thing with counter-parries.

3.   He will take a series of simple and counter-parries without announcing them in advance, and his partner will deceive them by sight. The cadence of these movements should be varied. A full stop should be made between each group of parries so as to encourage clean-cut play.

CHAPTER III
Simple and Compound Attacks

Fig. 21 - The feint

The Feint

The feint is the simulation of an attack by the action of the fingers and the extension of the arm without a lunge, in order to force the opponent to take a parry. The feint, therefore, is simply an arm movement, which is to be made without exaggeration and without jerking the shoulder, as these faults will upset balance and make it more difficult to recover the guard position if it is necessary to parry. In a compound attack made in motion, the first feint must be coordinated and completed simultaneously with the foot movements.

It is a good practice to make some feints at the beginning of a bout in order to "feel out" what kind of fencer the adversary is, whether or not he will respond to a feint, and to decide where, against that particular opponent, you will find your best openings.

As soon as the arm is fully extended in a feint, you are in the attack position.

Keep in mind that on the short distance it is possible to be touched by a feint.

The Attacks

The attack is that movement or combination of movements by means of which the fencer seeks to touch his adversary. Attacks are either simple or compound. The attack is simple when it is executed as a single motion; it is compound in all other cases. The attack may be executed in place or in motion, with or without any preparation.

When made immediately after a parry, it is known as a riposte. There are three simple attacks: the straight thrust, the disengage and the cut-over (coupe).

In every case, you must not lunge until the point of the foil is already in its final line and the right arm is fully extended. You should lunge only if it is necessary to do so in order to hit. The right hand should be raised during the attack to the height of the right shoulder, the point slightly below the level of the hand, so as to get the maximum protection against a stop-thrust during your attack.

The thrust terminating the attack must be made with a slight opposition to the outside or inside, depending upon the line you have chosen for it. That slight opposition will close the line to the deadly direct riposte.

The Straight Thrust

The straight thrust is a thrust executed without any change in line. It is executed by extending the arm and lunging to touch with opposition. This attack is made when the line of engagement is open.

It is seldom possible, however, to find an opening wide enough for a touch to be made by a straight thrust without preparation, since fencers will always try to keep their line of engagement closed. In combat, therefore, the straight thrust is

29

generally preceded by a beat, press, glide or expulsion. It can be executed in any line.

The Disengage

The disengage is an attack ending in a line other than that of the engagement. To execute the disengage use your fingers to direct your point by the shortest possible distance to the line in which you expect to touch, extending your arm as in the straight thrust. Lunge and touch with opposition.

In disengages from high line to high line, your point passes under your adversary's blade; from low line to low line, over the blade. Two disengages can be made from each line. Those recommended are the disengages from high line to high line, and high line to low line. Disengages from low line to low line are not practical.

The Cut-Over (Coupe)

The cut-over is a disengage over the adversary's point. To execute the cut-over, raise the point of your blade vertically only as far as is necessary to clear your opponent's point, using the thumb and index finger and slightly relaxing the grip of the last fingers. Then, with the aid of your wrist, direct the point in to the line opposite that of the engagement, extend your arm with opposition, and lunge.

There is no cut-over from low to low line.

Compound Attacks

Compound attacks are those made up of more than one movement. In compound attacks, the first feint or feints must be made as far forward toward the opponent as is possible without disrupting the guard position. The feints should be made in progression so that the distance will gradually be closed and the attack terminate successfully.

The judicious use of the feint will make it possible for you to predict whether your opponent will take a simple lateral parry

30

or a counter-parry. You must know this in order to know how to proceed with your attack. Feints made close to the blade will probably provoke counter-parries. Wide feints will probably provoke lateral parries. Such wide feints, however, must not go past the limits of the body, or they will get no response at all, except possibly a stop-thrust. It is to be noted that the kind of compound attack executed depends upon the parries taken. For example, if you intend to execute a 1-2, and your opponent takes a counter-parry on your first feint, the 1-2 cannot be followed through; instead, you must use the double.

The following paragraphs list the most useful compound attacks from two to four movements. While one- and two-movement attacks are the most useful in the bout, the three- and four-movement attacks given are valuable in developing judgment and suppleness of fingers, wrist and arm.

Some Two-Movement Attacks

1.   The straight thrust, disengage: a feint straight thrust, followed by a disengage deceiving a simple parry.

2.   The straight thrust, deceiving a counter-parry: a feint straight thrust, followed by a disengage deceiving a counter-parry.

3.   The 1-2: a feint disengage to the high or low line, followed by a disengage to the high or low line, deceiving a simple or half-circular parry.

4.   The cut-over, disengage: a feint cut-over, followed by a disengage deceiving a simple parry.

5.   The double cut-over: a feint cut-over, followed by a cut-over deceiving a simple or counter-parry.

6.   The double: a feint disengage, followed by a disengage in the same line, deceiving a counter-parry.

31

7. The double to the low line: a feint disengage followed by a second disengage ending in the low line, after deceiving a counter-parry in the high line.

Some Three Movement Attacks

1. The straight thrust, 1-2: a feint straight thrust, followed by a 1-2, deceiving two simple parries.

2. The 1-2-3: two feint disengages, followed by a disengage, deceiving two simple or half-circular parries.

3. The cut-over, 1-2: a feint cut-over, followed by a 1-2, deceiving two simple or half-circular parries.

4. The disengage, cut-over, disengage: a feint disengage, followed by a cut-over disengage, deceiving two simple parries.

5. The double, disengage: a feint double, followed by a disengage in the high or low line, deceiving first a counter-parry and then a simple or half-circular parry.

6. The triple: a feint double followed by a disengage, deceiving two counter-parries.

Some Four Movement Attacks

1. The 1-2-3-4: three feint disengages, followed by a disengage, deceiving three simple or half-circular parries.

2. The cut-over, 1-2-3: a feint cut-over followed by three disengages, deceiving three simple or half-circular parries.

3. The double, 1-2: a feint double, followed by a 1-2, deceiving first a counter-parry, then two simple or half-circular parries in the high or low lines.

4. The quadruple: a feint triple, followed by a disengage, deceiving three counter-parries in the high or low lines.

5.   Triple, disengage: a feint triple, followed by a disengage, deceiving two counter-parries, then a simple or half-circular parry.

6.   Double in both lines: a feint double followed by a double in the opposite line, deceiving a counter-parry, a simple parry and a counter-parry.

The above-listed compound attacks are only a few of the many possible combinations. You may prefer to use combinations of your own.

All the above attacks are predicated on a quarte or sixte guard, as these are the only engagements normally used.

CHAPTER IV
The Riposte and Counter-Riposte

The Riposte

The riposte is the attack which follows the parry. It is a direct riposte when it takes place in the same line as that in which the parry was taken. When the direct riposte immediately follows a parry made by beat, it takes the name of "tac-au-tac" riposte, and should be executed with the greatest rapidity. When the direct riposte is executed after a parry by opposition, it takes the name of "riposte by opposition," and should be made with a slight elevation of the hand in opposition. Whenever the line is changed, the riposte is still simple if it is executed in a single motion. The riposte is a compound riposte when it is executed in more than one movement.

The delayed riposte is one which does not follow immediately after the parry. The degree of delay is determined by the adversary's movements.

Fig. 22 - Riposte against a flèche with hand in tierce position

34

The "tac-au-tac" riposte should be ma<le in place; the others can be executed in place, with the lunge, or during the advance or retreat.

The direct riposte is ordinarily the best since it travels through the shortest distance and is the fastest. It should be used against any opponent at first, until actual practice proves that it will not work against him. If it does fail, it means that your opponent is at least as fast as you are and that he is coming back on guard protecting himself in the same line as that in which the parry was taken. If he continues to do this, try the riposte by disengage or cut-over, as the opposite line will then be open.

Fig. 23 - Riposte to the low line on the close distance, hand in prime

The riposte by cut-over can be executed in two ways: (1) By giving a preliminary beat in taking the parry and then, as your adversary answers the beat or recovers his guard, making the cu t-over vertically from the position of the parry. (2) By one continuous looping motion. The parry here is given by the first half of the cut-over, by sliding upwards with opposition to the tip of the adversary's blade, and then making the riposte down the other side of his foil (coupe a la mouche). While the cut-over

35

riposte may occasionally be used with great effect, it is slower than the direct riposte.

Against an opponent who keeps his hand in the middle of two lines while returning on guard, the 1-2 is effective. Against an adversary who makes a change of guard by a circular movement while recovering his position, use the riposte by the double. A double to the low line would add an element of surprise and would therefore be likely to prove more effective.

The Counter-Riposte And Second Counter-Riposte

The counter-riposte is the attack which follows the parry of the riposte. As in the case of the riposte, it can be direct, compound or delayed. The counter-riposte may be made in place or in motion, or, whenever necessary, from the lunge position of the original attack. The second counter-riposte is the attack following the parry of the counter-riposte, and follows the same principles as the riposte and counter-riposte.

Redoubling Of The Riposte

Redoubling of the riposte consists of two immediately consecutive ripostes against an adversary who, after parrying the first riposte or merely avoiding it, fails to counter-riposte but retreats or fails to keep his line closed. Between the riposte and the redoubling of the riposte there should be no break in time, even when the redouble is made with a lunge.

The Phrase (Phrase D'Armes)

A phrase is an entire group of movements—attacks, parries, ripostes and counter-ripostes—given and received without interruption, ending either decisively or indecisively.

CHAPTER V
Preparations to the Attack

Preparation To The Attack

The preparation to the attack is the movement or movements made before the attack to assure its greater success. Preparations are begun with the arm bent; in some, the arm will finally become extended. Those in which the arm is kept bent include change of guard, double change of guard, invitation to an attack, the press, beat and opposition; those in which the arm is finally extended include the expulsion, the glide, the feint bind and the various feints executed for the purpose of preparation.

Preparations may be made from the guard position, or on the advance and retreat.

If you generally use preparations, it is good practice to attack occasionally directly from the guard position without preparation, simply to vary the game and to surprise an opponent who is anticipating the usual preparation.

Preparations Striking The Blade: The Beat: The Expulsion

Preparations striking the blade are those executed by contacting the adversary's blade sharply in order to deflect with force a threatening point or to facilitate an attack by strongly opening a line. The contact is not maintained.

The beat: The beat is a quick sharp blow executed with the middle of your blade against your opponent's foible so as to open a line for your attack. It is executed chiefly by the action of the fingers, which alternately squeeze and relax on the grip. Only slight aid is rendered by the wrist. The blade should remain at the point where the beat was given.

The beat can be effected in the line of engagement or with a change of line; in the latter case it is called a counter-beat. When the beat is to be followed by a straight attack, it should be strong enough to open the line. It should be lighter when it is to be followed by a disengage. Otherwise, when you disengage, you will find that by hitting your adversary's blade too hard, you have closed the line against yourself. In attacking, the arm should be extended only after the beat, and not during its execution.

A wide beat is easily deceived.

Since a beat opens up the line, a beat given by your opponent should be answered. Be careful how you respond, as your adversary may be waiting to deceive your response with a disengage.

To practice the beat, get on guard facing another fencer, and return his simple beats, from both engagements. Then take turns with counter-beats. Occasionally, you should deceive each other's beats, to see if your points are being kept within the limits of the body.

The expulsion (froissement): The expulsion is a sharp, continually increasing, slightly diagonal pressure exerted with the middle of the blade all the way down the opponent's blade from his foible to his forte, resulting in the expulsion of his blade from the line and opening up a line of attack. At the end of the movement, the arm is extended. The expulsion is executed against an extended arm. It may be made in the line of engagement or with a change of line (counter-expulsion).

The expulsion should not be over-emphasized, as it is wide and therefore dangerous to execute. It is better to use a beat or a press as a preparation.

Preparations Maintaining The Blade: The Press; Opposition; The Glide

Preparations maintaining the blade are those in which contact is made with the adversary's blade without shock and is maintained for an appreciable length of time. They are used to push aside a threatening point and to facilitate an attack by engaging and maintaining the adversary's blade.

The press: The press is a pressure exerted against the foible of the adversary's blade in order to remove it from the line, once contact of his blade has been established. It should be executed smoothly, not jerkily, and without warning the opponent in advance by any conspicuous finger- and wrist-play. The foil should remain at the place where the press was given, and the position of the arm will remain the same. As with the beat, it is intended to open the line of engagement, and if the opponent responds, to take advantage of his response by disengaging.

The press may also be executed after an opposition, a change of guard or a double change of guard. It can be made in the line of the engagement or with a change of line (counter-press).

To practice the press, get on guard with another fencer, and practice answering each other's simple presses, from both engagements. Then change to alternative counter-presses, from both engagement. As with the beat, deceive each other's presses occasionally by a feint disengage.

Opposition: Opposition is the maintenance of the adversary's blade outside the limits of the target by exerting continual and sufficient resistance to his blade. Contact is made without a beat.

When opposition is used as a preparation to an attack, it may be taken in the same line or with a change of line (counter-opposition).

Opposition is a good preparation to use, but it is a dangerous one for beginners, as they are apt to make their hand movements too wide laterally. In executing opposition, the hand and point should never go beyond the limits fixed for the engagements.

The glide (coulé): The glide is like the feint straight thrust, but is made with contact of the opponent's blade. Slide your blade forward along your adversary's foil by extending the arm. At the end of the glide, your forte should be at the middle of his blade, so that you will be able to overcome his opposition.

Be careful not to press too strongly laterally in executing the glide. Its purpose is to enable you to close in on an opponent by maintaining contact of forte against foible. This close position will give you the advantage in your own attack and superiority over an opponent who decides to make an attack on your preparation. After the glide, it is best to execute a straight thrust, keeping your opponent's blade sufficiently outside by a slight opposition to open the line. If your adversary responds to your glide, disengage.

Fig. 24 - Invitation to the attack

The Invitation To The Attack (Absence D' Épée)

The invitation to the attack is a deliberate and exaggerated opening of a line so as to encourage the adversary to attack in a line in which you wish him to attack. It should be executed with extreme care.

The invitation is useful against an opponent who does not wish to attack, or against one who is stronger on the defensive than on the offensive.

40

Fine precision and an accurate sense of distance and timing are necessary to execute the invitation successfully. In effect, you are pitting your judgment against that of your opponent. He knows what you are doing. He will not attack until he believes that you have misjudged, that you have made the invitation too wide to be able to defend yourself in time. It's up to you to make him believe so, without actually passing the thin margin of safety.

Closing In On The Opponent (Se Loger)

You close in on your opponent by any series of movements which drives the point of your foil closer and closer to your adversary's target, so as to make his parry of your final attack more difficult and to assure the ultimate success of your attack.

Deceiving The Preparation To The Attack: The Avoidance; The Attack On A Preparation

The preparation to an attack may be deceived by either of two methods: by removing your blade from your opponent's control, or by a surprise attack as he begins his.

The avoidance (derobement): Avoidance is the deception of the opponent's blade by a feint disengage just at the moment he starts to execute a preparation for his attack. At the end of the avoidance your arm is extended.

Avoidance may be used as an exercise, student versus student.

The attack on a preparation: The attack on a preparation is one which is begun from a state of complete immobility in such a way as to surprise the adversary in the preparation of his own attack. It may be used against any preparation. It is generally made by a simple movement, whether or not it is preceded by a preparation.

Many fencers confuse the terms "avoidance," "attack on a preparation," "stop-thrust" and "time-thrust."

The avoidance is a deception of your opponent's blade, without a lunge.

The attack on a preparation is a surprise attack deceiving your opponent's preparation to his own attack.

The stop-thrust is an attack made on your opponent's attack, not on his preparation.

The time-thrust or time-attack is an attack with opposition, fulfilling at the same time the functions of parry and riposte, executed against an attack by your opponent.

CHAPTER VI
Special Attacks

The False Attack

The false attack is an attack made in one or several movements without any intention of touching the opponent, accompanied by a simulated lunge in which the right foot is brought forward a short distance.

At the end of the false attack, you have several alternatives:

1. If your opponent does not respond, either recover the guard position and try again, or make a straight thrust or a disengage to the low line.

2. If he responds by taking a simple or counter-parry, deceive that parry by a disengage to the high or low line.

3. If he responds by taking a parry and then making a riposte, parry his riposte and counter-riposte yourself with a lunge.

The false attack can, of course, be preceded by a preparation.

You should begin a bout against a new opponent by using a false attack; it will enable you to "feel out" the strength and ability of your adversary. In addition, it will enable you to close in on him.

The false attack is useful to draw out a fencer who generally fights on the defensive.

The Stop-Thrust (Coup D' Arrêt)

The stop-thrust is a straight thrust executed with or without a lunge against the opponent's attack, with the intention of scoring a touch cleanly before his attack arrives. It is used if before the attack the opponent makes several feints, or when, during an attack, he abandons the blade or keeps his line open during the advance. In order to avoid a double touch, the thrust must be made at the very beginning of the adversary's attack, or when he starts to raise his foot to advance.

To create an opportunity to use the stop-thrust, provoke your adversary to advance by retreating on his attack. The stop-thrust is most effective against such an advancing attack.

The stop-thrust is not recommended for beginners until they have mastered all the attacks and ripostes.

Fig. 25 - The stop-thrust executed against a cut-over

The Time-Attack

The time-attack is an attack which fulfills at the same time the functions of parry and riposte, by extending the arm as much as is necessary to touch and simultaneously closing the line in which the adversary's attack is expected to terminate. It must always be made with opposition, without a lunge or with a half-lunge. The time-attack always consists of a single movement, and is much more effective when used against a compound attack than against a single-movement attack. It is easier to execute in the outside line than in the inside line.

44

In general, the greatest caution must be exercised in judging just when to launch the time-attack. The timing must be exceptionally well gauged.

The following are examples of time-attacks:

1. From an engagement in quarte, when the opponent disengages or executes a cut-over to sixte, extend the arm with sixte opposition and touch.

2. From an engagement in sixte, when the adversary disengages, drop the point of your foil by a motion similar to the cross and touch in the low line with low sixte opposition.

3. From an engagement in sixte, when the adversary disengages to the low line, drop your point, extend your arm and touch with low sixte or seconde opposition.

4. From an engagement in quarte, when the opponent disengages to the low line, drop your point, extend your arm and touch with opposition in low quarte.

5. From an engagement in sixte, on the first feint of a 1-2, take the opposition in the same line, and when the adversary disengages, extend the arm and touch with sixte opposition.

6. From an engagement in sixte, on the first feint of a 1-2 (if you feel certain that your opponent is about to use this attack), extend your arm directly with opposition in sixte the moment he starts his attack, then touch with a part-lunge.

7. From an engagement in quarte, on the first feint of a 1-2, take sixte opposition; when your opponent disengages back to quarte, drop your point over his blade and touch, maintaining the opposition in low sixte.

8. On the same attack from the same engagement, if you feel certain that your adversary is about to use this attack, do

not move during the first feint but on his second disengage drop your point over his blade and touch in the low line, maintaining low sixte opposition.

9. From an engagement in quarte, on the first feint of a double, take the opposition of counter-quarte, extend your arm on the right-hand side during the time that your adversary is continuing his second disengage of the double, and touch with opposition.

10. From an engagement in quarte, on the first feint of a double, counter-disengage by extending the arm on the right-hand side, and touch with opposition.

11. From an engagement in sixte, on the first feint of a double, take the opposition of counter-sixte, drop the point over his blade, and touch in the low line, maintaining the opposition in low sixte.

12. From an engagement in sixte, on the first feint of a double (if you feel certain that your opponent is about to use this attack), drop the point over his blade and touch, maintaining the opposition in low sixte.

Mastery of the time-attack is not to be expected before the end of the second year.

Fig. 26 - The time-attack against a 1-2 (inside, outside)

The Counter Time-Attack

The counter time-attack is one executed against an adversary who starts to make a stop-thrust or a time-attack. It follows any provocation which makes your opponent take a time-attack; and on his time-attack you make a simultaneous parry and counter-riposte, maintaining the opposition.

The best way to execute a counter time-attack is to provoke a stop-thrust or a time-attack by making a false attack, or by raising the right foot to simulate an advance.

The counter time-attack requires the utmost speed and fine judgment. In general, only the advanced fencer will be able to execute it properly.

Redoubling

Redoubling is a second attack made from the lunge position immediately after an opponent fails to riposte after parrying. It can be executed in two ways:

1.   If the line is closed, retake the blade by a beat and touch by a straight thrust, a disengage, a cut-over, or a compound attack.

2.   If the line is open, do not retake the blade, but seek to touch by a straight thrust, a disengage, a cut-over, or a compound attack.

To protect yourself against an opponent who redoubles, do not foil to riposte, and do so with opposition by maintaining your opponent's blade.

The Remise

The remise is a second attack made from the lunge position against an adversary who makes a riposte; it fulfills at the same time the functions of a parry and a counter-riposte. It is merely a time-attack executed from a different position and against a riposte from your opponent. The time-attack is made from the guard position; the remise, from the lunge position. The

Fig. 27 - The remise against a disengage riposte

time-attack is made against an opponent who attacks; the remise, against one who makes a riposte.

Many fencers and judges confuse the remise and the redouble. It is important to remember that the remise is made against an opponent who ripostes; the redouble, against one who fails to riposte. The remise is always executed in the same line as that in which the parry was taken; the redouble may involve a change of line.

As much as possible, the remise should be executed against a riposte ending in your outside line. A remise executed against a riposte terminating in your inside line will expose you too much to a double touch. If it is executed in such a case, however, the opponent's blade should be stopped in the low line by a remise similar to the cross. For example, if your opponent parries quarte and starts to riposte by a 1-2, execute a cross on his final movement, and touch with opposition in the low line.

The best way to avoid the remise is to riposte by maintaining the opposition, and to use the direct riposte or a simple disengage to the low line. Since the remise is very difficult to execute, no importance should be assigned to it during the beginner's first year of fencing. A counter-riposte gives the same result and is much safer and easier to execute.

The Delayed Attack

If for any reason the attack is slowed down or temporarily interrupted by the attacker, thus causing a loss of time in its execution, it is called a delayed attack. Such an attack almost always results in the loss of the right of way.

It is therefore obvious that the attack should not be made too slowly and should be made without halting, so as to avoid giving your adversary the time to make a stop-thrust against you before the end of your attack.

In certain circumstances, the delayed attack may be used intentionally as a preparation for the final touch. In this case, you must be careful not to be hit by a stop-thrust.

The Circling Cut (Tour D' Épée)

The circling cut is a single-movement attack begun as a cut-over; but once the adversary's point is cleared, the point is brought back to its starting position by a circular movement. At the end of the movement, the arm will be extended so as to force the opposition taken to open the line slightly. It should be executed as one continuous motion.

The circling cut may be executed both as an attack and as a parry and riposte; it is more effective as an attack, however.

The Bind (Liement)

The bind is a single-movement attack in one continuous motion, in which the adversary's extended blade is contacted with opposition and, maintaining that contact, is transferred from low to high line, or high to low line, where the attack will terminate.

1.   From a high to a low line, from an engagement in sixte: when your opponent extends his arm in quarte, take the opposition in quarte, pass the forte of your blade over the foible of your adversary's foil, maintaining contact with his blade; your point will pass above your adversary's hand and will describe a half-circle from high to low line, so that your blade now takes the opposition of low sixte. By the time you have taken this opposition your arm is extended. Lunge with opposition in the low line.

2.   From a high to a low line, from an engagement in quarte: when your opponent extends his arm in sixte, make your half-circle in the other direction, and follow through in the same manner as above.

3.   From a low to a high line, when your adversary extends his arm in the low line: execute in the same way as in the

50

high line, except that here the direction is reversed and your point will end in the high line. The forte of your blade will of course go under his foible. If your adversary starts his feint in low sixte, your bind will carry your blade to a final attack in quarte. If your opponent starts in low quarte, you will end in sixte.

Occasionally, on the short distance, the bind may be executed from high to low line, with the hand finishing in the seconde position; or, from low to high, in tierce.

Since the bind is most effectively executed when your opponent has his arm extended, this movement may be considered as a simultaneous execution of an attack with a parry and riposte.

After a counter-parry, the bind can be made by opposition in the high line. In this case, the bind will begin as a continuation of the counter-parry and will touch with opposition on the opposite side. In former times the feint bind executed sharply to the low line was used to disarm an opponent as he was extending his arm. A disarmament in those days was considered equivalent to a touch. Since the disarmament has lost its scoring value, there is no point today in disarming an opponent.

To parry a bind made by your adversary, bend your arm and take a simple opposition in the same line as that in which the bind is intended to end. In other words, the bind is parried by opposition, which continues through the riposte.

The bind is best deceived by a disengage executed at its very beginning.

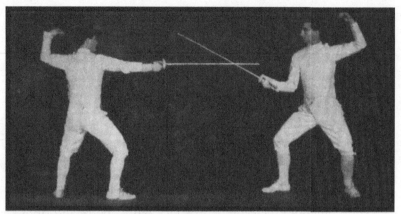

Fig. 28 - The bind(a.) Opposition of quarte against a feint inside

Fig. 29 - The bind(b.) Going into opposition of low sixte

Fig. 30 - The bind(c.) Extended arm, lunge to low line

52

The Double Bind

The double bind is merely the continuous execution of two consecutive binds, ending in the same line as that in which they began. To execute, contact your opponent's blade as for the bind, with a simple or counter-opposition. Describe a complete circular movement, maintaining continuous contact with his blade, from the high line to the low line and back again to the high line, where the touch is scored with opposition.

It is possible to execute a double bind starting from the low line, but it is not recommended, since continuous contact cannot be so effectively maintained.

Like the bind, the double bind should not be executed against a bent arm.

The Cross (Croisé)

The cross is a transverse movement from high to low line, fulfilling at the same time the functions of parry and riposte, made without a lunge. The line is kept closed all the time during the parry and the riposte is made with opposition. The cross is executed against the final movement of the adversary's attack

The cross should not be confused with the bind; the bind is an attack made against the adversary's extended arm, while the cross is a parry and riposte executed on your opponent's attack.

The Envelopment

The envelopment is a transverse movement from low to high line, fulfilling at the same time the functions of parry and riposte, made without a lunge. The line is kept closed all the time during the parry and the riposte is made with opposition. The envelopment is executed against the final movement of the adversary's attack.

It will be noted that the envelopment is the same movement as the cross, made in the opposite direction.

The Flèche

The flèche is a running attack executed in the following manner:

1. The arm is extended with opposition, the point directed at the target.

2. The weight is shifted from the left to the right leg, and the left foot is brought up to a position slightly in front of the right foot.

3. From this position, the arm and shoulder stretch out as far as they will go, the body inclines forward until it is almost off-balance, and the distance is closed with a rush, preventing the opponent from riposting.

The placing of the left foot in front of the right will enable you to keep facing your opponent as you run forward. You may make your rush directly forward, in which case you limit it so as not to come into bodily contact with your adversary, or you may pass him to either side. Passing him to the left is preferable. If possible, avoid running off the strip, for the moment you do so any subsequent action on your part during the phrase is nullified; whereas your opponent is allowed one immediate riposte, which is valid even if you are off the strip.

The flèche is most effectively executed just as your opponent is recovering his guard position from some action of his.

The best defense against the flèche is the parry; do not try to stop-thrust, as his opposition and the force of his rush will push your blade aside.

The flèche is more generally used in the épée than in the foil. While tolerated in foil, it is generally frowned upon; in close decisions the benefit of the doubt is generally given to the defender.

Retaking The Attack (Reprise D' Attaque)

Retaking the attack is the act of going on the offensive after any inconclusive phrase.

CHAPTER VII
Exercises

Some Alternative Exercises

The alternative exercises given here have for goal the preparation of the beginning fencer for the actual bout. The first exercise should be executed in this manner: two fencers should get on guard so that their blades cross just below the tips. One makes a feint disengage (no lunge); the other takes a simple parry and ripostes with a feint disengage. The first then parries this riposte with a simple parry and counter-ripostes in a like manner, and so on. As the movements proceed without interruption, the distance should be gradually shortened by very short steps forward and the speed increased until a touch is scored to end the exercise.

The exercises given here should be executed first without lunges, and then with lunges as the fencers become more familiar with the movements. In this case, the ripostes will be coordinated with the recoveries of the guard position.

The movements must be clean-cut at all times. Correctness of execution must not be sacrificed to speed. In the long run, it will be seen that the correct way to execute any given movement in fencing is also the fastest wav.

The parries in the following alternative exercises may be taken by opposition or beat. With some of the exercises, the beat given at the end of the parry must be answered to allow the exercise to proceed. For example, in #8, the parry is taken by two counter-parries. The final movement of these two parries will be a beat. This beat will have to be answered by the original attacker, that is, he will have to push slightly against the beat and thus deliberately open up his line to enable his partner to disengage and begin his double.

The two fencers executing these exercises are referred to as the "instructor" and the "pupil." They may be executed by any

56

two fencers in any stage of advancement, however; an occasional check by the instructor would be sufficient to insure correctness of execution.

Start all the following alternative exercises from sixte; then from quarte, changing parries to suit the action.

Some Alternative Exercises

Instructor's Attack	Pupil's		Instructor's
	Parry	Riposte	Parry
1. Disengage	Quarte	Disengage	Sixte (Repeat until a touch is scored)
2. Disengage to low sixte	Low Sixte	Disengage to Sixte	Sixte
3. Disengage	Quarte	Disengage to Low Quarte	Low Quarte
4. Disengage	Counter-Sixte	Disengage	Counter-Sixte
5. 1-2	Quarte, Sixte	1-2	Quarte, Sixte
6. 1-2 (first to low line, then to high line)	Low Sixte, Sixte	1-2, Low, High	Low Sixte, Sixte
7. 1-2	Quarte, Counter-Quarte	1-2	Sixte, Counter-Sixte
8. Double	Two Counter-Sixte	Double	Two Counter-Sixte
9. Double	Counter-Sixte, Quarte	Double	Counter-Quarte-Sixte
10. Triple	Three Counter-Sixte	Triple	Three Counter-Sixte

Some Counter-Riposte Exercises

Pupil's Feint	Instructor's Parry	Instructor's Riposte (no lunge)	Pupil's Parry of Riposte	Pupil's Counter-riposte (lunge)
1. Straight thrust	Sixte	Straight thrust	Sixte	Straight thrust
2. Disengage (or cut-over)	Quarte	Disengage	Counter-quarte	Disengage
3. Disengage	Counter-sixte	Disengage	Counter-sixte	Disengage
4. 1-2 (or cut-over, disengage)	Quarte, sixte	Disengage	Counter-sixte	Disengage
5. 1-2 (or cut-over, disengage)	Quarte, Sixte	1-2	Quarte, sixte	Disengage to low line
6. Beat, disengage	Counter-sixte	Disengage	Quarte	1-2 to low line
7. Press, 1-2	Quarte, sixte	1-2	Quarte, sixte	1-2
8. Double	Two counter-sixte	Double	Two counter-sixte	Disengage
9. Double	Two counter-sixte	Double	Two counter-sixte	Double
10. Beat, disengage (or cut-over)	Counter-sixte	1-2	Quarte, sixte	Double
11. 1-2-3, low, high, low	Low sixte, sixte, low sixte	Disengage to high line	Sixte	1-2-3
12. Cut-over, 1-2	Quarte, sixte, quarte	Disengage	Counter quarte	Cut-over
13. Disengage to low line	Low sixte	Disengage to high line	Sixte opposition	Bind
14. Disengage	Quarte opposition	Feint bind	Low sixte opposition	Bind
15. On instructor's feint disengage, pupil takes quarte opposition, double bind, disengage	Quarte opposition, sixte	Disengage	Quarte opposition	Double bind, disengage

NOTE: All the movements listed in the first column, when done without the lunge, are feints; with the lunge, these same movements arc attacks. They may be done in either way. All the parries, ripostes and counter-ripostes may be executed in the guard position, the lunge position, or while recovering the guard position from the lunge.

Some Second Counter-Riposte Exercises

Instructor's Feint	Pupil's		Instructor's		Pupil's	
	Parry	Riposte (no lunge)	Parry of Riposte	Counter-riposte (lunge)	Parry of Counter-riposte	Second Counter-riposte (with lunge)
1. Disengage	Quarte	Straight thrust	Quarte	Straight thrust	Quarte	Straight thrust
2. Cut-over	Quarte	Straight thrust	Quarte	Straight thrust	Quarte	Disengage (or cut-over)
3. Glide, disengage	Counter-sixte	Disengage	Counter-sixte	Disengage	Quarte	Straight thrust
4. 1-2	Quarte, sixte	Disengage to low line	Low sixte	1-2	Sixte, quarte	1-2
5. Cut-over, disengage	Quarte, sixte	Disengage	Counter-sixte	1-2	Quarte, sixte	Disengage
6. 1-2, high, low	Quarte, low quarte	1-2	Quarte, sixte	1-2	Quarte, sixte	1-2, low, high
7. Disengage	Counter-sixte	1-2	Quarte, sixte	Disengage	Quarte opposition	Bind
8. 1-2-3	Quarte, sixte, quarte	Disengage	Counter-quarte	1-2-3	Sixte, quarte, sixte	Disengage
9. Double	Two counter-sixte	Disengage	Counter-sixte	Double	Two counter-sixte	Disengage
10. Double	Two counter-sixte	Double	Two counter-sixte	Double	Two counter-sixte	Disengage to low line
11. Double	Two counter-sixte	Double	Two counter-sixte	Double	Two counter-sixte	1-2
12. 1-2, low, high	Low sixte, sixte	1-2, low, high	Low sixte, sixte	1-2, low, high	Low sixte, sixte	Double
13. Disengage	Quarte opposition	Bind	Low sixte opposition	Disengage to high line	Sixte opposition	Bind
14. 1-2, low, high	Low sixte, sixte	Disengage	Counter sixte	Disengage	Counter-sixte opposition	Double bind

NOTE: All the movements listed in the first column, when done without the lunge, are feints; with the lunge, these same movements are attacks. They may be done in either way. All the other movements may be executed in the guard position, the lunge position, or while recovering the guard position from the lunge.

59

CHAPTER VIII
Lessons

The Lesson

It is not difficult to learn the mechanics of a movement. What will be difficult for you to attain is the ability to use the movement with effect at the proper time. The chapters before this have been dedicated to the explanation of the movements used in fencing with the foil and to the demonstration of these movements by means of photographs. This chapter contains eighteen lessons, used by the author during many years of coaching in Europe and the United States, which will train you to use these movements at the proper time and to get results with them. They have been drawn up with special attention to the problem of making you think for yourself, rather than rely on verbal instruction from the coach. Ina bout, you can receive no instruction from your coach, but must rely on your own senses of sight and touch. It should be your aim, throughout these lessons, to train these senses.

You should learn, for example, to make a straight thrust upon any movement opening up the line of engagement; to disengage on a press, beat, expulsion or change of guard; to use a cut-over against a low point; to base your decision whether or not to lunge with your attack or riposte on the distance between you and your opponent; and to do this on your own initiative. It is these things, and not definitions, that will help you in the bout.

For these lessons, take the engagement in the high line. Practice each exercise in both sixte and quarte, so as to develop both lines equally.

Train yourself to recover your guard, after your lunge, on the same side as that in which the final movement of your attack or riposte was parried; in other words, on the same side as the instructor's blade.

Unless instructed to the contrary, recross blades before beginning a new movement.

The Make-Up Of A Complete Lesson

The following order of progression has given the author the most satisfactory results in teaching the foil.

1.   On guard, advance, retreat, lunge, change of guard, double change of guard. These fundamental movements serve a double purpose, in that they give you a chance to warm up gradually and allow the instructor to catch any departures from correct form.

2.   Simple attacks.

3.   Simple and counter-parries; ripostes.

4.   Attacks deceiving simple or counter-parries, beginning with two and going to four movements. Although the instructor will explain the phrase in advance, he will allow your initiative as full play as possible, by not informing you precisely what parries you will have to deceive.

5.   Two- to four-movement parries for the above attacks, with a simple or compound riposte.

6.   A counter-riposte exercise, such as the ones given in "Some Counter-Riposte Exercises."

7.   A second counter-riposte exercise, such as the ones given in "Some Second Counter-Riposte Exercises."

8.   Exercise in speed attacks, parries and ripostes. In these exercises, the instructor will indicate beforehand precisely what attack, parry and riposte arc to be taken. Emphasis here is upon speed.

9.   Explanation and demonstration of new movements. This will give you a rest after the exertions of the speed exercise.

10.   Correction of the fundamental positions, reassembling and salute.

If it is desired to spread the following lessons over a period of three years, they should be divided as follows:

1st year:	Lessons 1-7.
2nd year:	Lessons 1-14.
3rd year:	Lessons 1-18.

It may be seen from the above that no fencer is so far advanced that he can afford to stop practicing fundamentals.

Lesson 1

1.   The foil
2.   Holding the foil
3.   Taking the guard position
4.   The advance; the retreat.
5.   Reassembling
6.   Finger-, wrist- and arm-play
7.   Extension of the arm; coming back on guard
8.   The lunge; recovery of the guard position
9.   Explanation of the lines
10. Explanation of the feint
11. Engagement in sixte; quarte; change of engagement and double change of engagement
12. The parry positions: sixte; quarte; low sixte; low quarte; tierce; prime; seconde; quinte
13. The straight thrust
14. Forward recovery of the guard position after the lunge
15. Explanation of the attacks
16. Reassemble and salute

NOTE: This lesson should be repeated until the student can execute all the movements with facility. It should be stressed for at least two weeks (three lessons per week).

Lesson 2

1.   The guard position, the advance, the retreat, the lunge.
2.   Explanation of the three simple attacks: the straight thrust, the disengage, the cut-over.
3.   Execute the above three simple attacks in two counts: feint straight thrust, lunge; feint, disengage, lunge; feint cut-over, lunge.
4.   Attack exercise: instructor will create openings for the pupil; the latter will take advantage of them by sight or touch, without verbal instruction. When the instructor opens a line, the pupil will lunge with a straight thrust; when the instructor presses or beats, pupil will disengage.
5.   Parry exercise:
    a. From engagement in sixte and upon disengage to quarte: parry quarte.
    b. From engagement in quarte and upon disengage to sixte: parry sixte.
    c. From engagement in sixte and upon disengage to low sixte: parry low sixte.
    d. From engagement in quarte and upon disengage to low quarte: parry low quarte.
6.   Explanation of the riposte.
7.   Attack exercise: the cut-over, executed as a single motion, developing the student's senses of sight and touch.
8.   Parry and riposte exercise:

Instructor's Attack	Pupil's Parry	Pupil's Riposte
a. From sixte, disengage (or cut-over)	Quarte	Straight thrust
b. From quarte, disengage (or cut-over)	Sixte	Straight thrust
c. From sixte, disengage (or cut-over)	Counter-sixte	Straight thrust
d. From quarte, disengage (or cut-over)	Counter-quarte	Straight thrust

9.   Parry and riposte exercise:

Instructor's Attack	Pupil's Parry	Pupil's Riposte
a. From sixte, disengage to low line	Low sixte	Straight thrust to low line
b. From quarte, disengage to low line	Low quarte	Straight thrust to low line

It should be realized that a parry should not be made from sixte to low quarte, or from quarte to low sixte, as the line attacked is left

64

open too long before the blade is deflected, and the defender may be touched in spite of his parry.

10. A counter-riposte exercise: Exercise #1.

11. A second counter-riposte exercise: Exercise #2.

12. The speed exercise, attacks: the straight thrust, ten times, to both lines. The instructor will leave open the line he desires the student to attack. If he wishes the student to lunge in sixte, he will move his blade to quarte; and so on.

13. The speed exercise, parry and riposte: five disengages to each line by the instructor; the pupil takes five sixte or five quarte parries, depending on the line in which the disengage ends, and ripostes with straight thrusts.

14. Explanation of the point in line; distance; deceiving a parry.

15. Reassemble and salute.

NOTE: The first and second lessons are the most important. The student should master all the movements included in them before he is allowed to pass on to the following lessons.

The three simple attacks, with the two simple and counter-parries, form the basis of fencing. In the speed exercises, the student's ripostes should be allowed to touch. When the instructor advances on his attack, the pupil should riposte without the lunge.

Lesson 3

1. The guard position, the advance, the retreat, the extension, the lunge.
2. Attack exercise: review the three simple attacks, executed as single-movements, developing the senses of sight and touch.
3. Parry and riposte exercise:

Instructor's Attack	Pupil's Parry	Pupil's Riposte
a. From sixte, disengage	Quarte	Disengage, low line
b. From quarte, disengage	Sixte	Disengage, low line
c. From sixte, disengage	Counter-sixte	Disengage, low line
d. From quarte, disengage	Counter-quarte	Disengage, low line

4. Explanation of compound attacks; two-movement attacks.
5. Attack exercise: execute some two-movement attacks, deceiving a simple or counter-parry, developing sight and touch.
6. Parry and riposte exercise:

Instructor's Attack	Pupil's Parry	Pupil's Riposte
a. From sixte, disengage	Quarte	Disengage, high line
b. From quarte, disengage	Sixte	Disengage, high line
c. From sixte, disengage	Counter-sixte	Disengage, high line
d. From quarte, disengage	Counter-quarte	Disengage, high line

7. A counter-riposte exercise: Exercise #2.
8. A second counter-riposte exercise: Exercise #2.
9. Speed exercise, attack: Pupil executes five disengages in quarte, five to sixte, five cut-overs to quarte, five to sixte.
10. Speed exercise, parry and riposte: Instructor will make five disengages and five cut-overs to each line; pupil will parry counter-quarte or counter-sixte, as required, and riposte with a straight thrust.
11. Explanation of the preparation to the attack; the beat; the press; the expulsion.
12. Explanation of, and distinction between, the 1-2 and the double.
13. Alternative exercise: five or ten minutes should be spent on one or two of the exercises in "Some Alternate Exercises".
14. Reassemble and salute.

NOTE: In Exercise #10 above, the speed exercise for the parry, the instructor should try to touch the pupil by progressively increasing the speed of his attack.

1. The guard position, the advance, the retreat, change of guard, the lunge.
2. Attack exercise: the three simple attacks, deceiving a change of guard.
3. Parry and riposte exercise:

Instructor's Attack	Pupil's Parry	Pupil's Riposte
a. From sixte, disengage	Quarte	Cut-over
b. From quarte, disengage	Sixte	Cut-over
c. From sixte, disengage	Counter-sixte	Cut-over
d. From quarte, disengage	Counter-quarte	Cut-over

4. Attack exercise: execute some two-movement attacks, deceiving a simple or counter-parry.
5. Parry and riposte exercise:

Instructor's Attack	Pupil's Parry	Pupil's Riposte
a. From sixte, 1-2	Quarte, sixte	Straight thrust
b. From quarte, 1-2	Sixte, quarte	Straight thrust
c. From sixte, double	Two counter-sixte	Straight thrust
d. From quarte, double	Two counter-quarte	Straight thrust

6. A counter-riposte exercise: Exercise #3.
7. A second counter-riposte exercise: Exercise #3.
8. Speed exercise, attack: execute the 1-2 ten times, starting five times from sixte and five times from quarte.
9. Speed exercise, parry and riposte: Instructor executes ten 1-2's as above; pupil parries quarte, sixte or sixte, quarte, as required, and ripostes with a straight thrust each time.
10. Explanation and execution of opposition.
11. Reassemble and salute.

NOTE: Beginning with the next lesson, the instructor, in the parry exercises, will have the student execute some preparation such as a beat or a press; the instructor will deceive this on his attack, which the pupil will then parry. For example, the pupil gives several beats in sixte; the instructor deceives any one of these, thus adding an element of surprise, by disengaging to the open line, in this case quarte. The pupil must parry quarte before riposting.

This exercise has several advantages. In the first place, the pupil will learn to beat or press without throwing his point ou t of line. In the second place, he will learn to come back to a parry immediately after being deceived by an attack. This exercise trains the pupil to react exactly as he should in fencing combat.

Lesson 5

1. The guard position, the advance, the retreat, the combination of the lunge with the advance and retreat.
2. Attack exercise: the three simple attacks with the advance, deceiving a beat.
3. Parry and riposte exercise:

Instructor's Attack	Pupil's Parry	Pupil's Riposte
a. From sixte, 1-2	Quarte, sixte	Disengage
b. From quarte, 1-2	Sixte, quarte	Disengage
c. From sixte, 1-2	Quarte, counter-quarte	Disengage
d. From quarte, 1-2	Sixte, counter-sixte	Disengage

4. Attack exercise: Student will execute some two-movement attacks with the advance, deceiving a simple or counter parry.
5. Parry and riposte exercise:

Instructor's Attack	Pupil's Parry	Pupil's Riposte
a. From sixte, double	Counter-sixte, quarte	Disengage
b. From quarte, double	Counter-quarte, sixte	Disengage
c. From sixte, double	Two counter-sixte	Straight thrust
d. From quarte, double	Two counter-quarte	Straight thrust

6. Counter-riposte exercise: Exercise #4.
7. Second counter-riposte exercise: Exercise #4.
8. Speed exercise, attack: Student will execute the double, five times in both lines.
9. Speed exercise, parry and riposte: on the instructor's attack five times in each line with the double, the student will make two counter-parries, and will riposte straight.
10. Explanation and execution of the bind, from high to low line.
11. Reassemble and salute.

In any lesson, when the parries are taken on the advance or the retreat, the parries up to the final one should be taken by opposition, that is, by contacting the opponent's blade without a beat and maintaining that blade outside the limits of the body. This opposition must be taken by the time that the advance or the retreat is completed.

Lesson 6

1. The guard position, the advance, the retreat, combination of the advance and the retreat with a change of guard.
2. Attack exercise: the three simple at tacks with the retreat, deceiving a press.
3. Parry and riposte exercise.

Instructor's Attack	Pupil's Parry	Pupil's Riposte
a. From sixte, beat, disengage	Quarte	1-2
b. From quarte, beat, disengage	Sixte	1-2
c. From sixte, press, disengage	Counter-sixte	1-2
d. From quarte, press, disengage	Counter-quarte	1-2

4. Attack exercise: Student will execute some three-movement attacks, deceiving two parries, simple or counter.
5. Parry and riposte exercise:

Instructor's Attack	Pupil's Parry	Pupil's Riposte
a. From sixte, 1-2-3	Quarte, sixte, quarte	Straight thrust
b. From quarte, 1-2-3	Sixte, quarte, sixte	Straight thrust
c. From sixte, 1-2-3	Quarte, sixte, counter-sixte	Disengage
d. From quarte, 1-2-3	Sixte, quarte, counter-quarte	Disengage

6. Counter-riposte exercise: Exercise #5.
7. Second counter-riposte exercise: Exercise #5.
8. Speed exercise, attack: Student will execute five attacks in each line with the disengage, cut-over, disengage.
9. Speed exercise, parry and riposte: on the instructor's attack with the disengage, cut-over, disengage, five times in each line, the student will parry sixte, quarte, sixte, or quarte, sixte, quarte, and will riposte with a disengage each time.
10. Explanation and execution of the false attack.
11. Reassemble and salute.

In this lesson, the student should retreat while parrying.

69

Lesson 7

1.   The guard position, the advance, the retreat, the combination of the advance and the retreat with a double change of guard.
2.   Attack exercise: the student will execute some two-movement attacks, deceiving a change of guard.
3.   Parry and riposte exercise:

Instructor's Attack	Pupil's Parry	Pupil's Riposte
a. From sixte, 1-2	Quarte, sixte	Circling cut
b. From quarte, 1-2	Sixte, quarte	Circling cut
c. From sixte, double	Counter-sixte, quarte	Disengage, low line
d. From quarte, double	Counter quarte, sixte	Disengage, low line

4.   Attack exercise: the student will execute some three-movement attacks, deceiving two simple or counter-parries.
5.   Parry and riposte exercise:

Instructor's Attack	Pupil's Parry	Pupil's Riposte
a. From sixte, 1-2-3, high, low, low	Quarte, low quarte, low sixte	Straight, low line
b. From quarte, 1-2-3, high, low, low	Sixte, low sixte, low quarte	Straight, low line
c. From sixte, double, disengage, high, low, low	Counter-sixte, low sixte, low quarte	Straight, low line
d. From quarte, double, disengage, high, low, low	Counter-quarte, low quarte, low sixte	Straight, low line

7.   Counter-riposte exercise: Exercise #6.
8.   Second counter-riposte exercise: Exercise #6.
9.   Speed exercise, attack: Student will execute the 1-2-3, five times in each line.
10.   Speed exercise, parry and riposte: on the instructor's attack with the 1-2-3, five times in each line, the student will parry quarte, sixte, quarte, or sixte, quarte, sixte, and will riposte with a disengage each time.
11.   Explanation and execution of avoidance, and the glide.
12.   Reassemble and salute.

In #10, the avoidance or derobement, the instructor should have his pupil deceive a beat, a press, an expulsion, a bind and a change of guard, by a feint disengage. In the instructor's execution of a double change of guard, the pupil should not react during the instructor's first movement, but should deceive the second movement by a feint disengage.

For the double in the low line, see "Some Two-Movement Attacks."

70

Lesson 8

1. The guard position, the advance, the retreat, the combination of the advance and retreat with a change of guard and a double change of guard.
2. Attack exercise: the three simple attacks preceded by a beat.
3. Parry and riposte exercise:

Instructor's Attack	Pupil's Parry	Pupil's Riposte
a. From sixte, disengage	Quarte	1-2, low line, high line
b. From quarte, disengage	Sixte	1-2, low line, high line
c. From sixte, disengage to low line	Low sixte	1-2, low line, high line
d. From quarte, disengage to low line	Low quarte	1-2, low line, high line

4. Attack exercise: the student will execute some three-movement attacks, low, high, low line, deceiving a half-circular parry and a simple parry.
5. Parry and riposte exercise:

Instructor's Attack	Pupil's Parry	Pupil's Riposte
a. From sixte, 1-2-3, low, high, low	Low sixte, sixte, low sixte	Disengage to high line
b. From quarte, 1-2-3, low, high, low	Low quarte, quarte, low quarte	Disengage to high line
c. From sixte, triple	Three counter-sixte	Disengage to low line
d. From quarte, triple	Three counter-quarte	Disengage to low line

6. Counter-riposte exercise: Exercise#7.
7. Second counter-riposte exercise: Exercise #7.
8. Speed exercise, attack: double, disengage, executed five times by the student in each line.
9. Speed exercise, parry and riposte: on the instructor's attack with a double, disengage, five times in each line, the student will parry counter-sixte, quarte, sixte, or counter-quarte, sixte, quarte, and will riposte straight in each case.
10. Explanation and execution of the tierce parry and riposte, and the attack on a preparation.
11. Execution of the bind and parry of the bind, from the high line to the low line, and vice versa.
12. Reassemble and salute.

In the tierce parry exercise, #10 above, the instructor should remain on the lunge or should retake the forward guard position in order to shorten the distance between him and the pupil. At this close distance, the student will parry sixte or tierce if the instructor's blade is on the right side; counter-sixte or counter-tierce, if on the left. The student should then riposte, maintaining the opposition, with his hand in tierce position.

Lesson 9

1. The guard position, the advance, the retreat, the combination of the advance and the retreat with a change and double change of guard.
2. Attack exercise: the three simple attacks preceded by a change of guard.
3. Parry and riposte exercise:

Instructor's Attack	Pupil's Parry	Pupil's Riposte
a. From sixte, 1-2	Quarte, sixte	1-2
b. From quarte, 1-2	Sixte, quarte	1-2
c. From sixte, double	Two counter-sixte	1-2
d. From quarte, double	Two counter-quarte	1-2

4. Attack exercise: the student will execute some three-movement attacks; he will begin the attack deceiving a change of guard by the instructor and two parries, simple or counter.
5. Parry and riposte exercise:

Instructor's Attack	Pupil's Parry	Pupil's Riposte
a. From sixte, double, disengage	Counter-sixte, quarte, sixte	Straight thrust
b. From quarte, double, disengage	Counter-quarte, sixte, quarte	Straight thrust
c. From sixte, double, disengage	Counter-sixte, quarte, counter-quarte	Straight thrust
d. From quarte, double, disengage	Counter-quarte, sixte, counter-sixte	Straight thrust

6. Counter-riposte exercise: Exercise #8.
7. Second counter-riposte exercise: Exercise #8.
8. Speed exercise, attack: the student will execute a cut-over, 1-2, five times in each line.
9. Speed exercise, parry and riposte: on the instructor's attack with a cut-over, 1-2, five times in each line, the student will parry quarte, sixte, quarte, or sixte, quarte, sixte, and will riposte with a disengage.
10. Explanation and execution of the cross and the envelopment.
11. Reassemble and salute.

In the parry exercises of this lesson, the instructor should tell his student to execute a change of guard, and then deceiving this change of guard, the instructor should begin his attack, which the student will then parry.

Also, the instructor should stop now and then in the middle of his attack, and stop his student at the same time. In this way he can check to see if the student is keeping his point in line as he parries.

73

Lesson 10

1. The guard position, the advance, the retreat combination of the advance and the retreat with the lunge, and with a forward guard.
2. Attack exercise: the three simple attacks preceded b, a double change of guard.
3. Parry and riposte exercise:

Instructor's Attack	Pupil's Parry	Pupil's Riposte
a. From sixte, beat, disengage	Quarte	Double
b. From quarte, beat, disengage	Sixte	Double
c. From sixte, press, disengage	Counter-sixte	Double
d. From quarte, press, disengage	Counter-quarte	Double

4. Attack exercise: the student will execute some three-movement attacks; he will begin his attack by deceiving a double change of guard by the instructor and two simple or counter-parries.
5. Parry and riposte exercise:

Instructor's Attack	Pupil's Parry	Pupil's Riposte
a. From sixte, triple	Three counter-sixte	Straight thrust
b. From quarte, triple	Three counter-quarte	Straight thrust
c. From sixte, triple	Three counter-sixte	Disengage
d. From quarte, triple	Three counter-quarte	Disengage

6. Counter-riposte exercise: Exercise #9.
7. Second counter-riposte exercise: Exercise #9.
8. Speed exercise, attack: the student will execute a cut-over (high line), 1-2 (low line, high line), five times in each line.
9. Speed exercise, parry and riposte: on the instructor's attack with the cut-over high line), 1-2 (low line, high line), five times in each engagement, the student will parry quarte, low quarte, and quarte (or vice versa if the attack starts from the quarte engagement), and will riposte straight.
10. Explanation and demonstration of the invitation to an attack, and redoubling.
11. Reassemble and salute.

Remember that counter-quarte parry can be executed only on a disengage starting from the quarte position, and counter-sixte from the sixte; in other words, you cannot go from sixte to counter-quarte, or vice versa. This will help in figuring out from what engagement the attack began.

To deceive a double change of guard, the student should keep in mind that he is to keep his foil stationary on the instructor's first change of guard, and will begin his attack by deceiving the instructor's second change of guard.

At first, the student should be taught to redouble with simple movements on simple attacks made by the instructor.

Lesson 11

1.   The guard position, the lunge, the forward guard, the retreat, and the advance.
2.   Attack exercise: the three simple attacks with the advance, deceiving a change of guard.
3.   Parry and riposte exercise:

Instructor's Attack	Pupil's Parry	Pupil's Riposte
a. From sixte, 1-2, low, high	Low sixte, sixte	Disengage
b. From quarte, 1-2, low, high	Low quarte, quarte	Disengage
c. From sixte, double	Two counter-sixte	Disengage, low
d. From quarte, double	Two counter-quarte	Disengage, low

4.   Attack exercise: the student will execute some three-movement attacks with the advance, deceiving the instructor's change of guard with the first feint, and then deceiving two simple or counter parries.
5.   Parry and riposte exercise:

Instructor's Attack	Pupil's Parry	Pupil's Riposte
a. From sixte, triple, low	Two counter-sixte, low sixte	Straight, low line
b. From quarte, triple, low	Two counter-quarte, low quarte	Straight, low line
c. From sixte, triple	Three counter-sixte	Disengage, low line
d. From quarte, triple	Three counter-quarte	Disengage, low line

6.   Counter-riposte exercise: Exercise #10.
7.   Second counter-riposte exercise: Exercise #10.
8.   Speed exercise, attack: the student will execute the triple, five times from each engagement.
9.   Speed exercise, parry and riposte: on the instructor's attack with the triple, five times from each engagement, the student will parry by three counter-sixte five times, or three counter-quarte five times, and will riposte straight in each case.
10.   Explanation and demonstration of the stop-thrust.
11.   Reassemble and salute.

At the very beginning, in teaching the stop-thrust, the instructor should start with a three-movement attack, on the advance, and should train his pupil to begin his stop the instant the instructor starts to raise his right foot for the advance.

Lesson 12

1. The guard position, the advance, the retreat, the change and double change of guard.
2. Attack exercise: the three simple attacks with the retreat, deceiving a change of guard.
3. Parry and riposte exercise:

Instructor's Attack	Pupil's Parry	Pupil's Riposte
a. From sixte, 1-2	Quarte, sixte opposition and the cross	
b. From quarte, 1-2	Sixte, quarte opposition and the cross	
c. From sixte, double	Counter-sixte, quarte opposition and the cross	
d. From quarte, double	Counter-quarte, sixte opposition and the cross	

4. Attack exercise: the student will execute some four-movement attacks, deceiving three simple or counter-parries.
5. Parry and riposte exercise:

Instructor's Attack	Pupil's Parry	Pupil's Riposte
a. From sixte, 1-2-3-4	Quarte, sixte, quarte, sixte	Straight
b. From quarte, 1-2-3-4	Sixte, quarte, sixte, quarte	Straight
c. From sixte, double, 1-2	Counter-sixte, quarte, sixte, quarte	Straight
d. From quarte, double, 1-2	Counter-quarte, sixte, quarte, sixte	Straight

6. Counter-riposte exercise: Exercise #11.
7. Second counter-riposte exercise: Exercise #11.
8. Speed exercise, attack: the student will execute the 1-2-3-4, five times from each engagement.
9. Speed exercise, parry and riposte: on the instructor's attack with the 1-2-3-4, five times from each engagement, the student will parry quarte, sixte, quarte, sixte (or vice versa), and will riposte straight each time.
10. Explanation and demonstration of the time-attack.
11. Reassemble and salute.

In the time-attack exercise, in the beginning the time-attack should be executed on a two-movement attack whose final movement ends in the right or outside line. The time-attack is more difficult to execute in the inside line.

77

Lesson 13

1. The guard position, the retreat, change of guard, advance, double change of guard, the lunge.
2. Attack exercise: the bind, in the four lines.
3. Parry exercise: parry the bind, in the four lines.
4. Attack exercise: execute some four-movement attacks preceded by a change of guard, deceiving three simple or counter-parries.
5. Parry and riposte exercise:

Instructor's Attack	Pupil's Parry	Pupil's Riposte
a. From sixte, triple, disengage	Two counter-sixte, quarte, sixte	Straight
b. From quarte, triple, disengage	Two counter-quarte, sixte, quarte	Straight
c. From sixte, 1-2-3-4	Quarte, sixte, quarte, counter-quarte	Straight
d. From quarte, 1-2-3-4	Sixte, quarte, sixte, counter-sixte	Straight

6. Counter-riposte exercise: Exercise #12.
7. Second counter-riposte exercise: Exercise #12.
8. Speed exercise: Alternative exercise #4, first without the lunge, and then with the lunge. Five minutes.
9. Explanation and execution of retaking the attack , and closing in on the opponent.
10. Reassemble and salute.

Lesson 14

1. The guard position, the lunge, the forward guard, the lunge, the advance, the retreat.
2. Attack exercise: the three simple attacks executed with a false attack.
3. Parry and riposte exercise:

Instructor's Attack	Pupil's Parry	Pupil's Riposte
a. From sixte, 1-2-3, low, high, high	low sixte, sixte, counter-sixte	Disengage, low line
b. From quarte, 1-2-3, low, high, high	low quarte, quarte, counter-quarte	Disengage, low line
c. From sixte, double to the low line, disengage, low	counter-sixte, low sixte, low quarte	Disengage
d. From quarte, double to the low line, disengage, low	counter-quarte, low quarte, low sixte	Disengage

4. Attack exercise: the student will execute some four-movement attacks preceded by a double change of guard, deceiving three simple or counter-parries.
5. Parry and riposte exercise:

Instructor's Attack	Pupil's Parry	Pupil's Riposte
a. From sixte, 1-2, deceiving a counter-parry, then disengage	Quarte, counter-quarte, sixte, counter-sixte	Straight
b. From quarte, 1-2, deceiving a counter-parry, then disengage	Sixte, counter-sixte, quarte, counter-quarte	Straight
c. From sixte, triple, disengage	Three counter-sixte, quarte	Disengage, low
d. From quarte, triple, disengage	Three counter-quarte, sixte	Disengage, low

6. Counter-riposte exercise: Exercise #13.
7. Second counter-riposte exercise: Exercise #13.
8. Speed exercise: Alternative exercise #5, first without the lunge, then with the lunge. Five minutes.
9. Demonstration and execution of the remise. The difference between the remise and redoubling should be brought out.
10. Reassemble and salute.

79

Lesson 15

1. The guard position, the double change of guard, the lunge, the forward guard, the retreat, and the advance.
2. Attack exercise: the three simple attacks preceded by a glide; then the three simple attacks preceded by an expulsion.
3. Parry and riposte exercise:

Instructor's Attack	Pupil's Parry	Pupil's Riposte
a. From sixte, triple to the low line, disengage to high line	Two counter-sixte, low sixte, sixte	Straight
b. From quarte, triple to the low line, disengage to high line	Two counter-quarte, low quarte, quarte	Straight
c. From sixte, 1-2-3, low, high, high, then deceiving a counter-parry	Low sixte, sixte, two counter-sixte	Straight
d. From quarte, 1-2-3, low, high, high, then deceiving a counter-parry	Low quarte, quarte, two counter-quarte	Straight

4. Attack exercise: the student will execute some four-movement attacks, deceiving the instructor's double change of guard, and then deceiving three simple or counter-parries.
5. Parry and riposte exercise:

Instructor's Attack	Pupil's Parry	Pupil's Riposte
a. From sixte, triple	Three counter-sixte	1-2
b. From quarte, triple	Three counter-quarte	1-2
c. From sixte, double, 1-2	Two counter-sixte, quarte, sixte	Straight
d. From quarte, double, 1-2	Two counter-quarte, sixte, quarte	Straight

6. Counter-riposte exercise: Exercise #14.
7. Second counter-riposte exercise: Exercise #14.
8. Speed exercise: Alternative exercises #8 and #9, first without the lunge, then with the lunge. Five minutes.
9. Execution of the time-attack.
10. Reassemble and salute.

Lesson 16

1. The guard position, the lunge, the forward guard, the retreat, the lunge, the guard position, the lunge, the retreat and the advance.
2. Attack exercise: the student will execute the three simple attacks, deceiving a double change of guard; then the same, deceiving an expulsion.
3. Parry and riposte exercise:

Instructor's Attack	Pupil's Parry	Pupil's Riposte
a. From sixte, 1-2-3	Quarte, sixte, quarte	Opposition and the cross
b. From quarte, 1-2-3	Sixte, quarte, sixte	Opposition and the cross
c. From sixte, double, disengage	Counter-sixte, quarte, sixte	Opposition and the cross
d. From quarte, double, disengage	Counter-quarte, sixte, quarte	Opposition and the cross

4. Attack exercise:

Instructor's Attack	Pupil's Parry	Pupil's Riposte
a. From sixte, feint 1-2	Quarte, sixte	Opposition and the bind
b. From quarte, feint 1-2	Sixte, quarte	Opposition and the bind
c. From sixte, feint 1-2, high, low	Quarte, low quarte	Opposition and the bind
d. From quarte, feint 1-2, high, low	Sixte, low sixte	Opposition and the bind

5. Parry and riposte exercise:

Instructor's Attack	Pupil's Parry	Pupil's Riposte
a. From sixte, 1-2, high, low	Quarte, low quarte	Opposition and envelopment
b. From quarte, 1-2, high, low	Sixte, low sixte	Opposition and envelopment
c. From sixte, double, low	Counter-sixte, low sixte	Opposition and envelopment
d. From quarte, double, low	Counter-quarte, low quarte	Opposition and envelopment

6. Counter-riposte exercise: Exercise #15.
7. Second counter-riposte exercise: Exercise #15.
8. Speed exercise: Alternative exercises #1,2, 3 and 4. Five minutes.
9. Execution of the stop-thrust on a two-movement attack accompanied by an advance. Explanation and execution of the double bind.
10. Reassemble and salute.

Lesson 17

1.   The guard position, the double change of guard with the advance and the retreat, and some slow-motion movements.
2.   Attack exercise: the student will execute some double binds, first from the sixte engagement, then from quarte.
3.   Parry exercise: the student will parry the double bind, in both high lines, by re-bending the arm and parrying with simple opposition on the instructor's final attack. The student will riposte with a disengage.
4.   Attack exercise: the student will execute some double binds, 1-2 in the high line, from both engagements.
5.   Parry and riposte exercise: on the instructor's attack with a double bind, 1-2, the student will parry by re-bending his arm and taking three simple parries by opposition. The student will riposte with a disengage. The attack should be made from both engagements.
6.   Counter-riposte exercise: Exercise # 16.
7.   Second counter-riposte exercise: Exercise # 16.
8.   Speed exercise, attack: the student will execute a double bind, disengage, five times from each engagement.
9.   Speed exercise, parry and riposte: on the instructor's attack with a double bind, disengage, five times from each engagement, the student will rebend his arm, take a simple opposition and a counter-parry. The pupil will riposte with a 1-2.
10.   Some parry and riposte exercise by the pupil while in the lunge position.
11.   Explanation and execution of the counter time-attack.
12.   Reassemble and salute.

In Exercise #3 above, it should be noted that the double bind is executed on the pupil's extended arm; it is therefore necessary for him to rebend his arm to meet the final movement of the double bind with opposition in the line in which the final movement will end.

82

Lesson 18

1. The guard position, the double change of guard during the retreat, the lunge, and some slow-motion movements.
2. Attack exercise: the student will execute the three simple attacks, deceiving a double change of guard during the retreat.
3. Parry and riposte exercise:

Instructor's Attack	Pupil's Parry	Pupil's Riposte
a. From sixte, disengage	Counter-sixte	Double
b. From quarte, disengage	Counter-quarte	Double
c. From sixte, cut-over	Counter-sixte	Double, low
d. From quarte, cut-over	Counter-quarte	Double, low

4. Attack exercise: the student will execute some four-movement attacks, deceiving a double change of guard during an advance.
5. Parry and riposte exercise:

Instructor's Attack	Pupil's Parry	Pupil's Riposte
a. From sixte, beat, 1-2-3-4	Quarte, sixte, quarte, counter-quarte	1-2
b. From quarte, beat, 1-2-3-4	Sixte, quarte, sixte, counter-sixte	1-2
c. From sixte, press, double, 1-2	Counter-sixte, quarte, sixte, counter-sixte	1-2
d. From quarte, press, double, 1-2	Counter-quarte, sixte, quarte, counter-quarte	1-2

6. Counter-riposte exercise: any of these exercises that have been giving difficulty.
7. Second counter-riposte exercise: any of these exercises that have been giving difficulty.
8. Speed exercise: Alternative exercises #8, 9 and 10.
9. Execution by the student of the time-attack on the instructor's attack with the double, first to the outside line, then to the inside line.
10. Some slow-motion movements for corrective purposes.
11. Reassemble and salute.

After the student has mastered these eighteen lessons, he may then be advanced to concentrate on the counter-riposte, the second counter-riposte and the alternative exercises; in addition, if more lessons are required, the student or the instructor can make up his own combinations.

It should be remembered, however, that the beginning lessons are the most important, for advanced students as well as beginners, and should be repeated over and over again. These beginning lessons contain instruction on the type of movements actually used in tournaments; the complicated three- and four-movement attacks and parries given in the latter lessons are little used in tournament play, and are intended solely to perfect the student's form, accuracy and timing

CHAPTER IX
Practical Advice

General Advice On The Bout

The following remarks pertain to the bout itself and should be useful to the fencer who is beginning tournament play. It would be advisable to re-read this paragraph from time to time.

Until you are an experienced strong fencer, stick to the book. That is, do not use unorthodox positions and movements until you have mastered the orthodox ones. The latter would not have become standard practice if they were not generally effective. From time to time, check your positions with the book. For example, if you are often touched through your parries, you may be justified in assuming that they are not being correctly executed; your hand may not have been enough to the side, or you may be omitting to maintain the opposition during your riposte.

While there are fencers who have achieved good results by concentrating on defensive play in the foil bout, it may be said in general that offensive play gives better results. Perhaps one reason for this is the fact that it takes less time for a point to penetrate a line that is open than it does for the hand or fingers to move to take a parry. This does not mean that you should attack all the time. Not only would your opponent soon solve your style, but you would become exhausted. Your style should be a judicious mixture of offensive and defensive play, with emphasis on the offensive.

When you attack, attack hard, with the greatest confidence and determination. The fear that most beginners have, that the opponent will pull a rabbit out of a hat, will <lo something to upset the attack, reveals a false attitude of mind. Against a properly executed simple attack there are no effective tricks. Once you have taken your opponent's blade you may go in with the knowledge that all he can do is to parry and riposte. If

you recover your guard position quickly, covering the line in which the parry was taken, you are reasonably safe.

Single-movement attacks, preceded by some preparation, arc the best in combat. To their execution, however, must be added a fine sense of timing and judgment of distance. Complicated attacks will generally be upset by slop-thrusts and time-attacks; they require too much planning and often lose their effectiveness through the confusion of the attacker himself. The best fencer the author has ever known personally used such simple play, straight thrusts, disengages, cut-overs preceded by beats, presses, opposition, and glides, interspersed with 1-2's, doubles and other two-movement attacks. When properly executed, nothing is more effective than these.

If your opponent will not respond to feints, try a false attack.

In the attack, the foil must not be held too tightly, for the fingers must not be contracted if they are to move freely. The arm when extended should be relaxed. Any stiffness in the arm or shoulder will cause the point to miss.

If your adversary retreats, recover your guard position forward, thus gaining the distance he has lost and facilitating your reprise attaque.

Keep moving. Do not freeze in any position for any length of time. Make yourself hard to hit by using short steps to change the distance between you and your opponent. In this manner you will make him misjudge and you will prevent him from getting set for an attack.

Do not "telegraph" your attack. If you will ·watch fencers engage in combat, you will find that there are many who give away their intention to attack by crouching a little lower, by tensing their body and arm, by leaning forward, and so forth. At all times that your opponent is within reaching distance, you should be tense without stiffness, in a perfect guard position ready for either attack or parry. Start from this position without give-away movements, with perfect economy of gesture, and you will find that your opponent never knows what to expect. At your slightest movement of finger and point, he will brace himself for an attack; he will be continually tensing and relaxing and will become tired. In addition, he will sometimes misjudge and will be relaxed instead of tense when you do attack, and his parry will be insufficient.

Do not remain on the lunge unless to redouble or remise, when you do recover, do so rapidly and with your feet at the normal guard distance, so that you will be able to lunge immediately if necessary, or to retreat. This correct position of the feet is often neglected in the excitement of a bout.

While the advancing attack is effective, you must learn to vary you r attacks so as to execute some without the advance. If your opponent is sure you will advance with every attack, he will soon learn to stop-thrust every time your right foot begins to move.

If you have made a feint or a series of feints without attacking, simply to feel out your opponent's reaction, do not proceed immediately afterward to go through exactly the same motions in a real attack, as your opponent will have had time to prepare himself for them.

In a wider application, never do the same thing twice in succession. If you have been successful in making a bind to the low line, let us say, do not do it again until you have tried something else; otherwise, your opponent will be waiting for you. On the other hand, if you will go one step further, you will generally be successful in an immediate repetition. Suppose you were to touch with a beat in quarte, disengage to sixte. Immediately afterward, try a beat in quarte, 1-2. Your opponent, determined not to let you do the same thing again, will probably throw everything he has into his sixte parry, permitting you to touch easily in quarte.

Without underestimating your opponent, try to keep one step ahead of him in the battle of wits.

Keep your eye on your opponent's hand. Observe whether he has the tendency to "telegraph" his attacks.

It is sometimes advisable to retreat against a superior opponent to avoid being touched; at other times, a retreat may be used to deceive the distance. In general, however, a fencer who always retreats will never gain confidc11ce in his parries and ripostes.

Against a fencer who reveals a strong wrist, (1) engage the blades foible to foible, since any pressure can be most easily neutralized at that point; the entire blade acts as a lever, the hand being the fulcrum, and the leverage will act in your favor; or (2) avoid any attack of his on your blade by deceiving his blade whenever possible; or (3) keep your blade in constant motion, so that he will be unable to dominate it.

In defensive play, the hand should be tensed only when actually taking a parry. If it is necessary to parry an attack of several movements, try to refrain from following your opponent's blade. Parry as late as you dare. The lack of response to his feints will weaken his attack. But if you must follow his blade several times, do it by tensing and relaxing the hand as many times as there are feints in the attack, and actually parry only on the final movement when the adversary lunges.

Vary your parries as much as possible in both lines so that your opponent will not be able to anticipate the position of your blade. Do not continually engage in sixte; if you favor one engagement, you will become weak in the parries on that side. By engaging sometimes in sixte and sometimes in quarte, you will develop your parries on both sides.

Against an adversary who redoubles or executes remises, riposte with a simple movement, such as a straight thrust or a disengage, in the high line.

Do not advance aimlessly into your opponent's point. Keep out of his reach until you are ready to attack; then close the distance rapidly and lunge.

Some fencers have acquired the habit of retreating to the end of the strip before deciding to launch their attack. Be prudent against such a fencer; take your time. When he approaches the encl of the strip, make a false attack; since he cannot retreat any more, he will be expecting an attack and will probably try a stop-thrust. This extension of his arm is just what you want. Take his blade with a beat, with opposition, or with a bind, and lunge.

To become a good fencer, two qualities are essential: (1) instantaneous judgment, which in turn requires good condition and well-tempered nerves; (2) muscular strength and speed.

Left-Handed Fencers

For left-handed fencers, the "inside" line is on the right, and the "outside" line is on the left of his left hand. The left-handed fencer will of course have to make his own adaptations to the directions given in this book. His counter-sixte parry, for example, will be made counter-clockwise, and his counter-quarte parry will be made clockwise, just the opposite of these movements as made by a right-handed fencer. "Left" leg will have to be substituted for "right" leg, and so on. The exercises and the lessons will have to be modified, for if a left-handed fencer is fencing against a right-hander, the right-hander should be in the engagement of quarte.

Generally, a left-handed fencer will prefer sixte guard to quarte. The left-hander usually has a strong and fast quarte parry and hence a right-hander should avoid this parry as much as possible in a bout with him. This quarte parry is executed in the sixte line of the right-hander, who is not accustomed to receive so strong a parry on that side and is therefore often disarmed, or his weapon is temporarily dislocated in his hand. The right-hander should make his attack end in the left-hander's outside line as much as possible.

The left-handed fencer also enjoys the advantage that he is accustomed to meeting right-handed opponents, but right-handers are not equally used to fight against left-handers, since most fencers are right-handed. The right-hander, match ed against a left-hander, will suddenly find everything reversed; to succeed in his attacks, he must be able to forget the routine order in which he practiced his attacks and must think out and execute his attack differently. A left-hander pitted against another left-hander, however, finds himself in the same predicament.

The best attack or riposte against a left-handed fencer is one terminating in sixte or low sixte. The right-handed fencer should avoid making his final attack movement in quarte.

A left-handed fencer will often riposte in the low line, so a right-hander should remember to keep his low line protected in a bout.

It is a good idea for a right-hander to go out of his way, if necessary, to get in a little practice with a left-hander; otherwise, he may find himself unpleasantly surprised in a bout.

Women Fencers

For some time, participation in fencing was followed exclusively by men. The error of this practice has been clearly demonstrated by the results that women have attained in intercollegiate, national and international meets. In general, a man fencer will defeat a woman fencer within their respective categories; but there are many women fencers today who can easily defeat many advanced men fencers.

In most competitive fencing, however, women will fence against women, in which case the muscular advantage that men enjoy is obviated.

In the opinion of the author, fencing is the most complete and attractive of all sports for women. The poise and suppleness of the female body lend themselves admirably to the requirements of fencing, and, on the other hand, the exercise followed in the guard position and the lunge will have beneficial results on carriage of the shoulders and hips. There is no more graceful sport than fencing, and none that will so effectively lead to grace in the participant. In addition, fencing will add to the self-confidence, will improve wind and judgment.

Women fencers practice the foil almost exclusively. The épée blade is too stiff and dangerous, and sabre is too rough. The woman's foil should have a #4 blade with a light guard and a light pommel. The fencing jacket should have some special aluminum breast protection for maximum security against injury.

Book II: The Épée

CHAPTER I
Preliminary Phases

The épée, or dueling sword, consists of a blade triangular in cross-section, broad at the forte and diminishing to a flattened round tip upon which is super-imposed a "pointe d'arret," and a mounting formed of three pieces: the guard, the grip and the pommel. The pointe d' ârret is composed of three sharp prongs whose function it is to make the touch more evident. In the electric épée, the point d'arret serves as an electric button which registers the touch.

For competition, the rules prescribe that the overall length of the épée must be less than 43.3 inches and its total weight, ready for use, less than 27 ounces.

The épées used in competition today exhibit the greatest possible variations within the limits prescribed by the rules. Out of ten épées it is seldom that two are found mounted in the same fashion. Many mountings in use today are not designed to give the best results.

For example, there is the question of the guard. A modern development is the off-center guard, where the perforation in the bell for the passage of the blade falls not at the center but about one-third of the distance from the inside edge of the guard. Thus, two-thirds of the bell are on the right of the blade and the grip, that is, they cover the outside line. While it is true that this gives increased protection to the outside of the forearm, the use of the correct sixte position will protect the hand and forearm quite adequately without displacing a goodly portion of the guard from the inside line. Since most attacks in épée are started from the inside line, the off-center guard leaves this line woefully weak.

Since, moreover, the off-center guard displaces the center of gravity, the point becomes harder to control, resulting in a lack of precision in both attacks and parries. In parrying counter-sixte, for example, or in moving from seconde to sixte, the point will tend to rise; and the hand must fight the off-center balance in taking quarte, counter-quarte, seconde and counter-seconde.

The center of gravity of the guard should fall in the axis of the épée itself, regardless of the angle of tilt of the guard, and regardless of what type of grip is used. The guard may be tilted at an angle, but it should not be off-center.

An épée of the following make-up will yield very good results:

Fig. 1 - The épée

1.   A blade of medium weight.

2.   A center-guard, within the limits prescribed by the rules.

3.   A grip 6 to 6 ½ inches in length, corresponding in shape to the French foil grip, but slightly larger; a pommel 1½ to 2 inches long.

4.   An oval aluminum wedge, 1 inch by ¾ inch, having a width of ¼ inch on one side and ⅛ inch on the other. This wedge is inserted in front of the épée guard, between the guard and the heel of the blade, the thicker part of the wedge toward the inside.

5.   A thin cushion or thumb pad between the guard and the grip.

The top of the grip should be slightly filed so that when the grip is in the hand, the higher part is on the right. There should be a difference of ⅛ to 3/16 of an inch between the two sides.

94

When assembled, the blade and grip should fall in the same prolongation and should both pass through the center of the guard. The blade will automatically fall slightly inside, approximately 1 to 1½ inches. The point will fall very slightly below the level of the heel of the blade at the guard.

This type of épée will protect the forearm perfectly without forcing the fencer to move his hand far to the right. If the épée is then held so that the forearm is in prolongation with the épée itself, the guard will be found tipped sufficiently to give perfect protection to the hand and forearm; the blade will fall slightly inside and down, and yet will be perfectly balanced and adapted for both parry and attack.

A General Discussion Of Épée Fencing

Of the three weapons, the épée has changed least of all through the years. It has never been, and probably never will be, so closely subjected to rules and regulations as the foil and the sabre. The épée is the living image of the duel. Since it is not so restricted by rules, it is more dangerous to handle, both for the fencer who has not received special instruction in épée and for the amateur who does not believe special instruction is necessary.

To learn to fence épée well, it is necessary to practice certain special movements until they become automatic-movements, moreover, that will not be useful in foil or sabre. A list of these movements follows.

1. The épée fencer must make almost all his attacks, parries and ripostes by opposition maintaining the blade. His guard is almost exclusively in the outside line, between sixte and low sixte. The foil fencer, however, does not limit his hand to any one guard, and uses attacks striking the blade as well as opposition.

2. Almost all the attacks in épée are directed to the arm.

3. Since in épée the guard position is taken with the arm almost fully extended, thereby shortening the distance

between the targets, the guard distance automatically becomes greater than in foil or sabre. If the foil or sabre guard distance were used, there would be no need to lunge to touch the arm.

4. The principal attacks used in épée are the stop-thrust, re-doubling and the remise; these are used sparingly in foil.

5. The weight of the épée requires more wrist-play than the foil.

These five distinctions serve to indicate how different épée is from foil and sabre. For a further discussion of this point, refer to Chapter VII, The Principle of the Épée.

In épée fencing, just as in the duel, all parts of the body and clothing of the adversary are valid targets. A hit anywhere counts, from the sole of the foot to the crown of the head.

Épée bouts are generally decided in three touches. The element of time, and not that of right of way, is of paramount importance. If two touches are scored, and there is an appreciable difference of time between them, only the first touch is counted. When there is no distinct time difference, or whenever the director has no clear opinion as to the priority, both touches are counted (a double touch). If the score is 2-1 and a double touch is awarded, the score becomes 3-2, and a full defeat is registered for the contestant with the lower score. If before the double touch the score was 2-2, both contestants receive a full defeat.

Only touches with the point count. Since épée movements are generally short and lightning fast, it is very difficult for the judges to see whether a thrust directed, for example, to the wrist reached with the point or was flat. Accordingly, a drop of red ink is usually placed between the prongs of the point d'arret; this will show up on the body of the contestant only if the hit was made with the point.

The use of the electric épée will obviate this difficulty. Only hits made with the point send an electric impulse to the scoring machine. The first touch to arrive, moreover, even if the difference of time is as short as $1/15^{th}$ of a second, closes the circuit to the other touch; the problem of time, of ten extremely difficult for the director to decide, is thus automatically solved by the electric épée.

The épée bout is fought on the same strip as the foil and sabre bouts. The jury is composed of a director or referee and four judges. The director stands midway between the two contestants, about four yards from the strip; the judges form a quadrangle about the contestants, one at each side of each contestant, at least a yard from him and behind him. The two judges flanking Fencer A will watch Fencer B, and the two flanking Fencer B will watch Fencer A.

The two contestants assume their places at the two ends of the strip. They are in the position preparatory to coming on guard. At the director's command to fall on guard, both execute the salute and fall on guard a short distance from the center of the strip. The director, after asking if the contestants are ready, gives the command "Fence!" The two contestants are now free to conduct their combat in any manner consistent with the rules of fencing. (For a full exposition of these rules, see the book "Fencing Rules" published in New York by the Amateur Fencers' League of America.) After any decisive phrase the director will call "Halt!" and call for a vote of the jury. Each of the four judges of the jury has one vote; he may vote on the materiality of any action, that is, whether any attack actually arrived. The director has 1 ½ votes; he is the only one who may vote on validity, that is, time. To the vote of the jury the director will add his own vote and render the decision. After the decision, the director will place the two contestants on guard again, and the play will continue in this manner until one of the two has scored two touches. At this point, the two contestants will change sides on the strip, when one of the two has scored three touches and the last decision has been announced, the contestants salute each other, remove their masks and shake hands.

There are several conventions regarding the flèche, which is much used in épée.

Flèche attacks ending in a collision that jars the opponent are classified as unnecessary roughness, and the touch, if any, is annulled.

The normal flèche, executed without a corps-a-corps, even if it involves running beyond the opponent, is not forbidden. The director may not call a halt so soon that the other fencer loses his right to an immediate riposte. A fencer who fails to hit on his flèche and crosses the boundaries of the strip in its execution must be penalized. If he crosses the boundaries of the strip, end or side, with both feet, he is warned once and thereafter during the course of the same bout is penalized one touch for each subsequent offense. A legitimate riposte against such an offending fencer counts, without prejudice to the warning. If the fencer executing the flèche does not score until he is off the strip, that touch does not count; it does count, however, if it is scored while the fencer is on the strip, even if he runs off afterward.

It may be seen, therefore, that while the flèche is allowed, its failure or improper execution is penalized.

It is proper here to introduce a brief digression on épée fencing in this country. The tendency has unfortunately been to subordinate épée fencing and to base its exercise on the principles of the foil. The author has always felt that the beginner does not have to learn the foil before he takes up the épée, although some coaches have this opinion; in fact, along certain lines the practice of the foil will be harmful to the practice of the épée. A good foil-man may, of course, become a good épée fencer; but such a fencer would have reached the same level in the épée without having first practiced the foil. The result of basing the practice of épée on that of foil is that the épée is the least understood of the three weapons in this country.

The practical value of special training in épée was strikingly shown years ago during the famous Dreyfus-Picard affair in France, from 1896 to 1903. This famous trial split Paris into two camps-one which insisted upon the innocence of Dreyfus, the other upon the integrity of the accuser, Picard. More than a thousand duels took place in France alone during this period.

In Paris at this time there was a fencing master, M. B., who specialized in épée. His claim that épée was a special art distinct from foil was opposed to the accepted opinion of the day. But when one of his pupils, a young unknown épée fencer, defeated in a duel one of the best foil-men of France, a great deal of attention was attracted to the claims of this presumptuous maitre d'armes; the matter even got into the newspapers, which hotly debated the question of épée vs. foil. During the time that the trial lasted, this fencing master's épée pupils succeeded in winning (in what was considered at that time a bizarre fashion) nearly all their combats, over 350 duels. A pupil would come to M. B- and tell him that he had to fight a duel in a day or two and ask for special instruction. M. B. had so much confidence in his distinctive technique that if his student lost, he would pay nothing for the instruction; if he won, on the other hand, he would pay for a year's membership in M. B.'s fencing club. This special technique proved so successful that M. B. soon left his old quarters for a larger salle and increased his staff from one assistant to five, who were kept busy day and night. M. B. was eminently successful because he was one of the first to initiate, in this period of foil predominance in France, the true, highly individualized principles of the épée.

Épée fencing has changed very little since M. B.'s time, except hat more importance is given to touches to the arm, more emphasis is placed on speed and effectiveness, and less on orthodoxy of movement.

Holding The Épée

The grip of the épée is held in such a way that it lies across the second phalanx of the index finger, with the convex curve of the grip against the palm. Place the ball of the thumb flatly on the wider upper surface of the grip near the épée guard; the other fingers will encircle the grip so that the third phalanx of each finger will be on the left side of the grip. The grip should be maintained firmly in the hand, but should be pressed strongly only at the moment of executing an opposition or a beat. The weight of the épée being much greater than that of the foil, it is even more important that the direction of the épée be maintained in line by the action of the last three fingers and the wrist.

Ordinarily, the grip is held in the center of the hand; the pommel is maintained against the forearm as much as possible. In the parries of tierce, seconde and quinte, where the palm is down, the pommel will have to be separated slightly from the forearm and will fall slightly to the right of the wrist.

Finger-, Wrist- And Arm-Play

In the attacks, the action of the thumb and index finger must predominate to direct the point of the épée, while the last three fingers and the wrist must be used to maintain the direction of the blade. Take care that an excessive relaxation of the last three fingers does not cause the point of the blade to deviate from its line. In any attack or parry along the low line, as well as in the tierce parry, however, the last three fingers must be relaxed more.

In the lateral parries of quarte and sixte, as well as in those in the low line, the action of the forearm is important. The main thing to remember is not to deviate too much from the line of sixte. The right arm, in the attacks and parries, should stay as close as possible to the line of sixte. In taking quarte parry, only the forearm should be displaced to the left , and then only slightly.

The counter-quarte and counter-sixte parries, on the other hand, are taken by the fingers and wrist. The seconde, tierce and quinte parries are made using both wrist and forearm. Low quarte (septime) and low sixte (octave) are executed using the wrist only.

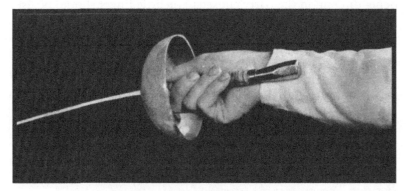

Fig. 2 - Holding the épée: the guard position or low sixte

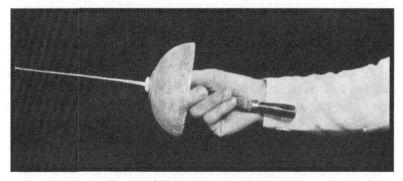

Fig. 3 - Holding the épée: sixte and quarte

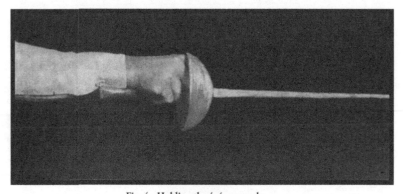

Fig. 4 - Holding the épée: seconde

The circular or counter-parries are made by squeezing and relaxing the last three fingers, and, with the help of the wrist, by describing a complete circle of the smallest possible circumference. The point will travel in a clockwise or counter-clockwise direction, depending upon the parry chosen. The little finger should be used to keep the pommel as close as possible to the forearm. In the low line parries, the little finger may be relaxed a little.

The wrist also comes into play in the bat, the press, the expulsion, the bind, the double bind, in seconde, quinte, tierce, in taking opposition, and in the half-circular parries.

The forearm should always be protected as much as possible behind the épée guard.

Position Preparatory To Coming On Guard

To take up the position preparatory to coming on guard, place the feet, heels together, at right angles to each other, the right toe pointing toward your opponent. Extend the right arm fully, obliquely downward and directly in front of the body, the épée in line with the arm. The thumb is at 1 o'clock. The point is a few inches from the strip. The head is facing front, and the body is turned well to the left. The left arm is extended fully and obliquely downward so that the hand is about fifteen inches from the left thigh. The palm of the left hand is turned upward in a natural manner.

The Guard Position

Coming on guard is executed in three counts, which are to be practiced until they flow into each other.

Count 1. Being in the preparatory position, raise the épée, keeping the arm extended, directly to the front and stopping the hand at the height of the chin. The nails are turned up slightly, and the épée is in a prolongation of the arm. The head is still facing front.

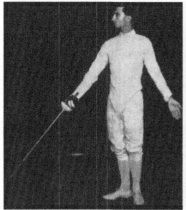

Fig. 5 - Position preparatory to coming on guard

Fig. 6 - The guard position

Count 2. Bend the arm until it is about three-fourths extended and at the same time lower it until it is now level with the right breast. The thumb is at 1 o'clock. The forearm is perfectly protected behind the épée guard. The point is slightly inside and slightly downward, level with the lower part of the épée guard. Simultaneously with the right arm, the left arm describes an arc upward to the rear and the elbow bends until the hand is at the height of the top of the head; the hand is arched.

Count 3. Bend at the knees, separating them; the right foot moves forward a distance approximately two shoe lengths from the left heel. The right leg from the knee down is almost perpendicular to the ground. A perpendicular dropped from the left knee will fall just inside the arch of the left foot. The two heels are in line, at right angles to each other. The body is erect on its haunches and presents as small a target as your physical make-up will allow.

Reassembling

Reassembling is the movement by which the fencer assumes, from the guard position, the position preparatory to coming on guard. To reassemble to the rear, (1) extend the right arm directly in front of you and drop the left as in Count 1of coming on guard; (2) at the same time, straighten out your knees

103

and move your right foot backward to its original place in the position preparatory to coming on guard; (3) drop your right arm to its place in the preparatory position.

To reassemble forward, follow the same movements except for (2), which consists of moving the left foot forward to the preparatory position.

Reassemble whenever the instructor gives a brief rest period during a lesson; at the end of your lesson, followed by a salute; and at the end of a bout, followed by a salute.

The Salute

Being in the preparatory position of the épée guard, bend the right arm, moving the hand (thumb at 3 o'clock) to the height of the chin, about five inches in front of it. The épée will then be vertical. Then lower the blade forward in an arc, slowly, while completely extending the arm and stopping when the point is about five inches from the strip. The hand is now directly forward, the nails are up and the blade is in a prolongation of the arm.

From this position, to salute to the left, raise the right hand back to the level of the breast, nails up, with the tip of the épée falling outside the left limit of the body at the height of the eyes. Turn the head to follow the blade.

From here, to salute to the right, turn the nails down, and move the right hand horizontally across the body to the right breast. The tip of the épée will then fall outside the right limit of the body at the height of the eyes. Turn the head to follow the blade.

The Advance

Since the épée fencer should be on the move at all times during the bout, the advance and retreat will of course play a very important role in his fighting. To advance, move the right foot forward and follow up with the left to the proper guard distance, without otherwise disturbing the guard position. The step is short and light; balance is not disturbed. Advance with caution. All movements of the arm should be coordinated with the foot movements, and must be completed with the completion of the advance.

The Retreat

To retreat, move the left foot to the rear and follow immediately with the right until the proper guard distance has been attained; the guard position is otherwise undisturbed.

During the retreat in an épée bout, the arm should be extended rather than bent back (as with the foil), since the retreat may be combined with a stop-thrust.

Jumping Forward

The jump forward is used as a quick, disconcerting means of shortening the distance, and, when used in conjunction with an attack, as a source of speed and power for the attack.

The jump forward should be very short, preferably less than fifteen inches. The shorter the distance covered, the faster the attack and the easier the maintenance of balance. At the end of the jump forward, both feet strike the strip lightly, simultaneously and flatly. The guard position is not otherwise disturbed.

Jumping Backward

The jump backward is used to regain the proper guard distance from the opponent. It is generally used, rather than the simple retreat, after a full lunge in which some distance was lost because of sliding, and in coping with a flèche attack. As in the jump forward, the feet strike the floor flatly and at the same time, and the guard position remains unchanged.

Foot-Signals

To execute the foot-signal, tap the strip lightly with the right heel and follow immediately with a heavier stamp of the entire right sole. The weight of the body is shifted slightly to the left leg. Do not otherwise disturb the guard position.

Use foot-signals to check your balance while on guard, or during a bout to attract the attention of the judges to the fact that you have a request to make.

Distance

In épée combat, the proper distance is such that with a full lunge you can touch your opponent in the middle of his forearm, and with a half-lunge on the wrist. Be careful that in the excitement of a bout you do not forget to maintain this distance.

Before a competition, test out your judgment of distance by taking a few full lunges against an opponent.

In practice, train yourself to maintain this distance at all times by following the advances and retreats of your partner with corresponding movements, until the maintenance of the proper distance becomes automatic with you.

Fig. 7 - Extension of the arm

Extension Of The Arm

Extend the arm horizontally without jerking and without moving the shoulder. The nails will be up, the thumb at 1 o'clock. The épée will be in a prolongation of the arm and on a level with the shoulder: the point will be directed two or three inches above that part of the target where it is desired to touch. The body rests firmly upon its haunches. The arm should be extended without muscular contraction; there should be no stiffness.

Coming Back On Guard After Extension Of The Arm

To come back on guard, bend the arm without jerking and without moving the shoulder, and take up the correct guard position.

The Thrust

The thrust is the carrying of the point of the épée to the target. It is made with opposition, that is, by simultaneously closing the line in which the attack terminates. The opposition is taken by moving the right arm slightly to the right or left during the execution of the thrust, depending upon whether the thrust is given to the outside or inside line.

In épée, the thrust is more precipitate, more sudden, than in the foil. It is most frequently directed to the nearest part of the target, the hand, cuff, arm or leg. The thrust is usually directed to the body only as a riposte or as a special attack called the "flèche" or "rush."

The Lunge

The lunge is the extension given to the guard position in an at· tempt to touch the opponent. To lunge, first extend the right arm as indicated above. Then snap open the left leg until it is fully extended, keeping the sole pressed flat against the strip; simultaneously move the right foot forward, skimming closely over the strip such a distance that when the right sole lands flat on the strip, the right leg from the knee down will be perpendicular to the floor and also in line with the left heel. At the same time, sweep the left arm down, stopping it about fifteen inches from the left thigh, palm up and fingers extended. The body will rest firmly on its haunches and will be slightly forward. The left shoulder is pulled back as much as possible, and the hips are in a line coincidental with the line of the lunge.

Proportion your lunge to the distance to be covered. If the distance is short, use a half-lunge; if long, use the full lunge. Lunges in épée are usually shorter than lunges in foil, closer to half-lunges; but even in these half-lunges the left leg should be snapped fully open, as the speed and force of the lunge come chiefly from this action.

Fig. 8 - The lunge

Recovery Of The Guard Position After The Lunge

The recovery of the guard position after the lunge is, like the lunge, a combination of distinct movements of arms, body and legs that must be mastered to split-second timing to be effective. In the lunge position the weight of the body is slightly forward. The first movement of the recovery is the bending of the left leg and the flexing upwards of the left arm; these simultaneous movements start the body weight backwards. Immediately after, the right foot pushes against the strip, thus completing the shifting

108

of the weight to the rear, and the right foot skims backwards over the strip to its original guard position. After all these movements are completed—and not before—the right arm bends back to the guard position.

The maintenance of the extension until the recovery is complete keeps the line closed and makes it difficult for your opponent to riposte. This seemingly minor point is very important, and is one of the chief points of difference between the épée and the foil.

It is also possible to recover the guard position forward after a lunge. Such a recovery will gain for you any distance lost by the opponent during his retreat. The occasional use of this movement will disconcert your opponent. In the forward recovery, the weigh t of the body is held forward on the right leg, which does not move, while the left leg is brought forward to the proper guard distance.

The Lines

The lines are those parts of the body where definite parries are made and to which attacks and ripostes are directed.

Since these lines are relative to the position of the hand, this position will be determined first. In foil, where both sixte and quarte guard positions are permissible and the body is the only target, the hand is arbitrarily set in the center of the body to fix the lines; in épée, however, only the sixte guard position is recommended, and the position of the hand to set the lines for épée is more to the right, at a point directly above the right knee at the height of the right breast. Everything above that hand will be the high line; the portion of the target below that hand will be the low line; the target to the right of the hand will be the outside line; to the left, the inside line. Since the hand is set to the right of center and since in épée the arm is more extended than in foil, there will obviously be very little of the target in the outside line. In Chapter V, it will be seen that each of these quadrangles—

109

outside high, outside low, inside high and inside low—has its appropriate parries.

	Outside Line	Inside Line	
High			Line
Low			Line

Fig. 9 - The lines

The Point In Line

When the arm is extended and the point is in the direction of the target, the point is then said to be "in line."

With the foil and sabre, the extension of the arm with the point in line generally confers the right of way upon the fencer who takes this action; all other things being equal, the right of way will decide the priority of one touch over another. This is not so with the épée; time is the only valid factor. The first touch to arrive is the only one allowed, regardless of the action preceding it.

Engagement

Engagement consists in contacting the adversary's blade three or four inches under his point with the foible of your own blade, the body being in the guard position.

Engagement is recommended only during the early stages of instruction, in order to facilitate the task of the instructor. During the actual bout the arm should be protected as much as possible behind the épée guard, which means that engagement will be voluntarily abandoned. The engagements recommended for purposes of instruction are those of sixte and quarte.

The Engagement In Sixte

Contact the adversary's blade on the outside of his blade and maintain it outside the limit of your right arm. Your hand is level with your right breast. Your thumb is at 1 o'clock. Your right elbow is inside. Your point is level with your right shoulder. In this position, your outside line is kept closed.

The Engagement In Quarte

Contact the adversary's blade on the inside of his blade and move your hand only slightly to the left. Your thumb is still at 1 o'clock. Your elbow has not moved, your point only a few inches to the left. In this position, your inside line is kept closed.

Change Of Engagement

The change of engagement is the passing of your point under your adversary's blade from sixte to quarte or vice versa; the trajectory of the point is as short as possible.

The change of engagement is not recommended except for instruction, as no contact of the blades is advised for the épée bout.

CHAPTER II
Simple and Compound Attacks

The Feint

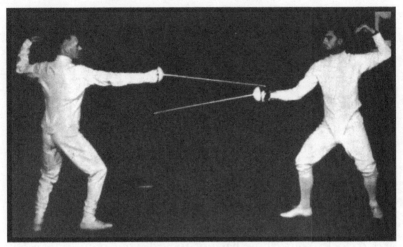

Fig. 10 - Feint to the wrist

The feint is a stimulation of an attack made by extending the arm without lunging, in order to force the opponent to take a parry.

Whether the feint is in the high or low line, the arm should be in almost the same position, that is, with the hand held high enough to keep the forearm protected by the bell. The point can be high or low, according to the direction desired, and is controlled by the fingers. Care must be taken that perfect balance is maintained at all times. The body should be erect, left shoulder back, and the arm extended without exaggeration.

In a compound attack made with an advance or a retreat, the feint or feints must be executed simultaneously with the foot movements.

It is a good practice to make some feints at the beginning of a bout to "feel out" what kind of fencer your opponent is, to discover whether or not, for example, he will respond to a feint, and to decide where, against that particular adversary, you will find your best openings.

Remember that as soon as your arm is extended, you are in the attack position.

Many touches are scored without lunging, that is, by a feint, since the target is much closer in épée than in foil.

The Attacks

The attack is that movement or combination of movements by which the fencer seeks to touch his adversary. Attacks are either simple or compound; simple attacks are single-movement attacks, compound attacks are multiple-movement attacks in which the final movement is preceded by at least one feint.

The attack may be made in place or may be combined with some foot movement, such as the lunge, the half-lunge, the jump, the advance or the retreat. It may be executed after one or several changes of guard, after a preparation, or after a parry. When executed immediately after a parry, the attack takes the name of a return or riposte. In every case, however, the fencer must have his point in the final line and his right arm extended before lunging, the point two or three inches above the part of the target it is expected to touch.

The following suggestions should be kept in mind:

1. During the attack the forearm should be fully protected behind the épée guard by keeping the arm in the same direction as the hand. Take a light opposition also on the same side as that on which the opponent's blade is located until your point reaches its destination.

2. Direct the point by the action of the first two fingers.

3.   To avoid a double touch, prepare your attack by using some movement such as the false attack, to make sure that your adversary will not attack you at the same time.

4.   When you precede your attack by a preparation, you must be ready to go back to the defensive in case your opponent should decide to launch his attack by deceiving your preparation.

5.   In executing a two-movement attack, you should not make the first feint so pronounced as in the foil, as you would be inviting a stop-thrust to the arm.

6.   Do not attempt attacks to the low line (to the leg and foot) except when an element of surprise is certain. Single-movement attacks to the low line should be preceded by a beat in sixte or in tierce, and two-movement attacks should be preceded by a feint to the high line before disengaging to the low line.

7.   Attacks to the body should be executed as flèche attacks and these, whenever possible, should be directed to the upper part of the right arm or shoulder and only as a last resort to the body.

In fact, one rule for developing the best technique for the épée is to concentrate on touching the nearest part of the target exposed. Occasionally, you may touch to the body, as on the short distance or on the riposte, where it is less likely that you will be stopped. Otherwise, it is dangerous to aim your attacks to the body.

The Straight Thrust

The straight thrust is a thrust executed without any change in line. It is executed by extending the arm and lunging to touch with opposition. Since in the sixte guard the inside line is always left open, it is possible to execute a straight thrust to the inside high line, to the upper part of the arm, body or mask, whether or not you take your opponent's blade.

114

When your adversary maintains his sixte guard, the straight thrust should be given without bothering to take his blade. When the adversary leaves his sixte guard to close his inside line or to move his hand more toward the center of his body, the straight thrust should be preceded by a beat, press, expulsion, or by opposition.

Fig. 11 - Disengage to underside of forearm, hand in seconde position

The Disengage

The disengage is an attack ending in a line other than that of the engagement. To execute the disengage, use your fingers and wrist lo direct your point through the shortest possible distance to the line in which you expect to touch, extending your arm as in the straight thrust. Lunge and touch with opposition.

Since disengages to the low line (underside of the forearm, leg and foot) expose the attacker's forearm during the execution, such disengages should be used only for surprise attacks. They should be preceded by a beat in sixte or in tierce.

To execute the disengage under the forearm, which is a special attack, turn the hand to the position of seconde before

115

extending the arm. In this attack, when the hand is in the position of seconde, the point should be directed by the help of the wrist, which will then of course have to be bent upward.

The Cut-Over

While the cut-over can be executed with the épée, it is not recommended, as it exposes the forearm too much and invites a stop-thrust.

Two-Movement Attacks

The following are some examples of two-movement attacks:

1. Deceiving a simple parry: This attack will consist of a feint straight thrust followed by a disengage, deceiving a simple parry in the high or low line.
    a. Feint straight thrust to the inside line, disengage to the outside or underside of the forearm, arm or shoulder.
    b. Feint straight thrust to the outs.de line, disengage to the inside or underside of the arm or shoulder.
    c. Feint straight thrust to the inside line, disengage to the underside of the forearm or to leg.
    d. Feint straight thrust to the outside line, disengage to the underside of the forearm or to leg.
2. Deceiving a counter-parry: This attack will consist of a feint straight thrust followed by a disengage, deceiving a counter-parry in the high or low line. The attacks in (1) above can be used if the opponent takes a counter-parry instead of a simple parry.
    a. Feint straight thrust to the arm, disengage to the arm.
    b. Feint straight thrust to the arm, disengage to the underside of the arm, turning your hand in the seconde position.
    c. Feint straight thrust to the forearm, disengage to the leg.

116

3.   The 1-2: The 1-2 is an attack consisting of a feint disengage followed by a disengage, deceiving a lateral parry. (Remember that the word "feint" applies only to an arm movement, hence there is no lunge; "disengage," however, implies a lunge.)
   a. Feint disengage to the mask or body, disengage to leg. (Or, vice versa, feint to leg, disengage to body or mask.)
   b. Feint disengage to arm, disengage to leg (or vice versa).
   c. Feint disengage to the outside line, disengage to the inside line (or vice versa).
   d. Feint disengage to the low line, disengage to the low line.

These movements may also be executed without deceiving a parry, if your opponent made no attempt to parry your feint.

4.   The double: The double consists of a feint disengage followed by a disengage, deceiving a counter-parry in the same line.
   a. Feint disengage to the inside or outside line, followed by a disengage to the forearm, arm or shoulder, deceiving a counter-quarte or a counter-sixte parry.
   b. The double to the low line. A feint disengage to the imide or outside line, followed by a disengage to the low line, deceiving a counter-parry in the high line.
5.   The bind, disengage: This is a feint bind, followed by a disengage, deceiving a simple parry.

Three-Movement Attacks

Three-movement attacks are not recommended in épée, but if you wish to practice some to improve your timing, use a two-movement attack as a feint and follow immediately with a simple attack. Three-movement attacks, then, consist of two feints followed immediately by a simple attack.

CHAPTER III
Preparations to the Attack

Preparations To The Attack

The preparation to the attack is the movement or movements made before the attack to assure its greater success. Preparations are all begun with the arm three-fourths extended; in some, the arm will finally be completely extended. They may be made from the guard position or during an advance or retreat.

The preparations in which the arm is kept three-fourths extended include the change and double change of guard, the beat, the press, opposition and the invitation to the attack. Those in which the arm is finally completely extended include the expulsion, the glide and the feints of the various attacks.

These preparations must be used with great prudence, as the fencer who uses too many preparations to his attack or who uses them continually will be met by a stop-thrust.

Preparations Striking The Blade: The Beat; The Expulsion

Preparations striking the blade are those executed by contacting the adversary's blade sharply in order to deflect with force a threatening point or to facilitate an attack by strongly opening a line. The contact is not maintained.

The beat: The beat is a quick sharp blow executed with the middle of your blade against the opponent's foible, so as to open a line for your attack. It is executed chiefly by the action of the fingers and wrist. The blade remains where the beat was given, while the beat can be given in all lines, it is used in épée chiefly to open the line allowing a touch to be made to the forearm or leg.

The beat should be strong when it is to be followed by a straight thrust, in order to open the line sufficiently; it should be light when it is to be followed by a disengage, in order to avoid placing your adversary's blade in the line in which you are finally going to attack.

If your adversary answers your beat, disengage immediately.

The arm should not be extended with the beat, for if your beat is deceived, you will no longer be in a position to take a parry. An exception can be made in the case of the beat, straight thrust, however; here, whether the beat is deceived or not, the attack should continue. If your arm is extended and your point has not gone out of line, you are at least on equal footing with your opponent in regard to time.

Since a beat opens a line strongly, any beat given by your adversary must be answered by a heat, so as to close the line opened.

If the beat is executed with a change of line, it takes the name of "counterbeat."

On a feint to the inside high line, the beat in seconde position may be used to cut the opponent's line, sending his blade past the outside low line; this breaks up his attack and exposes his forearm.

If you wish to continue with an attack, after such a beat in seconde, there are two very effective possibilities: either continue with a straight thrust to the underside of the forearm, or disengage to the sixte position, turning the nails up, and touch in the outside high line.

The expulsion (froissement): The expulsion is a sharp, continually increasing, slightly diagonal pressure exerted with the middle of the blade all the way down the opponent's blade from his foible to his forte, resulting in the expulsion of his blade from the line and opening up a line of attack. At the end of the movement the arm is extended. The expulsion is executed against an extended arm. It may be made in the line of engagement or with a change of line (counter-expulsion).

119

During the execution of the expulsion, be careful to keep your point in line as much as possible; in making this movement it is very easy to have your point go far beyond the limit of the target.

If the expulsion is accompanied by an advance or a retreat, it should be completed simultaneously with the foot movement.

A beat may be executed against an opponent who keeps his point either above or below his épée guard, but an expulsion can be made only against a point that is above the guard.

Since the expulsion tends to open up the line strongly, the natural reaction of your opponent is to try to come back to his original position. When this reaction begins, take advantage of it by disengaging. If the reaction does not begin immediately, make a straight thrust.

Both the beat and the expulsion require a strong wrist. Since the element of surprise is an important factor in their successful execution, be careful not to "telegraph" them by drawing back the hand, arm or blade, or by any other movement.

It is not necessary to be in contact with the opponent's blade in order to give a beat or expulsion.

Both these movements may be learned by practicing with a partner an alternative exercise consisting of consecutive beats and expulsions.

Preparations Maintaining The Blade: The Press; Opposition; The Glide

Preparations maintaining the blade are those in which contact is made with the adversary's blade without shock and is maintained for an appreciable length of time. They are used to push aside a threatening point and to facilitate an attack.

The press: The press is a pressure exerted against the foible of the adversary's blade in order to remove it from line, once contact of his blade has been established. It should be executed

120

smoothly, not jerkily, and without warning the adversary in advance by any conspicuous finger- or wrist-play. The épée will remain at the place where the press was given and the position of the arm will remain the same. As with the beat, it is intended to open the line of engagement, and if the adversary responds, to take advantage of his response by disengaging.

The press may also be used after an opposition or a glide. It can be made in the line of the engagement or with a change of line (counter-press).

The same system of alternative exercises as with the beat and expulsion may be used to learn the press. The press is done properly when it is executed with alternative pressure, relaxation, pressure, relaxation of the hand.

Fig. 12 - Low quarte opposition, straight thrust to leg, executed at the beginning of an attack to low line

Opposition: Opposition is the maintenance of the adversary's blade outside the limits of the target by exerting continual and sufficient resistance to his blade. Contact is made without a beat.

Opposition is very important in épée. Most of the parries in épée are taken by opposition, and most of the attacks rely on

121

the opposition taken to protect the forearm from a stop-thrust during their execution.

You should precede your attack, against an opponent who has his arm in a normal épée guard position, by taking a light opposition with a lateral or circular movement; in other words, by a light simple or counter-opposition. If your adversary's arm is bent more than normally, it is unwise to take opposition, as then you will have to take it with your foible and will have difficulty controlling his blade.

Against an opponent who is beginning his attack, the best time to take your opposition is the moment when he is extending his arm.

If your opponent does not answer your opposition, execute a straight thrust; if he does, disengage.

Opposition is most useful against an opponent who does not wish to attack or against one whose strength lies in his parry and riposte.

The glide (coule): The glide is like the feint of a straight thrust, but is made with contact of the opponent's blade. Slide your blade forward along your adversary's blade by extending your arm. At the end of the glide, your forte should be at the middle of his blade, so that you will be able to overcome his opposition.

Since in épée engagements are not recommended, contact will have to be made with the adversary's blade before the glide can be executed.

If your opponent answers your glide by an opposition, disengage.

If he does not answer your glide, continue and touch.

The Invitation To The Attack (Absence D' Épée)

An invitation is a deliberate, exaggerated opening up of a line so as to encourage an adversary to attack in a line in which

122

you wish him to attack. It should he made with extreme care. The invitation is useful against an opponent who does not wish to attack or one who is stronger on the defensive than the offensive.

Fig. 13 - Invitation to the attack, hand in position of quinte

Fine precision and an accurate sense of distance and timing are necessary to execute the invitation successfully. In effect, you are pitting your judgment against that of your opponent. He knows what you are doing. He will not attack until he believes that you have misjudged, that you have made the invitation too wide to be able to defend yourself in time. It is up to you to make him believe so, without actually passing the thin margin of safety.

Against a man who uses the invitation, precede your attack with a false attack or with some preparation in order to make his blade return to its normal position.

Closing In On An Opponent (Se Loger)

You close in on your opponent by any series of movements which drives the point of your épée closer and closer to your adversary's target, so as to make his parry of your final attack more difficult and to assure the ultimate success of your attack.

123

Deceiving The Preparation To The Attack: The Avoidance; The Attack On A Preparation

The preparation to an attack may be deceived by either of two methods: by removing your blade from your opponent's control, or by a surprise attack as he begins his attack.

Avoidance (derobement): Avoidance is the deception of the opponent's blade by a feint disengage just at the moment he starts to execute a preparation for his attack. At the end of the avoidance your arm is extended.

Avoidance may also be used as an exercise, student versus student.

The attack on a preparation; The attack on a preparation is one which is begun from a state of complete immobility in such a way as to surprise the adversary in the preparation of his own attack. It may be used against any preparation, against any feint outside the body, and against an opponent who closes in. It is generally made by a simple movement, whether or not it is preceded by a preparation.

CHAPTER IV
Special Attacks

The False Attack

The false attack is a preparatory attack, usually of one or two movements, made without any intention of touching the opponent. It is accompanied by a simulated lunge; the right foot is brought forward a short distance. Some of the possible alternatives are:

1. If your opponent does not respond to your false attack, complete the lunge with a straight thrust or a disengage to the low line.

2. If he responds to your false attack by taking a simple or counter-parry, deceive this parry by a disengage to the high or low line (underside of forearm or knee).

3. If he responds by taking a parry and then making a riposte, parry and then counter-riposte by a simple movement, or use a stop-thrust just as your opponent is beginning his riposte.

The false attack is especially valuable to use at the beginning of a bout in order to "feel out" the strength and the ability of your opponent. In fact, it is recommended that any bout against a new opponent be begun with a false attack.

It is also useful against an opponent who fights exclusively on the defensive, relying on the stop-thrust; the false attack will provoke a reaction from him without unduly exposing the attacker.

The false attack, of course, can be preceded by a preparation, such as a beat or a press.

If your opponent does not respond to the false attack, you may fall back on guard so as to make a second false attack from a closer distance. If he again fails to respond, you will now be more certain that your straight thrust or disengage to the arm or leg will reach.

Take extreme care to protect yourself during the false attack from a stop-thrust to the arm from your opponent.

The Stop-Thrust (Coup D' Arrêt)

The stop-thrust is a straight thrust executed with or without a lunge against your opponent's attack, with the intention of scoring a touch cleanly before your opponent's touch lands.

The stop-thrust is one of the most important attacks in épée, as almost any attack of the opponent can be stopped. Its correct execution requires a great deal of coolness and precision. It should be used whenever the opportunity arises, that is, whenever your opponent leaves a line open during his attack, even if only for a short time, and against an advancing attack.

In order to avoid a double touch, it is necessary that the stop-thrust (which is always executed as a straight thrust to the nearest part of the target) be begun the moment your adversary begins to raise his right foot for his advance, or the moment he begins his attack.

In certain circumstances, a special kind of stop-thrust is possible. If your opponent should attack low, that is, the leg or foot, reassemble backward out of reach, straightening both legs, extending the arm at the same time, and leaning slightly forward; direct your point to his arm, shoulder or mask.

Or, if the attack is to the underside of the forearm, straighten both legs without bothering to carry your right foot backward, extend your arm at the same time, and, leaning slightly forward, direct your point to his arm.

It is preferable to direct the stop-thrust to the upper surface of the forearm, the arm, shoulder or mask, as these portions of the target are closest. Remember that the stop-thrust

126

to the forearm requires fine precision, and necessitates special training.

When the stop-thrust is executed on a riposte or a counter-riposte, it is called a remise.

On any attack in the low line, it is better to use the stop-thrust than to parry and riposte, since the parries in the low line open the line too much and in addition are more difficult to execute.

The Counter Stop-Thrust

The counter stop-thrust is a stop-thrust executed on your adversary's stop-thrust. It should be made with opposition. For example, you make a false attack to the arm or leg; and your opponent tries to stop you; you disengage and counter-stop to the arm. Or, on your feint 1-2, if your opponent tries to stop you with a straight thrust, extend your arm with opposition and counter-stop to the arm.

Like the stop-thrust, the counter stop-thrust can be taken with a lunge or a half-lunge.

The Time-Attack

The time-attack is an attack which fulfills at the same time the functions of parry and riposte, by extending the arm as much as is necessary to touch and at the same time closing the line where the attack of the adversary ought to terminate.

The time-attack is practical with the foil but not recommended for épée, since it is more difficult to execute with the latter weapon. A time-attack well-made is a beautiful attack, but few fencers are able to use it effectively. It is very risky to use during the bout. A good simple attack, with or without a preparation, is generally better than a time-attack.

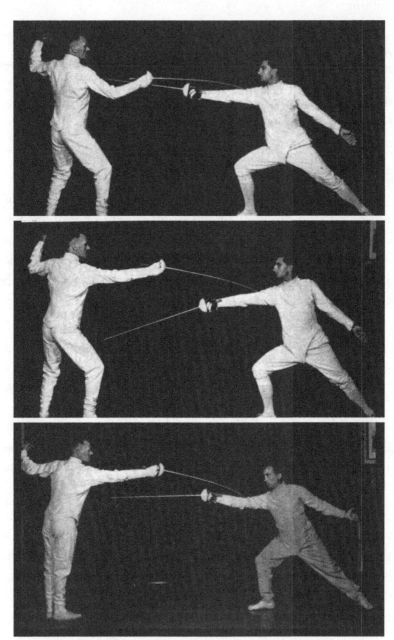

Fig. 14(Top) - Stop-thrust with quarte opposition against an attack to the
inside of the arm
Fig. 15(Center) - Stop-thrust on a disengage to leg
Fig. 16(Bottom) - Reassembling backwards wtih the stop-thrust to arm, against
against a disengage to low line

128

Fig. 17 - Straightening both legs with the stop-thrust inside the arm

Fig. 18 - The counter stop-thrust executed against a stop-thrust

The Counter Time-Attack

A counter time-attack is one made against an adversary about to execute a stop-thrust or a time-attack. Itis easier to execute a counter time-attack in épée than a time-attack.

A counter time-attack follows any provocation which makes your opponent take a time-attack; and on his time-attack, you make a simultaneous parry and counter-riposte, maintaining the opposition. For example, on your false attack, say a 1-2 (quarte, sixte), your opponent tries to touch you by extending his

129

arm with sixte opposition. Bend back your arm slightly, take sixte opposition, and make a straight counter-riposte to his arm.

Redoubling

Redoubling is a second attack made from the lunge position immediately after your opponent has parried but failed to make a riposte. You can redouble in two ways: (1) By retaking the blade with a beat and seeking to touch by a straight attack, a disengage, or a compound attack; (2) Without retaking the blade, and seeking to touch by a disengage or by a compound attack.

The redouble is always directed to the nearest part of the target.

In épée, no distinction of validity should be made between re-doubling and the remise, since time is the only criterion of the validity of any touch. ·whenever your attack misses, always try to replace your point. Regardless of whether your opponent parries, ripostes or does not riposte, try to touch again immediately, directing your attack to the upper or lower part of his arm, depending on where you consider you have the greater possibility of success. This second attack must be made from the lunge position, or, if your opponent gives you time, during the time you are recovering your guard.

Redoubling may be used immediately after a riposte as well as after an original attack. It is made against an adversary who, after parrying or avoiding the first riposte, fails to counter-riposte. It is usually made by a disengage under the guard or under the forearm.

The Remise

The remise in épée is slightly different from the remise in foil and sabre. It is the immediate continuation of the attack by a straight thrust given after your opponent's parry. The remise should be executed: (1) On any riposte or counter-riposte, simple or compound; (2) On a delayed riposte; or (3) On your opponent's abandoning your blade on a riposte.

130

As in the case of redoubling, the remise should be executed from the lunge position or during recovery of the guard.

In foil and sabre, the remise should be taken only in certain cases and is not recommended as a general practice; in épée, the remise is the general rule. It can be seen, therefore, that the whole principle of give-and-take with the épée is different from that of the foil and sabre, with radical differences in the method of fighting employed. Since the remise in épée can be directed to the arm and head, it can be executed in any line. For example, you attack in an outside line, your opponent parries simple sixte; on his riposte, maintain your lunge position and replace your point to his forearm, keeping a firm grasp on your épée. If the distance has been closed excessively, remise during the time you are recovering your guard.

Retaking The Attack (Reprise D' Attaque)

Since the offensive in épée yields better results than the defensive, retake the attack after any inconclusive phrase. After such an indecisive phrase, the fencers generally fall back on guard; retake the attack by some simple movement.

The Bind (Liement)

The bind is a single-movement attack in one continuous motion in which the adversary's blade is contacted with opposition and, maintaining that contact, is transferred from low to high line or high to low line, where the attack will terminate. It is executed only when the adversary has his arm extended or almost fully extended. To execute the bind, when your adversary extends his arm in the high line, take sixte or quarte opposition with the forte of your blade against his foible, arm still bent, and then with the help of the wrist, describe a half-circle downward (in sixte, this will be in a clockwise direction; in quarte, a counterclockwise direction), maintaining your blade above that of your opponent. After the opposition is taken, the arm is gradually extended as the half-circle is being described until, when the point

131

is in line at the end of the movement, the arm is completely extended. When the point is in line and the arm is fully extended, lunge without interruption and touch with opposition in the low line (preferably to the leg above the knee).

To execute a bind from the low to the high line, when your opponent makes a feint to the low line, take low sixte or low quarte opposition with the forte of your blade against his foible, arm still bent, and then with the help of the wrist, describe a half-circle upward (if low sixte, in a counterclockwise direction; if low quarte, clockwise), maintaining your blade under his, and stopping the movement when the point is in the direction of the arm. After the opposition is taken, the arm is gradually extended until, at the completion of the movement, the point will be in line and the arm will be fully extended. Then lunge with opposition and touch in the high line.

To execute a bind to the underside of your opponent's forearm, when he extends his arm in quarte, take quarte opposition and immediately begin reversing the hand to the seconde position, describing at the same time, with the help of the wrist, a half-circle downward and counterclockwise, maintaining your blade above his, and stopping your hand in the position of seconde, pommel to the right of the wrist. The point will be directed under the forearm by bending the wrist upward. At the same time, after the opposition has been taken, you are gradually extending your arm until the point is in line with the arm fully extended. Then lunge and touch under the forearm.

The bind can also be executed after a counter-party. It will then begin as a continuation of the counter-parry and will be directed to the underside of the forearm or to the leg. If directed to the leg, a slight opposition should be taken on the side opposite the counter-parry.

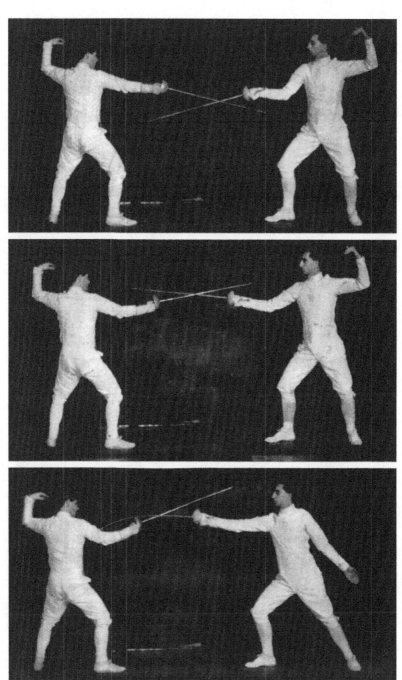

Fig. 19(Top) - The bind(a.) Low quarte opposition
Fig. 20(Center) - The bind(b.) Going into sixte opposition
Fig. 21(Bottom) - The bind(c.) Lunge to arm with sixte opposition

133

It is dangerous to attempt a bind against an adversary when he has his arm bent. Since the épée guard position is taken with the arm almost fully extended and since it is easy to provoke an extension, the bind finds frequent use in épée.

To deceive a bind, disengage at the moment your adversary is beginning his bind. If you have no time to deceive the bind and your blade is already taken, bend back your arm, take an opposition on the same side, and then make your riposte.

In general, a bind must be parried by an opposition at the final movement of the attack.

The Double Bind

The double bind is merely two immediately successive binds, ending in the same line as that in which they began. To execute, contact the adversary's blade in the manner described above, beginning with a simple or counter opposition. Describe a complete circle, maintaining continuous contact with his blade, from the high line to the low line and back again to the high line, where the touch will be scored with opposition. At the very beginning of the double bind, raise your point slightly to insure better contact with his blade.

There is no practicable double bind from low line to low line, as contact cannot be maintained so effectively and thus you are too exposed. The double bind should not be executed against a point that is too low, nor should it be made against a bent arm.

The parry of the double bind is the same as for the bind.

Most épée fencers take their guard with their arms almost completely extended and there are therefore many opportunities to execute a bind or a double bind.

Before attempting to execute a bind or a double bind, you should try to take your opponent's blade experimentally several times just to see if he is skilled in avoiding your blade. If he shows skill in doing so, precede the bind or double bind with a false attack.

Most binds and double binds fail simply because the fencer cannot contact his opponent's blade without a beat, or because he does not make his bind or double bind as a single continuous motion until the end.

The Cross (Croisé)

The cross is a transverse movement from high to low line, fulfilling at the same time the functions of parry and riposte, made without a lunge. The line is kept closed all the time during the parry and the riposte is made with opposition, maintaining the blade. In épée, the cross should be directed as much as possible to the leg. The cross may be executed after a counter-parry; the final opposition will then be taken on the side opposite to the counter-parry.

To make a cross in seconde on an attack ending in your high inside line, first parry with quarte opposition and then drive your opponent's blade to the low line by reversing your hand from quarte to seconde position. At the same time, extend your arm, maintaining slight opposition to the right, and touch to the leg or body. The cross in seconde is very effective against an opponent who makes flèche attacks to the high inside line.

The cross is the same movement as the bind except that with the cross there is no lunge. The bind is an attack; the cross is a parry and riposte.

The Envelopment

The envelopment is the same as the cross, except that it is executed from the low to the high line. It is still a parry and riposte, and is executed against an attack which finally ends in the low line. There is no lunge. The envelopment is generally directed to the arm, shoulder, or upper part of the body.

To execute an envelopment in seconde, on an attack terminating in either low line, parry with seconde opposition, and drive your opponent's blade in a counter-clockwise arc to the high line, with your hand still in seconde position. At the same time, extend your arm and direct your point inside by bending your wrist, and touch to the inside of the arm. To touch the shoulder or body, it is preferable to turn the palm up to the sixte position as you are making the riposte.

The Flèche (Or Rush)

The flèche is a simple attack executed by fully extending the arm with the point in line with that part of the target you wish to touch, then deliberately losing your balance by leaning forward, and finally closing the distance by running forward rapidly so that your opponent cannot make a riposte. To make your flèche attack more likely to succeed, get your point in line and as far forward as possible before. you begin to run forward. Also, launch your flèche from as short a distance as possible so as to get the fullest measure of surprise.

The flèche can be executed in two different ways:

1. By taking the blade with opposition when the adversary has his arm extended.

2. Without taking the blade, when the adversary's arm is bent, or when he is bending back his arm after having extended it, or—and this is to be preferred—when he is recovering his guard after missing his attack. It may also be executed on an invitation.

Both methods may be used with the hand in different positions. The following positions are recommended when the. blade is taken:

1. When your opponent makes a feint straight thrust to the inside line, take counter-sixte opposition by extending the arm and maintaining sufficient opposition to touch the arm, shoulder, or body by shortening the distance. Begin

136

to run forward (at the same time that you take the opposition) by moving the left foot forward slightly beyond and slightly to the left of the right foot. This will enable you to keep facing your opponent as you advance and also to pass him on your left. Limit the number of steps you take so that you will neither come into bodily contact with your opponent nor run off the strip.

2.   When your opponent makes a feint to the outside line, take sixte opposition and execute as described above.

3.   The above two methods of making the flèche carry the attacker to the outside of his opponent, and thus minimize the danger of a double touch.

4.   On a feint to the inside line, contact your opponent's foible with your forte, going above his blade by reversing your hand to quinte or seconde position. (If you wish to touch the body, take quinte; if the leg, take seconde.) Maintain his blade slightly outside the limit of your body, shorten the distance, and touch to the low line. This flèche carries you to your opponent's inside line; however, the risk of a double touch is greater.

The following positions are recommended when the. blade is not taken:

1.   When your opponent is recovering his guard after having missed an attack, execute a flèche to the inside of the elbow joint, to the shoulder or to the mask. Start just at the moment he is raising his right foot to recover his guard position. This is the best flèche attack, but requires special training to be executed effectively.

2.   When your opponent starts to parry your feint, deceive that parry and execute a flèche, maintaining opposition.

3.   When your adversary changes his position by taking some "open" parries-parries which are taken uselessly or as a preparation-wait and time the execution of your flèche for

the moment when his point is outside the limit of your body.

Fig. 22 - The flèche(a.) Quinte opposition is taken against a feint straight thrust. Body weight starts forward

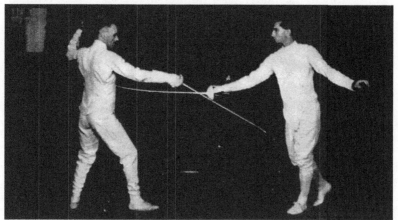

Fig. 23 - The flèche(b.) Run is continued past opponent's right side. Opposition in quinte is maintained, touch is made to low line

Flèche attacks from quarte opposition are recommended only for advanced fencers. These may be executed in the same way as from sixte. Great care should be taken that in this case the touch be made to the forearm or arm.

The best defense against a flèche attack is the parry; the stop-thrust is not recommend ed. Seconde parry is best. Any flèche to the inside line can be parried by seconde. If the flèche is high to the inside line, you will have to raise your point higher, keeping your elbow as close to the body as possible as a fixed pivot, until your point is about ten inches above your opponent's blade, to make certain of contacting his blade and also to secure the necessary leverage to deflect his blade down to the normal seconde position. Since your adversary is rushing upon you, all you have to do to touch is to maintain your point in line and extend your arm proportionately to your opponent's distance.

If you meet the flèche with a stop-thrust, be sure to maintain opposition.

Counter-sixte may also be used, but not so effectively as seconde. For the outside flèche attack, sixte parry will be used; for the outside low flèche attack, seconde parry will be used.

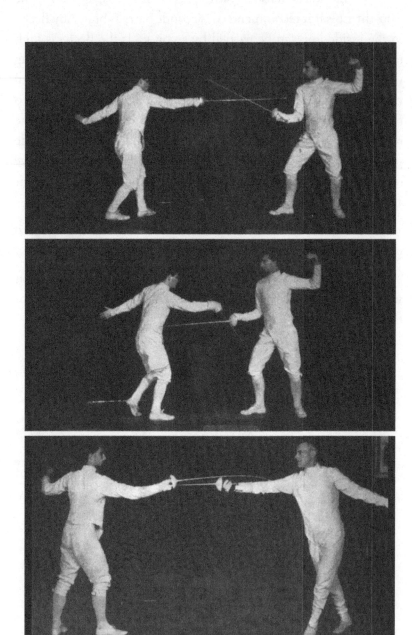

Fig. 24(Top) - Parry of inside flèche(a.) Quarte opposition
Fig. 25(Center) - Parry of inside flèche(b.) Going into seconde parry, with
riposte to low line
Fig. 26(Bottom) - Stop-thrust to arm, with quarte opposition, against inside flèche

CHAPTER V
The Parries

The Parries

The parry is the act of deflecting from the target the attack made by the adversary. It is executed by bringing the forte of your blade into contact with the foible of your opponent's blade. If the parry is in the high line, your point should be about five inches above your opponent's guard; if in the low line, your point should be the same distance below his guard. Parries are either lateral (simple), half-circular, or circular (counter-parries).

The parry is simple when it deflects the adversary's blade in the same line as that in which the attack terminated; half-circular, when, keeping the blade on the same side and describing a semi-circle, it ends in an opposite vertical line from that in which the attack ended; counter, when it deflects your adversary's blade by means of a full circle into the opposite horizontal line from that in which the attack ended.

Parries may be taken in two ways: by opposition (which is the better way in épée) and by beat. The parry is given by opposition when the opponent's blade is deflected from the target without any sudden shock pressure, and once contacted in this fashion, it is taken and maintained just outside the limit of the body. The parry is given by beat when the adversary's blade is deflected by means of a sharp tap given by the action of the fingers and wrist. Regardless of which of the two mean s is used, the point and wrist should stop at the limits fixed by the target. Keep in mind that all parries on the short distance in épée are taken by opposition and not by beat.

There are parries for each line, and in each line there are two possible positions for the hand. Since the target is arbitrarily divided into four lines, there are eight possible simple parries and eight corresponding counter-parries. The eight simple parries are:

141

- For the inside high line: Prime and Quarte.

- For the inside low line: Low Quarte and Quinte.

- For the outside high line: Tierce and Sixte.

- For the outside low line: Seconde and Low Sixte.

Prime, quinte, tierce and seconde (and their counter-parries) are made in pronation, that is, with the nails down; quarte, low quarte, sixte and low sixte (and their counter-parries) are made in supination, that is, with the nails up. Prime is not used in épée. Quinte as a parry finds no use in épée, but the quinte position for the hand may be used occasionally in executing a flèche attack. Tierce parry is not used, but the hand in tierce position may be used in an attack directed to the underside of the forearm. The low sixte and low quarte parries are not much used, because it is generally preferable to use the stop-thrust against a low attack. Quarte. sixte and seconde are the parries most used in épée.

The Quarte Parry

To take a quarte parry on an attack to your inside high line, first raise your point to about five inches above your opponent's guard, so as to insure contact with his blade, and then move the hand to your left no more than five inches from the sixte guard position (without changing the position of the fingers) and deflect the blade by taking opposition or by giving a beat. Remember that the basic position of the hand is low sixte; in the attacks and parries the hand should remain as close to this position as possible.

To take a counter-quarte parry on your adversary's disengage to sixte, pass your blade under his by describing a full counter-clockwise circle of the smallest possible circumference, stopping your point at the original position and deflecting his blade by maintaining opposition or by a beat.

The Sixte Parry

To take a sixte parry on an attack to your outside high line, first raise your point about five inches above your opponent's guard, and then move your hand to the sixte position (without changing the position of the fingers), and deflect the blade by opposition or beat.

To take a counter-sixte parry on a disengage to quarte, pass your blade under his by describing a full clockwise circle of the smallest possible circumference, stopping the point at the original position, deflecting his blade by opposition or beat.

The Low Quarte Parry

To execute a low quarte parry on an attack to the inside low line, bend the wrist down and in, and turn it so as to describe a clockwise half-circle downward, deflecting your opponent's blade by opposition or beat. The nails will still be up. When the

143

half-circle is completed and your point is in line with your opponent's waistline, your line is closed and you are ready for a riposte.

In the low line parries the little finger will have to be relaxed slightly and the pommel will be separated from the wrist.

Counter low quarte is not practical in épée. Low quarte parry itself is not much used, but the position of the hand in low quarte is useful in giving a beat as a preparation to an attack or to take opposition to begin a bind or an envelopment against an opponent who keeps his point low.

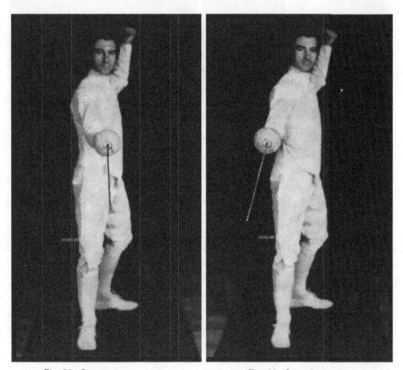

Fig. 29 - Low quarte parry   Fig. 30 - Low sixte parry

The Low Sixte Parry

To take a low sixte parry on an attack to the outside low line, describe a half-circle downward, counterclockwise. The nails are up. Keep the movement within the limits of the target. Deflect his blade by opposition or beat.

Counter low sixte is not practical.

The Tierce Parry

The tierce parry is seldom used as a parry in épée, but the hand in the tierce position is useful to facilitate a riposte at short distance.

Counter-tierce is not much used in épée.

The Seconde Parry

Seconde is a very useful parry in épée; it may be used to parry attacks directed to the outside low line or to inside line, high or low. If the attack is directed to the inside high line, seconde will have to be taken by opposition and the point at the start will have to be raised sufficiently above the adversary's blade, first of all to insure contact and then, once contact has been established, to make certain that by maintaining continuous contact his blade can be deflected in the outside low line. If the attack is directed to the inside low line, seconde can be taken either by opposition or by beat.

To execute seconde, then, on an attack to the inside line, describe a half-circle downward, counterclockwise, until the hand is on a level with the waist and at the right limit of your body. The half-circle was begun by going above the opponent's blade and ends with his blade to the right of yours. The point at the end of the parry will fall slightly below your own épée guard. The nails are down.

If your opponent makes a disengage to the inside line after you have parried seconde, take a counter-seconde parry by describing a complete circle in a counterclockwise direction, deflecting the blade by opposition or beat, stopping in the original position.

Fig. 31 - Tierce parry   **Fig. 32 - Seconde parry**

The Quinte Parry

To take a quinte parry on an attack to the inside line, turn the nails down, extend the arm almost fully, elbow in and with your blade diagonally across your body to the left and above and across your opponent's forte. Your point should be only slightly higher than your hand and outside the line. Either opposition or beat may be used. Riposte to the low line.

To take a counter-quinte parry on a disengage above your blade, describe a complete circle counter-clockwise above his blade, using the fingers and wrist and stopping at the original position.

Quinte parry is used in épée only to take the adversary's blade in going on a flèche attack.

146

Fig. 33 - Quinte parry

Notes On The Parries

The main thing to remember in executing a parry is to make it in such a way as to avoid a double touch on your riposte. In épée, where the first touch to arrive is the one that counts, it is of the greatest importance to prevent your opponent from redoubling. A final parry taken in an inside line will make it easy for your adversary to redouble, and may result in a double touch. Therefore, use as much as possible those parries which deflect your opponent's blade to the outside line, whence it will be much more difficult for him to redouble or remise.

The parries which will deflect your opponent's blade into the outside line are sixte, counter-sixte and seconde.

1.   On an attack to the outside high line, parry by sixte.

2.   On an attack to the inside high line, parry by counter-sixte.

3.   On an attack to the low line, parry by seconde.

It is of course understood that the above parries are flexible parries which must be altered slightly to adapt themselves to the

147

attack made. For example, if the attack is very high in the outside high line, the point will have to be raised more in executing sixte; if the attack is very high inside, as to the mask, then counter-sixte will have to be taken by describing the circle more to the inside and raising the point more; if the attack is directed to the underside of the forearm, then the seconde parry taken will be almost tierce; and if the attack is very low, as to the knee, the seconde taken will have to be made with the point lower than usual.

Since the attacks will be directed chiefly to the inside line, it is wise to vary your parries against those attacks so that your opponent will not be able to count on your taking a certain parry and thus be able to deceive that parry with a feint. Along the same line of reasoning, it is a good idea occasionally to parry an attack to the inside high line by taking seconde in the high line in such a way as to contact his blade early, and, maintaining contact, to deflect it to the normal seconde position outside the right limit of the body.

If you use quarte and counter-quarte now and then, be careful to riposte exclusively to the arm and shoulder.

Low quarte and low sixte should be used only against an adversary who keeps his hand high and his point low.

Quinte position should be used only against an opponent who keeps his arm extended, and then only as a preparation taking the blade or as a preparation to a flèche attack.

It is not necessary to answer a feint in quarte.

To make practical use of the parries listed above, the hand must nearly always be in the position of sixte and very seldom in quarte.

When raising your point to take a parry in the high line, be careful to do so at exactly the right moment, and to raise it only a few inches above your opponent's épée guard; this will facilitate your riposte, as it will tend to keep your point in line.

148

Remember that in the épée parries you do not have to move much laterally because the arm is more extended than in the foil, and the more the arm is extended the smaller is the arc you have to protect.

Deceiving The Parry

You deceive a parry when you avoid your opponent's blade by disengaging under it just at the moment he begins to execute his parry.

Deceiving the parry may be used as an exercise between two fencers; it is excellent for developing the eye and sense of timing. One fencer will attack the other, and at just the right moment will deceive the other's parry and continue to touch.

CHAPTER VI
The Riposte and Counter-Riposte

The Riposte

The return or riposte is the attack which follows the parry. It is a direct riposte when it is given in the same line as that in which the parry was taken. When the parry is made by a light beat, and when the direct riposte follows the parry immediately, it takes the name of "tac-au-tac" riposte, and should be executed with the greatest rapidity. When the direct riposte is executed after a parry by opposition, it takes the name of "riposte by opposition." Regardless of how the parry was taken, by beat or opposition, the riposte must be made with opposition, and should be directed to the arm, shoulder or leg. The riposte directed to the inside of the arm usually has the best chance of succeeding. If the distance is short, the riposte may be directed to the body for greater effectiveness. Whenever the line is changed by the riposte, the riposte is still simple if it is executed as a single-motion movement.

When there is a delay between the parry and riposte, the latter takes the name of delayed riposte. The extent of delay is governed by the adversary's actions.

The "tac-au-tac" riposte should be made in place; the others may be executed in place or with a lunge.

The riposte in épée is almost always given with the nails up. However, when the opponent closes the distance by a flèche or advance, it is advisable, if you have parried high tierce, to make your riposte with the hand in the same position, raising your hand proportionately to the closeness of the distance. The closer he has advanced, the higher you will have to raise your hand to keep your point on the target.

The riposte in seconde may also be used, without the lunge, if you have parried your opponent's lunge with a seconde parry.

The compound riposte, that is, one composed of more than one movement, is not effective with the épée, and is not recommended.

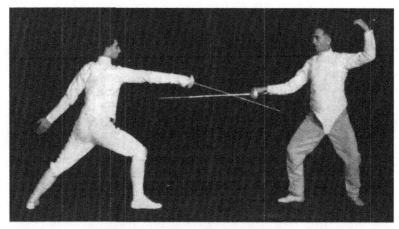

Fig. 34 - Seconde parry on attack to low line

Fig. 35 - Riposte to leg after seconde parry

The Counter-Riposte And Second Counter-Riposte

The counter-riposte is the attack following the parry of the riposte and is always given by the initial attacker. As in the case of the riposte, the counter-riposte may be simple (direct), compound or delayed. It can be made in place, with a lunge, or from the lunge position of the original attack. It is advisable to make the

151

counter-riposte to the forearm, since this will prevent your opponent from redoubling, a threat against which the fencer making the counter-riposte must always be on his guard.

The second counter-riposte is the attack following the parry of the counter-riposte made by the original attacker. The second counter-riposte is seldom used in épée, and is not recommended. This chapter, however, includes some second counter-riposte exercises, because they are invaluable in training the eye and sense of timing.

The Phrase (Phrase D' Armes)

The phrase is the term applied to the entire group of movements—the attacks, parries, ripostes and counter-ripostes—which are both given and received, executed without interruption and which may end decisively or indecisively. A phrase in épée is nearly always brief, since the stop-thrust, very often used with that weapon, puts a quick halt to any sequence.

Some Counter-Riposte Exercises

Pupil's Attack (No Lunge)	Instructor's		Pupil's	
	Parry	Riposte (no lunge)	Parry	Counter-riposte (With Lunge)
1. Feint straight	Quarte	Straight (shoulder)	Counter-sixte	Straight (shoulder)
2. Feint straight	Counter-sixte	Straight (arm)	Sixte opposition	Straight (arm)
3. Feint disengage	Sixte	Straight (arm)	Sixte opposition	Straight (arm)
4. Feint disengage (knee)	Low quarte	Disengage (arm)	Quarte by beat	Straight (shoulder)
5. Feint disengage (arm)	Counter-quarte	Straight (arm)	Quarte by beat	Disengage (arm, under or outside)
6. Feint straight (arm)	Counter-sixte	Straight (arm)	Sixte by beat	Disengage (arm, inside)
7. Feint disengage (arm)	Counter-quarte	Disengage (arm, outside)	Counter-quarte by beat	Disengage (arm, outside)
8. Feint straight (wrist)	Quarte	Straight (forearm)	Seconde opposition	Disengage to arm or shoulder (hand ending in sixte)
9. Feint disengage (low line)	Low quarte	Disengage (arm)	Seconde opposition	Disengage to arm or shoulder (hand ending in sixte)
10. Feint straight	Counter-sixte	Disengage (low line)	Low quarte opposition going in a bind from low to high line	
11. Feint 1-2 (low, high)	Low quarte, quarte	Straight (forearm)	Quarte opposition going into a bind from high to low line	
12. Feint straight	Quarte	Straight	Counter-sixte	Flèche attack outside
13. Double (arm, with lunge)	Two counter-quarte	Straight	Quite	Flèche attack front
14. Feint 1-2 (high, low)	Sixte, low sixte	Disengage (shoulder)	Sixte opposition going into a double bind	
15. 1-2 (low, high, lunge)	Low quarte, quarte	Disengage (knee)	Seconde by opposition and bind from low to high line	
16. 1-2 (low, high, lunge)	Low quarte, quarte	Disengage (knee)	Recovery of guard position	Stop-thrust to arm

All the above exercises may be preceded by a preparation, such as a beat, press, glide or the like. They may also be executed with a lunge or with an advance.

All the movements listed for the pupil in columns four and five may be replaced by recovery of the guard position with stop-thrust, as in Exercise 16.

153

Some Second Counter-Riposte Exercises

Instructor's Attack (No Lunge)	Pupil's		Instructor's		Pupil's	
	Parry	Riposte (no lunge)	Parry	Counter-riposte	Parry	Second Counter-riposte (Lunge)
1. Feint straight	Quarte	Straight to shoulder	Quarte	Straight to shoulder		Stop-thrust to forearm
2. Feint straight (wrist)	Counter-sixte	Straight	Sixte	Disengage (knee)		Stop-thrust to arm or shoulder
3. Feint disengage	Sixte	Straight	Sixte	Disengage under arm		Stop-thrust to forearm
4. Feint disengage (low line)	Low quarte	Disengage (arm)	Quarte opposition	Disengage to forearm		Stop-thrust to forearm
5. Feint straight (wrist)	Seconde	Disengage (arm)	Sixte opposition	Disengage (low line)		Stop-thrust to mask
6. Feint straight (wrist)	Counter-sixte	Disengage	Quarte	Straight		Quarte opposition going into a bind
7. Feint disengage (knee)	Seconde	Disengage (hand in sixte)	Sixte opposition	Disengage (low line)		Stop-thrust to arm
8. Feint straight	Quarte opposition, cross to seconde	Disengage (hand in sixte)	Sixte opposition	Disengage (high line)		Seconde or tierce opposition going into bind to inside of arm
9. Feint straight under forearm	Seconde	Disengage (inside forearm)	Counter-seconde	Disengage in sixte (hand in sixte position)	Sixte opposition	Straight to arm
10. Feint 1-2 (high, low)	Low quarte, quarte	Going into a cross to seconde	Seconde opposition	Disengage high, outside		Straight to arm
11. Feint straight	Quarte	Disengage, lunge (stay on lunge)	Sixte opposition	Straight to arm		Remise to arm from lunge position
12. Feint 1-2 (high, low)	Sixte, seconde	Disengage to sixte, lunge, stay on lunge	Sixte opposition	Disengage under forearm	Seconde	Straight to body, low line, from lunge position

13. 1-2 (low, high) lunge	Seconde, quarte	Disengage	Sixte	Feint bind	Low quarte opposition going into a bind	
14. Double, lunge	Two counter-quarte	Disengage to underside of forearm	Recovery of guard, sixte opposition	Stop-thrust to forearm	Sixte opposition	Flèche to shoulder
15. Feint disengage (low)	Low quarte opposition and envelopment		Sixte opposition	Cross to low quarte	Low quarte opposition	Straight to inside of forearm
16. Feint disengage (knee)		Stop to forearm	Sixte opposition	Disengage under forearm	Quinte opposition	Flèche to body

CHAPTER VII
Lessons

The Principle Of The Épée

It cannot be repeated too often that the principle of the épée is entirely different from that of the foil. The foil is a conventional weapon; that is, it is bound by the conventions arising from the limitations of the target and the equidistance, for all practical considerations, of all parts of the target from both opponents.

When two foil opponents each launch an attack at the same time, each properly made with a straight arm, it is obvious that both will arrive at the same time, or so nearly the same time that it is impossible, on the basis of time alone, to decide which of the two arrived first. Recourse is therefore had to the principle of action. The question is asked, which of the two had the right of way? With this question is born the principle of the foil, the convention requiring that an attack be parried before a riposte is made, that a riposte be parried before a counter-riposte is made, that a properly made attack have precedence over a stop-thrust, and so on. With the foil, time comes into question only when the action is faulty; that is, when an attack is delayed, or made with a bent arm, or made in several movements, so that a stop-thrust can take the time away from it.

Since the épée target is the entire body, it is obvious that all parts of the targets of the two opponents are not equidistant. Your opponent's wrist or knee, for example, is much nearer your point than your shoulder is to his point. This means that if your opponent launches a properly executed attack at your shoulder or body, you may stop-thrust him on the wrist appreciably before his attack would arrive; indeed, in a duel with uncovered points, this stop-thrust would, in all probability, effectively prevent his body-attack from arriving at all. What then happens to the principle of action? It is entirely lost and in its place is substituted the principle of time, which states that whoever hits first gets the award.

Starting from this principle, the practice of épée follows a different course from that of the foil. The foil precedence of attack over stop-thrust, attack over riposte, riposte over remise or counter-riposte, etc., has lost its value. With the épée all these actions have equal value. The stop-thrust is just as valid as the attack, provided both are properly made and provided one does not hit a nearer portion of the target than the other; and the remise is just as valid as the riposte. It is obvious then that with the épée it is advisable to stop-thrust whenever the opportunity presents itself, and to redouble or remise whenever your original attack misses or is parried.

The question now arises as to when it is advisable to stop-thrust. The reader is asked to look at Figures 6 and 7. Fig. 6 shows the épée guard position; Fig. 7, the position of épée, hand, and arm in an attack. In both of these figures the blade is in line and the point is threatening the target. A stop-thrust made against such an attack would hit the bell or miss the arm entirely, and would therefore be inadvisable.

If, however, your opponent's blade deviates from the line in any direction during an attack, whether it be high, low, left or right, it is possible to hit his forearm with a stop-thrust. If he drops his point downward and attacks your knee, the upper surface of his forearm comes into view long enough for you to hit it. If he raises his point to attack your mask, you can hit the underside of his forearm. The quarte guard leaves the outside of the forearm exposed; a wide sixte guard does the same for the inside of the forearm. So far as the forearm is concerned, what you can see, you can hit.

The first principle of the épée, therefore, is to attack with your blade in line, the forearm fully protected and in line behind the bell. The second principle is to replace your point or remise immediately if your original attack missed or was parried. The

157

third principle is to stop-thrust to the arm whenever your opponent fails to observe the first principle. If he does observe it, of course you must parry and riposte. Or, to put it another way, if you see an opening, attack in line; if you miss, replace or remise; if your opponent attacks in line, parry and riposte; if he attacks out of line, stop-thrust.

This, much simplified, is the theory of the épée. It is given here in this chapter of lessons rather than at the beginning of the book because the author feels that it is important for the beginner to have these principles fresh in his mind as he begins his lessons with an instructor. Only in this way can he develop the proper "épée reaction" until it is second nature to him.

Description Of A Complete Lesson

A complete lesson should include the following:

1.   The guard position, advance, retreat, and some slow-motion movements in the fundamental positions for corrective purposes.

2.   Single-movement attacks, with or without verbal directions.

3.   Single-movement parries and ripostes.

4.   One- to three-movement attacks, with or without verbal directions.

5.   One- to three-movement parries, with a simple riposte.

6.   The introduction of a new movement.

7.   Some counter-riposte exercises.

8.   Some second counter-riposte exercises.

9.   A speed exercise consisting of an attack, parry and riposte.

10.   Some slow-motion movements to taper off the exercise and for corrective purposes.

11.   Reassemble and salute.

No lesson should last more than fifteen to twenty minutes. At first there should be a maximum of movements executed with a minimum of speed.

Lesson 1

1. The épée.
2. Holding the épée.
3. Position preparatory to coming on guard. Coming on guard in three counts.
4. The advance; the retreat.
5. Reassembling.
6. Explanation of finger-, wrist- and arm-play.
7. Extension of the arm; coming back on guard.
8. Explanation of the lines; the point in line; the feint.
9. The lunge; recovery of the guard position.
10. Engagement of sixte; the engagement of quarte.
11. The positions of sixte; quarte; seconde; tierce; quinte; low sixte; and low quarte.
12. Explanation of the attacks.
13. The straight thrust to the shoulder and arm; student trained in proper sequence of extension of arm before going on lunge.
14. Reassemble and salute.

The student should be trained to take especially the positions of sixte, quarte and seconde, which are the positions most used in épée.

This lesson should be repeated two or three times before going on to the next lesson. Stress should be placed on the fundamentals of fencing.

During the first four lessons the student should take the engagement of sixte as a general rule, and quarte occasionally. This will facilitate understanding the various movements. After the fourth lesson, however, no contact of the blades will be taken, just as in a real bout.

If this course of lessons is to be spread over a number of years, or fencing seasons, they should be divided as follows:

Lessons 1-7, first year.

Lessons 1-14, second year.

Lessons 1-18, third year.

This division is predicated on the assumption that the pupil will take two or three lessons a week.

160

Lesson 2

1.   The guard position, advance, retreat, lunge (in two counts), reassemble, on guard, the forward guard.

2.   Explanation and execution of taking parries by opposition; by beat.

3.   Review of the sixte, quarte, low sixte and low quarte parries; execution of these parries by both opposition and beat.

4.   Explanation of the riposte; execution of straight ripostes to the shoulder or arm after parries of sixte, quarte, low sixte and low quarte.

5.   Execution of the feint straight thrust; explanation and execution of the feint disengage; explanation of facts contained in Notes on the Parries.

6.   Execution of some simple attacks, in two counts by command. The attacks will be some straight thrusts to the shoulder, some disengages to the arm and some to the leg. The commands should be given in two counts, in the following manner: 1. "Feint straight thrust" 2. "Lunge!" And 1. "Feint disengage" 2. "Lunge!"; and so on.

7.   Explanation and execution of tierce parry and seconde parry.

8.   Explanation of distance; method for securing the proper distance; its importance.

9.   Exercise for the different positions of the hand on the riposte:

Instructor's Attack	Pupil's Parry	Pupil's Riposte (by command and with lunge)
a. From quarte, disengage	Sixte opposition	Straight, to shoulder
b. From sixte, disengage	Quarte opposition	Straight, to shoulder
c. From sixte, disengage (knee)	Low sixte opposition	Disengage, to arm
d. From quarte, disengage (leg)	Low quarte opposition	Disengage, to arm
e. From sixte, disengage (low)	Seconde opposition	Disengage to arm, hand in sixte position
f. From quarte, disengage to outside of arm	Tierce opposition	Straight to arm, hand in sixte position

Exercise:#9 above should be repeated, with parries by beat.

10.   Explanation and execution of the stop-thrust.

Instructor's Attack	Pupil's Stop-Thrust
a. From quarte, feint disengage to low line	To upper surface of arm
b. From sixte, feint disengage to low line	To upper surface of arm
c. From sixte, feint straight to shoulder	To underside of arm
d. From quarte, feint straight, inside line	To inside of forearm
e. From sixte, feint straight, outside line	To outside of forearm

11.   Several full lunges for corrective purposes. The student should hold the lunge position until the corrections are made.

12.   Reassemble and salute.

This lesson should be repeated until the student can execute the movements with facility.

161

Lesson 3

1. The guard position, the advance, the retreat, jumping forward, jumping backward, some slow-motion fundamental movements for corrective purposes.

2. Single-movement attack exercises:
   a. From each line, straight thrust to arm when instructor begins to move his arm forward.
   b. From quarte, disengage to arm when instructor moves his hand to the left.
   c. From sixte, disengage to arm when instructor moves his hand to the right.
   d. From each line, disengage to underside of forearm when instructor begins to extend his arm in the high line.
   e. From each line, disengage to leg or arm when instructor drops his hand or moves it to the right.

3. Single-movement parry and riposte exercise:

Instructor's Attack (with advance)	Pupil's Parry (while retreating)	Pupil's Riposte (no lunge)
a. From sixte, straight thrust to arm	Sixte opposition	Disengage (low line)
b. From quarte, straight thrust to arm	Quarte opposition	Straight (arm)
c. From quarte, disengage to underside of forearm	Low quarte opposition	Straight (knee)
d. From sixte, disengage to underside of forearm	Low sixte opposition	Straight (leg)
e. From sixte, disengage to leg	Seconde opposition	Disengage (to arm, hand in sixte position)

4. Explanation and execution of preparations to the attack: opposition; the beat; the press.

5. Explanation of the counter-riposte and second counter-riposte.

6. Counter-riposte exercise: #1.

7. Second counter-riposte exercise: #1.

8. Explanation and execution of avoidance.

9. Speed exercise, attack: student will execute 5 straight thrusts, then 5 disengages, in both sixte and quarte, when the instructor opens these lines.

10. Speed exercise, parry and riposte: the instructor will attack 5 times in sixte and 5 times in quarte; the pupil will parry by opposition, and

will riposte straight to the shoulder. When the instructor makes 5 attacks by disengage, the student will take 5 counter-quarte or counter-sixte parries by opposition, and will riposte straight to the shoulder or arm.

11. Review of the different positions of the hand, taken in series of three's:
   a. Sixte, quarte, low quarte.
   b. Quarte, sixte, seconde.
   c. Tierce, quarto, sixte.
   d. Seconde, sixte, quarte.
   e. Sixte, low sixte, low quarte.
   f. Quarte, counter-quarte, seconde.
   g. Sixte, counter-sixte, seconde.
   h. Quarte, tierce, counter-tierce.
   i. Quarte, sixte, quinte.

12. Several slow-motion full lunges for corrective purposes.

13. Reassemble and salute.

Lesson 4

1. The guard position, the advance, the retreat, the lunge, the forward guard.
2. Attack exercise:
   a. From both engagements, straight thrust to arm when instructor begins to extend his arm.
   b. From both engagements, disengage to arm when instructor begin to move his arm to the left or right.
   c. From both engagements, disengage to underside of arm when instructor begins to move his arm forward in the high line.
   d. From both engagements, disengage to leg when instructor begins to drop his hand or moves it slightly to the right.
3. Parry and riposte exercise:

Instructor's Attack (with advance)	Pupil's Parry and Riposte
a. From both engagements, straight thrust to shoulder	Quarte or sixte opposition, riposte to shoulder
b. From quarte, disengage to shoulder	Tierce opposition, riposte to shoulder in sixte
c. From both engagements, disengage to knee	Seconde opposition, disengage to shoulder (hand in sixte position)
d. From quarte, disengage to sixte	Counter-quarte opposition, riposte to arm
e. No engagement, from sixte position, straight thrust to quarte	Counter-sixte opposition, riposte to arm

4. Stop-thrust exercise:

Instructor's Attack (Lunge)	Pupil's Stop-Thrust
a. From sixte, beat, straight thrust to arm	Stop to shoulder while straightening both legs (see Fig. 17)
b. From both lines, beat, disengage to leg	Stop while moving right foot extending point to forearm (see Fig. 16)

5. Explanation of how to deceive a parry.
6. Counter-riposte exercise: #2.
7. Second counter-riposte exercise: #2.
8. Speed exercise, attack: student will execute 5 beat, straight thrusts to knee. For a speed stop exercise, student will execute 5 stops to arm on instructor's execution of 5 beat, straight thrusts to knee.
9. Several slow-motion attacks to the body, first taking quarte, sixte, counter-quarte and counter-sixte oppositions, for corrective purposes.
10. Reassemble and salute.

164

Once the above attacks and parries have been mastered, they should be executed with the advance and retreat.

At the beginning, the instructor should expose himself obviously to a stop-thrust, but he should gradually expose himself less and less until he simulates the conditions of an actual bout.

*It may be noticed that when the attack is directed to the arm, the knees may be straightened during the stop-thrust without bringing the right foot back; the increase in height and reach thus afforded allow the stop-thrust to pass over the bell and sharply downward, making the touch arrive on the wrist. When the attack is directed to the leg or knee, it becomes necessary for the right foot to be drawn back while the stop-thrust is being made.

Lesson 5

Starting with this lesson, the instructor and pupil will assume the sixte position without engaging blades.

1. The guard position, some slow-motion fundamental movements for corrective purposes (with the advance and retreat).

2. Attack exercise (with opposition): the instructor will keep his blade in line, arm extended; the pupil will then be forced to take an opposition while lunging on the attack.

Instructor	Pupil's Attack
a. Arm in quarte	Straight thrust to arm, with quarte opposition
b. Arm in sixte	Straight thrust to arm, with sixte opposition
c. Arm in quarte	Straight to arm, with counter-sixte opposition
d. Arm in sixte	Straight to arm, with counter-quarte opposition

3. Parry and riposte exercise:

Instructor's Attack (advance)	Pupil's Parry	Pupil's Riposte (lunge)
a. Straight to shoulder	Quarte opposition	Straight to arm
b. Disengage to sixte (shoulder)	Sixte opposition	Straight to arm
c. Disengage to knee	Seconde opposition	Disengage to arm, hand in sixte position
d. Disengage to sixte	Counter-quarte opposition	Straight to arm
e. Straight to quarte	Counter-sixte opposition	Straight to arm

4. Execution of the stop-thrust on a feint:

Instructor's Feint	Pupil's Stop (with half-lunge)
a. Straight to mask	Under the arm, hand in tierce position
b. Disengage to sixte	To forearm
c. Disengage to underside of forearm (hand in seconde position)	High on forearm
d. Disengage to knee or foot	To shoulder or mask

5. Explanation and execution of the expulsion.

6. Counter-riposte exercise: #3.
7. Second counter-riposte exercise: #3.
For Exercises 8 and 9, the instructor's blade will be dead center, pointing at the body.
8. Speed exercise, attacks:
   a. Beat in sixte, straight to forearm, 5 times.
   b. Beat in quarte, straight to forearm, 5 times.
9. Speed exercise, parry and riposte:
On instructor's execution of #8a, pupil will parry sixte by beat, and riposte to arm;
On instructor's execution of #8b, pupil will parry quarte by beat, and riposte to arm.
10. Several slow-motion movements for corrective purposes.
11. Reassemble and salute.

After the pupil has parried, the instructor retreats so as to allow him room for the lunge with the riposte.

Lesson 6

1. The guard position (without engagement), several slow lunges with advances and retreats.

2. Stop-thrust exercise:

Instructor (Advance or half-lunge)	Pupil's Stop
a. Raise hand from low to high position and extend	To inside of forearm
b. Extend arm to left	To outside of forearm
c. Extend arm to left	To underside of forearm
d. Extend arm in low line	To wrist, straightening the knees

3. Parry and riposte exercise:

Instructor's Feint	Pupil's Parry	Pupil's Riposte (Lunge)
a. Straight thrust	Quarte opposition	Straight to forearm
b. Disengage to sixte	Sixte opposition	Straight to forearm
c. Straight thrust	Counter-sixte opposition	Straight to forearm
d. Disengage to sixte	Counter-quarte opposition	Straight to forearm

4. Explanation and execution of the bind; the double bind; redoubling; two-movement attacks.

5. Counter-riposte exercise: #4.

6. Second counter-riposte exercise: #4.

7. Speed exercise, attack: As instructor begins to move arm to left, preparing for an attack in the outside line, pupil will stop-thrust with lunge to inside of arm; 5 times. As instructor moves hand from low to high position, preparing for an attack in the high line, pupil will stop-thrust with lunge to inside of arm; 5 times.

8. Speed exercise, parry and riposte: When instructor makes a feint straight thrust to the inside of the arm, pupil will parry counter-sixte and riposte straight to arm; 5 times. When instructor makes a feint disengage to underside of the arm, pupil will parry seconde and riposte by disengage to arm (hand in sixte position); 5 times.

9. Several slow-motion movements for corrective purposes.

10. Reassemble and salute.

Lesson 7

1. The guard position, the advance, the retreat, pupil maintaining the proper distance as instructor advances and retreats.
2. Parry and riposte exercise:

Instructor's Feint	Pupil's Parry	Pupil's Riposte (Lunge)
a. Disengage to outside line	Sixte opposition	Straight to arm
b. Straight to inside	Quarte opposition	Straight to arm
c. Straight to inside	Counter-sixte opposition	Straight to arm
d. Disengage to outside	Counter-quarter opposition	Straight to arm

3. Compound attack exercise, deceiving a simple or counter-parry: the pupil will execute some two-movement attacks from the high line to the high line, from the high line to the low line, and from the low line to the high line.
4. Compound parry, simple riposte exercise:

Instructor's Attack	Pupil's Parry (Opposition or beat)	Pupil's Riposte
a. Feint straight and disengage	Quarte, sixte	Straight to arm
b. 1-2	Sixte, quarte	Straight to arm
c. Feint straight, disengage low	Quarte, low quarte	Straight to knee
d. 1-2, low, high	Low quarte, quarte	Straight to arm
e. 1-2, high, low	Sixte, seconde	Disengage to arm (hand in sixte position)

5. Explanation and execution of redoubling; the remise.
6. Counter-riposte exercise: #5.
7. Second counter-riposte exercise: #5.
8. Speed exercise, attack: instructor's blade is in line; pupil will beat and disengage to knee; 5 times.
9. Speed exercise, parry and riposte: instructor will attack with straight thrust and half-lunge; pupil will parry seconde, disengage to shoulder (hand in sixte); 5 times.
10. Several slow-motion 1-2 attacks to the body, with full lunge, for corrective purposes.
11. Reassemble and salute.

In the attacks, the student should be trained to execute the same movement against either a bent arm or an arm being extended in an attack.

Beginning with this lesson, in the compound parry and riposte exercises, for example, the student should be able to take his parries without verbal assistance.

169

Lesson 8

1. The advance, the retreat, some slow-motion lunges for corrective purposes.
2. Attack exercise: single-movement attack preceded by a beat.

Instructor's Attack	Pupil's Attack (Half-Lunge)
a. Raises his point from a low position	Beat in sixte, straight thrust to forearm
b. Raises his point from a low position	Beat in quarte, straight thrust to inside of forearm
c. Raises his point from a low position	Beat in sixte, disengage to underside position of forearm
d. Raises his point from a low position	Beat in sixte, disengage to knee

3. Parry and riposte exercise:

Instructor's Feint (Advance)	Pupil's Parry (Opposition or beat)	Pupil's Riposte (No lunge)
a. Straight to inside of forearm	Quarte by beat	Disengage to leg with opposition
b. Disengage to outside of forearm	Sixte by beat	Disengage to leg with opposition
c. Disengage to knee, lunge (stay on lunge)	Seconde opposition	Straight to body under the arm
d. Disengage to underside of forearm	Low quarte by beat	Straight to leg with opposition

4. Attack exercise: the pupil will execute several two movement attacks, deceiving a simple or counter-parry.
5. Parry and riposte exercise:

Instructor's Attack (Advance)	Pupil's Parry	Pupil's Riposte
a. 1-2	Sixte, counter-sixte	Straight to arm
b. Feint straight, disengage	Quarte, counter-quarte	Straight to arm
c. Feint straight, deceive a counter-parry	Two counter-quarte	Straight to arm
d. Double	Two counter-sixte	Straight to arm

6. Explanation and execution of the false attack; the cross; the envelopment.
7. Counter-riposte exercise: #6.
8. Second counter-riposte exercise: #6.
9. Speed exercise, attack: Five 1-2's in each line.
10. Speed exercise, parry and riposte: on instructor's attack with the 1-2, student will parry sixte, quarte or quarte, sixte, and riposte straight to the arm; 5 times in each line.
11. Several slow-motion double attacks with full lunges for corrective purposes.
12. Reassemble and salute.

170

Lesson 9

1. The guard position, the advance, the retreat, several slow lunges.
2. False-attack exercise: the pupil will make a false attack consisting ol a feint straight thrust with a half-lunge and follow up with a disengage to the high or low line. The instructor will vary his parries of the false attack so that the pupil will have to deceive various kin<ls of parries unexpectedly before making his final movement.
3. Parry and riposte exercise:

Instructor's Feint	Pupil's Parry	Pupil's Riposte with Opposition (Lunge)
a. Straight thrust to quarte	Quarte	Disengage to shoulder
b. Disengage to sixte	Sixte	Disengage to arm
c. Disengage to sixte	Counter-quarte	Disengage to arm
d. Disengage to quarte	Counter-sixte	Disengage to arm

4. Attack exercise: deceiving the instructor's press, the student will go into a two-movement attack; repeat several times, varying the two-movement attack.
5. Parry and riposte exercise:

Instructor's Attack	Pupil's Parries and Ripostes
a. 1-2, low, high	Low quarte and quarte opposition going into a cross
b. 1-2, low, high	Seconde and sixte opposition going into a cross
c. 1-2, high, low	Quarte and low quarte opposition going into an envelopment
d. 1-2, high, low	Sixte and seconde opposition going into an envelopment ending under the arm (hand in tierce position)

6. Execution of a bind after a seconde parry, with the final movement directed to the arm, nails up. On the instructor's extension of his arm and maintenance of that extension, the pupil will parry quarte by opposition; then, reversing his hand over the blade to the seconde position, he will deflect the instructor's blade to the position of seconde and will riposte under the forearm, his hand still in seconde position.
7. Explanation and execution of the invitation to the attack.
8. Counter-riposte exercise: #7.
9. Second counter-riposte exercise: #7.
10. Speed exercise, attack: on the instructor's extended arm, pupil will beat lightly in counter-tierce and disengage to the underside of the forearm (hand in tierce position); 10 times.
11. Speed exercise, parry and riposte: on the instructor's feint inside low, or inside, or outside low, pupil will parry seconde and riposte with a lunge to the shoulder, hand in sixte position; 10 times.
12. Several slow-motion movements using the bind and double bind with full lunges, for corrective purposes.
13. Reassemble and salute.

Lesson 10

1. The guard position, the advance, the retreat, the pupil maintaining the proper distance as the instructor advances and retreats.
2. Attack exercise: the student will execute some single-movement attacks by sight (when instructor presses on his blade, student will disengage without having to be told to do so, and so on).
3. Parry and riposte exercise:

Instructor's Attack (Advance)	Pupil's Parry	Pupil's Riposte
a. Straight thrust	Counter-sixte by beat	Disengage to underside of forearm (hand in tierce)
b. Disengage to sixte	Counter-quarte by beat	Disengage to underside of forearm (hand in tierce)
c. Disengage to knee	Seconde opposition	Straight to body (hand in seconde)
d. Disengage to knee	Low quarte by beat	Disengage to inside of forearm

4. Attack exercise: student will execute some two-movement attacks, by sight.
5. Parry and riposte exercise:

Instructor's Attack (Advance)	Pupil's Parry	Pupil's Riposte
a. Feint straight, disengage	Two counter-sixte opposition	Disengage to inside of arm
b. Double	Two counter-quarte opposition	Disengage to outside of arm
c. Feint straight, deceiving a counter-parry to the low line	Counter-sixte opposition, low sixte by beat	Disengage to forearm
d. Double to the low line	Counter-quarte and seconde opposition	Straight to body with opposition

6. Explanation and execution of the time-attack; the glide.
7. Counter-riposte exercise: #8.
8. Second counter-riposte exercise: #8.
9. Speed exercise, attack: 5 doubles to the low line, from each line (starting from sixte, then from quarte).
10. Speed exercise, parry and riposte: On instructor's double to the low line, starting from sixte, the pupil will parry counter-sixte, seconde opposition, and riposte by disengage to forearm; 5 times. On instructor's double to the low line, starting from quarte, the pupil will parry counter-quarte, seconde position, and riposte straight to body (hand in seconde position); 5 times.
11. Several slow-motion movements, such as the double, with full lunges, for corrective purposes.
12. Reassemble and salute.

Lesson 11

1. The guard position, the advance, the retreat, the forward guard, slow-motion movements for corrective purposes.
2. Attack exercise: single-movement attacks preceded by a beat.

Instructor (Guard Position)	Pupil's Attack (Lunge)
a. Raises his point from low position	Beat in sixte, disengage to knee
b. Keeps point down	Beat in low quarte, straight to leg
c. Keeps point down	Beat in low quarte, disengage to forearm
d. Raises his point	Beat in tierce, disengage to underside of forearm, hand in tierce.

3. Parry and riposte exercise: the parries here will be taken while retreating.

Instructor's Attack (Advance)	Pupil's Parry (Retreat)	Pupil's Riposte (Lunge)
a. Beat in quarte, straight to arm	Counter-sixte opposition	Straight to arm
b. Beat in quarte, disengage (arm)	Counter-quarte opposition	Straight to arm
c. Beat in quarte, straight to arm	Quarte opposition going into bind to leg	
d. Beat in quarte, disengage (arm)	Sixte opposition going into bind to leg	

4. Attack exercise: two-movement attacks.

Pupil's Attack	Instructor's parry of first feint
a. 1-2, mask, underside of forearm (hand in tierce position)	Sixte
b. 1-2, knee, shoulder with opposition	Low quarte
c. 1-2, arm, knee	Quarte opposition
d. 1-2, leg, underside of forearm (hand in seconde position)	Low quarte opposition

5. Parry and riposte exercise: compound parries, simple riposte.

Instructor's Attack (Advance)	Pupil's Parries	Pupil's Ripostes
a. 1-2, mask, underside of forearm and in tierce)	Sixte and seconde opposition	Straight to inside arm (hand in seconde)
b. 1-2, knee, shoulder with opposition	Low quarte and quarte opposition	Straight to shoulder with opposition
c. 1-2, arm, knee	Quarte and low quarte opposition	Straight to leg
d. 1-2, leg, underside of forearm (hand in seconde)	Low quarte and seconde opposition	Straight to arm with opposition (hand in sixte)

6. Explanation and execution of retaking the attack, using an attack of one movement followed by another single-movement attack after recovering the guard position forward.
7. Counter-riposte exercise: #9.
8. Second counter-riposte exercise: #9.
9. Speed exercise, attack: Five 1-2's, arm, knee. Five 1-2's, leg, underside of forearm (hand in seconde).

173

10. Speed exercise, parry and riposte: On instructor's attack with the 1-2, arm, knee, pupil will parry quarte, low quarte opposition and riposte straight to leg with opposition; 5 times. On instructor's attack with the 1-2, leg, underside of forearm (hand in seconde), pupil will parry low quarte, seconde and riposte straight to arm with opposition (hand in seconde); 5 times.

12. Several slow-motion movements using the 1-2 to the body so as to force full lunges, for corrective purposes.

13. Reassemble and salute.

Lesson 12

1. The guard position, the advance, the retreat, several slow-motion movements for corrective purposes.
2. Attack exercise: single-movement attacks preceded by a press (attack on a preparation).

Instructor (Guard Position	Pupil's Attack (Lunge)
a. Raises his point and presses in quarte	Answers press, straight to shoulder
b. Raises his point and presses in sixte	Deceives press, disengage to arm
c. Raises his point and presses in quarte	Deceives press, disengage to leg with opposition
d. Presses in low quarte	Answers press, disengage to arm

3. Parry and riposte exercise:

Instructor's Attack (Advance)	Pupil's Parries	Pupil's Ripostes
a. Press in quarte, disengage to arm	Answers press, sixte opposition	Straight to shoulder
b. Press in sixte, disengage to arm	Answers press, quarte opposition	Straight to arm
c. Press in low quarte, disengage to leg	Answers press, seconde opposition	Straight to body with Opposition (hand in seconde)
d. Press in low quarte, disengage to arm	Answers press, quarte opposition	Straight to arm

4. Attack exercise: some two-movement attacks in the high line, by sight. The attacks just below may be used.
5. Parry and riposte exercise:

Instructor's Feint	Pupil's Parry	Pupil's Riposte with Opposition (Lunge)
a. 1-2	Sixte and quarte opposition	Disengage to shoulder
b. 1-2	Quarte and sixte opposition	Disengage to arm
c. Feint straight, disengage	Counter-sixte, quarte opposition	Disengage to shoulder
d. Double	Counter-quarte, sixte opposition	Disengage to arm

6. Explanation and execution of the counter time-attack.
7. Counter-riposte exercise: # 10.
8. Second counter-riposte exercise: # 10.
9. Speed exercise, attack: Five 1-2's, low, high.
10. Speed exercise, parry and riposte: on instructor's attack with the 1-2, low, high, pupil will parry low sixte, sixte opposition and riposte straight to arm; 5 times.
11. Several slow-motion two-movement attacks to body with full lunges for corrective purposes.
12. Reassemble and salute.

175

Lesson 13

1. The guard position, the advance, the retreat, several slow-motion movements for corrective purposes.
2. Counter time-attack exercise:

Pupil's Feint	Instructor's Stop	Pupil's Counter Time-Attack
a.1-2	Attempt to stop at end of first feint	Beat in quarte, disengage to leg
b.1-2	Attempt to stop at end of first feint	Beat in sixte, disengage to arm
c. Feint disengage to low line, with advance	Attempt to stop to arm	Sixte opposition and bind to leg
d. Feint disengage to low line, with advance	Attempt to stop to arm	Quarte opposition and bind to leg

3. Parry and riposte exercise:

Instructor's Attack (Advance)	Pupil's Parries	Pupil's Ripostes
a. Disengage in sixte	Sixte by beat	Straight to forearm
b. Straight in quarte	Quarte by beat	Straight to forearm
c. Disengage in sixte	Counter-quarte by beat	Straight to forearm
d. Straight in quarte	Counter-sixte by beat	Straight to forearm
e. Disengage to leg	Seconde by beat	Straight to outside of arm (hand in tierce)

4. Attack exercise: some two-movement attacks with advance, preceded by beat (by sight).
5. Parry and riposte exercise: parries will be taken while retreating.

Instructor's Attack (Advance)	Pupil's Parries	Pupil's Ripostes (Lunge)
a. 1-2	Sixte and quarte opposition	Straight to arm
b. 1-2	Quarte and sixte opposition	Straight to arm
c. 1-2	Sixte, counter-sixte opposition	Disengage to arm
d. 1-2	Quarte, counter-quarte opposition	Disengage to arm

176

6. Explanation and execution of the flèche attack. The instructor will make a feint in quarte, the pupil will take counter-sixte opposition, and will run forward and outside on his flèche, touching to the shoulder, body or mask. On the same feint by the instructor, the pupil will take quinte opposition and execute a flèche forward to the body, hand in quinte. On the instructor's disengage in sixte, the pupil will take sixte opposition and execute a flèche outside to the shoulder, body or mask.

7. Counter-riposte exercise: # 11.

8. Second counter-riposte exercise: #11.

9. Speed exercise, attack: Five 1-2's, with an advance, in both lines.

10. Speed exercise, parry and riposte:
On instructor's attack with the 1-2, pupil will parry sixte, counter-sixte while retreating) and will riposte straight to arm with lunge; 5 times.
On instructor's attack with the 1-2, pupil will parry quarte, counter-quarte (while retreating) and will riposte straight to arm with lunge; 5 times.

11. Several slow-motion two-movement attacks preceded by a press, with full lunges, for corrective purposes.

12. Reassemble and salute.

Lesson 14

1. The guard position, the advance, the retreat, several slow-motion movements for corrective purposes.
2. Attack exercise: simple attacks preceded by an expulsion on an extended arm, accompanied by an advance.

Instructor	Pupil's Attack (Advance/Lunge)
a. Extends arm between two lines and retreats	Expulsion in sixte, straight to arm
b. Extends arm between two lines and retreats	Expulsion in quarte, straight to arm
c. Extends arm between two lines and makes expulsion	Deceives expulsion, disengage in sixte to arm
d. Extends arm in sixte and makes expulsion	Deceives expulsion, disengage in quarte to arm

3. Parry and riposte exercise:

Instructor's Attack (Advance)	Pupil's Parries	Pupil's Ripostes
a. Expulsion in quarte, straight to arm	Quarte opposition	Straight to arm
b. Expulsion in sixte, straight to arm	Sixte opposition	Disengage to arm
c. Expulsion, disengage in sixte, to arm	Sixte opposition	Straight to arm
d. Expulsion, disengage in quarte, to arm	Quarte opposition	Disengage to arm

4. Attack exercise: some two-movement attacks combined with a retreat (by sight).
5. Parry and riposte exercise:

Instructor's Attack (Advance)	Pupil's Parries	Pupil's Ripostes (With opposition)
a. 1-2, sixte, quarte	Sixte and quarte opposition	1-2, arm
b. 1-2, quarte, sixte	Quarte, sixte	1-2, shoulder
c. Double	Two counter-quarte	Double, forearm
d. Feint straight, disengage	Two counter-sixte	Double, arm

6. Explanation and execution of an attack on a preparation.
7. Counter-riposte exercise: #12.

178

8. Second counter-riposte exercise: #12.
9. Speed exercise, attack:
   On instructor's extension of arm, pupil will parry sixte by opposition (with advance) and disengage to underside of forearm, hand in seconde; 5 times. On instructor's extension of arm, pupil will parry counter-sixte by opposition (with advance) and disengage to underside of forearm, hand in seconde; 5 times.
10. Speed exercise, parry and riposte:
    On instructor's attack with the double, with an advance, pupil will parry two counter-sixte while retreating, and will riposte straight to arm; 5 times. On instructor's attack with the double, with an advance, pupil will parry two counter-sixte while retreating, and will riposte by disengage to arm; 5 times.
11. Several slow-motion movements for corrective purposes.
12. Reassemble and salute.

Lesson 15

1. The position preparation, to coming on guard, the guard position, the advance, the retreat.
2. Attack exercise: the double bind.

Instructor's Feint	Pupil's Attack
a. Feint disengage in sixte	Sixte opposition and double bind to shoulder
b. Feint straight thrust in quarte	Quarte opposition and double bind to shoulder
c. Feint straight thrust in quarte	Counter-sixte opposition and double bind to arm
d. Feint disengage in sixte	Counter-quarte opposition and double bind to arm

3. Parry and riposte exercise: instructor will attack while retreating, pupil will parry while advancing.

Instructor's Attack (Retreating, Attacking)	Pupil's Parries (Advancing)	Pupil's Ripostes (Lunge)
a. 1-2	Sixte, counter-sixte	Straight to arm
b. 1-2	Quarte, counter-quarte	Straight to arm
c. 1-2, low, low	Seconde, counter-seconde	Straight under wrist (hand in seconde)
d. Feint straight, disengage	Two counter-sixte	Disengage to arm
e. Double	Two counter-quarte	Disengage to arm

4. Attack exercise: some two-movement attacks, deceiving a beat on the first feint.
5. Time-attack exercise:

Instructor's Attack	Pupil's Parries	Pupil's Ripostes
a. Feint straight, disengage	Quarte opposition	Straight to arm with sixte opposition
b. 1-2	Sixte opposition	Low sixte over the blade, straight to knee with opposition
c. Double	Counter-quarte opposition	Straight to arm with sixte opposition
d. Feint straight, disengage	Counter-sixte opposition	Low sixte over the blade, straight to knee with opposition

180

6.   Explanation and execution of movements to be used against a left-handed opponent; two-movement attacks.
7.   Counter-riposte exercise: #13.
8.   Second counter-riposte exercise: #13.
9.   Speed exercise, attack: 5 doubles to the arm, in both lines.
10.   Speed exercise, parry and riposte:
        On instructor's attack with the double, pupil will parry two counter-sixte and riposte by disengage to the arm; 5 times.
        On instructor's attack with the double, pupil will parry two counter-quarte and riposte by disengage to the arm; 5 times.
11.   Several slow-motion movements for corrective purposes.
12.   Reassemble and salute.

Lesson 16

1. The guard position, the advance, the retreat, and some slow-motion movements.
2. Attack exercise: the false attack.

Pupil's False Attack (Half-lunge)	Instructor's Parry	Pupil's Final Attack (Lunge)
a. Feint straight in quarte	Quarte	Deceive parry, disengage to arm with opposition
b. Feint disengage to sixte	Sixte	Deceive parry, disengage to forearm with opposition
c. Feint straight in quarte	Quarte, riposte, straight to arm	Parry quarte, counter-riposte straight to arm with opposition
d. Feint disengage to sixte	sixte, riposte, straight to arm	Parry sixte, counter-riposte by disengage to arm, with opposition
e. Feint straight to knee	Low quarte	Deceive parry and disengage to knee

3. Parry and riposte exercise:

Instructor's Attack (Advance)	Pupil's Parry	Pupil's Riposte (No Lunge)
a. Beat, straight to forearm	Quarte by beat	Straight to forearm
b. Beat, disengage in sixte to arm	Sixte by beat	Straight to forearm
c. Beat in low line, straight to leg	Low quarte by beat	Disengage to forearm
d. Beat in low line, straight to leg	Seconde by beat	Disengage to forearm (hand in sixte)

4. Attack exercise: some two-movement attacks, with an advance, ending in the low line.
5. Counter-riposte exercise: student's parry of the riposte and his counter-riposte will be from the lunge position.

Pupil's Attack (Holding Lunge)	Instructor's Parries	Instructor's Ripostes	Pupil's Parry	Pupil's Counter-Riposte
a. 1-2	Sixte, quarte opposition	Disengage (arm)	Sixte opposition	Straight (arm)

182

b. 1-2	Quarte, sixte opposition	Disengage (forearm)	Quarte opposition	Straight (shoulder)
c. Double	Two counter-quarte by opposition	Disengage (arm)	Sixte opposition	Straight (shoulder)
d. Feint to sixte, disengage	Sixte, counter-sixte	Disengage (arm)	Quarte opposition	Straight (arm)

6.   The flèche attack during the time the instructor is recovering his guard position. The instructor will execute a 1-2 with a lunge, and the student will parry sixte, counter-sixte opposition; then, maintaining the opposition, he will start his flèche as the instructor begins to recover his guard position. On the instructor's feint to the knee, the pupil will parry low quarte going into an envelopment and will start his flèche maintaining the opposition.

7.   Counter-riposte exercise: #14.

8.   Second counter-riposte exercise: #14.

9.   Speed exercise, attack: Beat in tierce, disengage to knee, nails up; 5 times. Beat in tierce, disengage to underside of arm; 5 times.

10.   Some slow-motion movements, as a 1-2 or double, with full lunge, for corrective purposes.

11.   Reassemble and salute.

Lesson 17

1. The guard position, the lunge, the forward guard, the retreat, the lunge, on guard, the retreat, the advance, jumping forward, jumping backward.

2. Attack exercise, with the advance:

Instructor (Retreat)	Pupil's Attack (With Advance, Lunge)
a. Keeps arm between two lines, almost extended	Quarte opposition, straight to arm in one motion
b. Keeps arm between two lines, almost extended	Counter-sixte opposition, straight to shoulder in one motion
c. Keeps arm extended and takes quarte opposition	Deceive quarte opposition, disengage to arm
d. Keeps arm extended and takes sixte opposition	Deceive sixte opposition, disengage to arm

3. Attack on a preparation:

Instructor	Pupil's Attack
a. Beat in quarte	Answer by a straight thrust to forearm
b. Beat in sixte	Answer by a straight thrust to forearm
c. Beat in low quarte	Answer by a disengage to upper surface of forearm
d. Beat in low quarte	Answer by a straight thrust to knee

4. Attack exercise: some two-movement to wrist and forearm, preceded by a beat.

5. Parry and riposte exercise:

Instructor's Attack (Advance)	Pupil's Parries (Retreat)	Pupil's Riposte (Lunge)
a. 1-2, low, high	Seconde, tierce by beat	Straight to underside of forearm
b. 1-2, high, low	Sixte, seconde by beat	Straight to underside of forearm
c. Feint straight, disengage	Seconde over the blade, counter-seconde	Straight to underside of forearm
d. Feint straight, disengage	Counter-sixte, seconde over the blade	Straight to underside of forearm

6. Explanation of execution of the counter-riposte by bind:

184

Pupils' Attack (No lunge)	Instructor's Parries	Instructor's Ripostes (No Lunge)	Pupil's Counter-Riposte by bind
a. 1-2	Sixte, quarte opposition	Disengage to arm	Sixte opposition going into bind to knee
b. Feint straight, disengage	Quarte, sixte opposition	Disengage to arm	Quarte opposition going into bind to knee
c. 1-2, high low	Sixte, seconde opposition	Straight to leg	Seconde opposition going into bind to arm
d. 1-2, high, low	Quarte, low, quarte opposition	Straight to leg	Low quarte opposition going into bind to shoulder

7. Explanation and execution of the riposte at the close distance (see tierce, seconde); closing in on an opponent.
8. Counter-riposte exercise: #15.
9. Second counter-riposte exercise: #15.
10. Speed exercise, attack: Five 1-2's, in each line.
11. Speed exercise, parry and riposte: on the instructor's 1-2 attack in each line, pupil will parry and riposte to wrist or forearm.
12. Several slow-motion doubles and disengages to body, with full lunge.
13. Reassemble and salute.

185

Lesson 18

1. The guard position, the lunge, the forward guard, the retreat, the lunge, the guard position, the retreat, the advance, jumping forward and jumping backward.
2. Attack exercise: the double bind, first from sixte, then from quarte and finally from seconde.
3. Parry and riposte exercise: riposte by the cross.

Instructor' Attack	Pupil's Parries and Riposte (No Lunge)
a. 1-2	Sixte, quarte opposition and cross to leg
b. Feint straight, disengage	Quarte, sixte opposition and cross to leg
c. Double	Counter-quarte, sixte opposition and cross to leg
d. Feint straight, deceiving a counter-parry	Counter-sixte, quarte opposition and cross to leg

4. Redoubling exercise: two-movement attack.

Pupil's Attack (Holding the lunge)	Instructor's Parries (Retreat)	Pupil's Redouble (From Lunge Position)
a. 1-2	Sixte, quarte	Beat, straight to forearm
b. 1-2	Sixte, counter-sixte	Disengage to arm
c. 1-2	Sixte, counter-sixte opposition	Disengage to underside of arm
d. Feint straight, disengage	Quarte, counter-quarte opposition	Press, disengage to leg

5. Parry and riposte exercise: by envelopment.

Instructor' Attack (Advance)	Pupil's Parries and Riposte (No Lunge)
a. 1-2, high, low	Sixte, seconde opposition and envelopment to arm (hand in seconde)
b. 1-2, high, low	Quarte, low quarte opposition and envelopment to arm
c. Feint straight, deceiving a counter-parry by going to the low line	Counter-sixte, seconde opposition and envelopment to arm (hand in seconde)

186

d. Double to low line	Counter-quarte, low quarte opposition and envelopment to shoulder

6. Explanation and execution of the parries used against flèche attacks: see "The Flèche."
7. Counter-riposte exercise: #16.
8. Second counter-riposte exercise: # 16.
9. Speed exercise, attack: time attacks using stop-thrusts. Instructor will attack five times with the 1-2 (in both lines), advancing; then three times with the double (in both lines), advancing. In each case, pupil will take a simple opposition on the first movement and will then stop-thrust on the second movement.
10. Several slow-motion movements with full lunges, for corrective purposes.
11. Reassemble and salute.

Notes On Teaching The Épée

This paragraph contains a few remarks on teaching the épée, derived from many years of experience as a coach. It can have little interest for the beginning fencer, and he is advised to turn to the last chapter; nor is it designed for the professional fencing coach, who will have his own methods and short-cuts. But there are many advanced fencers who have obtained successful results in tournament play, who possess good style in fencing the épée, yet who find themselves at a loss when it comes to imparting to others the principles of their épée play. Such fencers are constantly besieged by beginners to show them a few pointers, to explain the reasons for any given movement; in short, to do some informal coaching. This section is for them.

I have found that most non-professional fencers can teach the foil and sabre adequately enough upon need, but when teaching the épée they fall into the error of starting with the assumption that the épée is like the foil, with a few exceptions. This false basis of instruction is enough to prevent any beginner from becoming a good épée fencer, unless he is good enough to do so in spite of his instruction. The épée should be considered as completely different from the other two weapons. It has its own technique and principles, its own "action" and "reaction," and should be so taught. And yet the épée is the simplest of the three weapons. Less time is required to develop a competent épée fencer than a foil or sabre fencer.

The reason for this difference lies in the uncomplicated nature of the épée. There is actually less to learn before a beginner begins to win bouts. It cannot be two of ten emphasized that simple play is the best; if the beginner will master the basic pattern of épée fencing, if he will learn to attack in line, to replace or remise when he misses or is parried, to parry attacks made in line and

187

to stop-thrust all others, he will have all he needs to be successful in his own class. As such a fencer becomes more experienced and continues to take instruction and to compete in tournaments, he will add finer points to his knowledge of the art; he will learn strategy; he will become adept in sizing up unfamiliar opponents; he will develop his own tricks and his own style, and may eventually begin to win championships.

But he must have the correct basis to start with. All the tricks in the world will be ineffective unless founded on the true principles of the épée. That these principles are imperfectly understood in this country is evidenced by the low calibre of épée fencing, at least in comparison with foil and sabre, to be seen in tournaments. I feel myself justified, therefore, in assuming that more generally disseminated knowledge of the special technique of the épée will result in better épée fencing, and accordingly am devoting several additional sections, of which this is one, to my book on the épée.

Let us assume that an advanced fencer who has participated in several major tournaments has been asked to act as amateur coach of some college fencing team. Such a fencer will find himself at the beginning of the fencing season with a score or more of aspirants to the team, most of whom have never fenced before. The coach is faced with the problem of sorting them out, that is, of deciding in each individual case which of the three weapons the beginner is best suited for. His correct solution of this problem will save him months of instruction, for I have found that in most cases the physical and temperamental make-up of any individual will predispose him toward one of the three weapons. I have known men who have worked several seasons with the foil, with no success whatsoever; and then have taken a half-dozen lessons with the sabre and blossomed out as championship material with that weapon. If such men had been correctly "diagnosed" at the beginning, much valuable time would have been saved and much discouragement avoided.

What to look for? How to proceed? I have found that the best way is to give the entire squad a few lessons, individually and in groups, in the fundamentals of the foil; not so many as to develop the foil "reaction" in the beginner and yet enough for the coach to size him up from the point of view of reflexes, muscular development, temperament, speed and intelligence. After these preliminary lessons, it should be possible to make three rough divisions in the squad, corresponding to the three weapons, and to pursue thorough instruction in each one.

Let us consider the sabre first. The sabre-man is usually muscular, with spring to his movements. His tendency is to hit hard, although after proper instruction this tendency should be converted to speed. Height makes no difference, nor is reach important. What counts is muscular tone, nervous energy and endurance. In many cases such a beginner will experience difficulty

188

in keeping his elbow sufficiently "inside" for foil or épée; the wider sabre guard position will set him at his ease. Men who like boxing will generally prefer the sabre. The foil fencer is the planner, the strategist, the trickster. He fights with his head. He employs a wide variety of methods and suits his play to the opponent of the moment, whom he must size up while he is fighting him. He needs speed rather than strength, nerve rather than muscle; he will generally be of medium height and wiry. A stout man will generally not be fast enough for foil.

The épée fencer is the cool fencer. He does not go in for tricks or a wide variety of methods. He sticks to a few time-honored principles. His constant striving is for accuracy of point. Ile does not fluster easily, nor react nervously to a feint. Physically, he will generally be tall and have a good reach.

Let us assume now that on the épée squad there is a pupil who has never fenced before, and one who has fenced previously with the foil. The coach will have to handle the two somewhat differently. In the first case, the first step in instruction is obviously that of teaching him the make-up of an épée, how to hold it, the guard, the lunge; in short, all the barest fundamentals as discussed in the earlier chapters of this book. In the second case, the pupil will be familiar with these fundamentals for the most part; but care must be taken to stress the points of difference between the foil and the épée. He must be trained to attack the arm rather than the body, and he must be taught to fall on guard midway between the sixte and low sixte positions, with the arm three-quarters extended and the point slightly lower than the hand; and so forth.

Our two pupils will now be on equal footing, with two important differences. The beginner will lack the foil fencer's experience and muscular training; but the foil fencer will have a series of automatic muscular and nervous reactions left over from foil, which he must change before becoming expert with the épée. Now both pupils should be taught the "épée action," which consists of two parts: l. To attack in line, the arm almost fully extended without stiffness, the point threatening the closest part of the target. 2. If the attack is avoided or parried, to redouble or remise immediately to the closest part of the target.

The foil fencer must be made to fight his tendency to raise his point in the guard position and to bend back his arm after an un successful attack, whereas the beginner, having no trained responses to adjust, will develop correct reactions with no difficulty.

The next step is to teach the pupil: the "épée reaction," which also consists of two parts: 1. To make a stop-thrust to the forearm against any feint or attack made with the point out of line. Here the beginner will also have the advantage. 2. To parry any attack made in line. In this the foil-man will have a great advantage over the beginner, as here he can use his normal foil reaction.

189

The only danger is his tendency to use it too much, at times when he should stop-thrust. This then is the broad outline of the course to be followed in teaching the épée. The non-professional coach will find the lessons included in this chapter of great use in breaking down the large amount of instruction necessary into correctly timed dosages.

A few hints. In giving lessons, first explain the lesson in advance to the pupil. The student should ordinarily be placed in the engagement of sixte, but from time to time, especially in the beginning, he should be placed in the engagement of quarte, without taking the blade. The instructor, in giving the lesson, should vary the position of his hand from time to time-a little too far to the right, or to the left, a little too high or a little too low, sometimes with his arm bent and sometimes extended-so as to prepare the pupil for any kind of opponent.

Use a pointe d'arret during the lesson.

When the pupil is introduced to a new movement, he should first master it in place, and only then should he be made to coordinate it with an advance or a retreat.

The student should be taught to disengage on any movement made by his opponent in an attempt to take his blade. The touch should be directed to the shoulder, arm or forearm.

The pupil should be taught to disengage and touch under the forearm on any forward movement, except a lunge, made by the instructor in the high line.

The student's first motion in any attack in the high line should be to raise his point above his instructor's épée guard. The height to which he must raise it will be governed by the height of the part of the target he wishes to touch. The second movement, which is executed at almost the same time, is to extend the arm. When the arm is extended, the position of the hand should be slightly above the point of the épée. He should then lunge with opposition.

To accustom the student to maintain, automatically, the proper distance at all times, the instructor should frequently advance and retreat without any verbal warning. The pupil will thus be forced to advance and retreat himself to keep the proper distance.

To make certain that the student understands the movements sufficiently to use them in a bout, the instructor should, from time to time, fight an actual bout with his student. During these bouts he should at first deliberately make errors to see whether or not the student is able to take quick advantage of them. Later, as the student progresses, the instructor should cease

190

making these obvious errors and force the student to open a line for himself by some preparation to his attack.

The coach should accustom his pupil to execute a stop-thrust immediately upon an attack to the low line, and to this end he should, from time to time during the course of the lesson, attack his pupil in the low line without any advance notice, to see whether or not the student is developing the proper reactions.

When the instructor wants his pupil to execute a stop-thrust on his attack, he should make his attack out of line. If he wishes his pupil to parry the attack, he should make his attack very close and in line, so as to force the student to take a parry.

The student should not be allowed to lunge in such a way as to gain distance by sliding. This is what happens when he tries to cover too much ground during a lunge. It is much better to close to within lunging distance before making the lunge. Otherwise the pupil will never be able to coordinate his point with his foot-work. If for any reason the pupil has lost his proper distance, he should be trained to recover it automatically.

It is a good idea to practice two-movement attacks in the lesson; but in the bout best results will be obtained from single-movement attacks, sometimes preceded by a preparation.

During the lesson the instructor may substitute an advance for his lunge. If he advances with his attack and stays on the advance, the pupil should realize for himself that he does not need to lunge to touch on the riposte. If the instructor wishes the student to lunge on the riposte, he should retreat before takin g his parry.

Start at the earliest possible moment to train the pupil to use his own eyes and his own head.

CHAPTER VIII
Practical Advice

General Advice On The Bout

The following remarks pertain to the bout itself and should be useful to the fencer who is beginning tournament fencing. It would be advisable to re-read this paragraph from time to time.

In general, with the épée, the offensive is more successful than the defensive; that is, emphasis on the attack gives better results than emphasis on the parry and riposte. Some attacks such as the stop-thrust, however, can be launched from a defensive position.

The crouch of the guard position is less marked in the épée than in the foil. The body should be turned sideways as much as possible, without hampering the ease of execution of any of the movements. The first movement in a bout should be to take a short step backward so as to get out of reach of your opponent.

Do not limit yourself to one type of attack. Your opponent will soon solve the problem of how to meet it. You should master a variety of attacks and adapt them to each opponent, after you have sounded out his capabilities in the preliminary skirmishes.

Keep your eyes on your opponent's hand; it will "telegraph" ample warning of danger.

Keep moving. Do not freeze in any position for any length of time. Make yourself hard to hit by using short steps to change the distance between yourself and your opponent. In this manner you will make him misjudge on his attacks and parries.

In the advance and retreat, your arm movements must be perfectly coordinated with your leg movements.

During the retreat, keep your arm almost extended (but without tenseness) and your point in line.

Do not advance aimlessly into your opponent's point. Keep out of your opponent's reach until you are ready to attack; then close the distance rapidly and lunge.

Do not give your opponent your blade, that is, do not engage blades. If he has been taught to handle the épée like a foil, this will disconcert him completely. Maintain your blade in line between the sixte and low sixte positions, with your épée guard slightly above the level of your opponent's guard and your point slightly below the level of your hand; in this manner you will have the maximum protection against a stop-thrust and will also be in a good position to execute one yourself.

If, however, you feel that your hand is stronger than your opponent's hand or that your point is surer, you may engage blades with the purpose of dominating his. Do not let yourself be fooled, however, many a wiry slender fencer has a stronger hand than would be assumed.

If your original attack misses or is parried, redouble or remise while you are recovering your guard.

If you prepare your attack with a feint, make i t in the opposite line from that in which your attack will terminate. Never allow your opponent to anticipate where your attack will land.

The best times to launch an attack are: 1. Whenever your adversary's point is out of line. 2. Whenever he bends his arm back for any purpose. 3. While he is recovering his guard.

Some fencers have acquired the bad habit of retreating to the end of the strip before deciding to launch their attack. Be prudent against such a fencer; take your time. When he approaches the end of the strip, make a false attack; he will be expecting an attack and will probably extend his arm to try to stop-thrust, and this extension of the arm is just what you want.

Take his blade with a beat, with opposition, or with a bind or double bind, and touch to the forearm or arm.

A fencer who makes spasmodic successive attacks while continually advancing often loses control over his own movements, and such a fencer can usually be successfully stopped.

If your opponent retreats during your attack, recover your guard position forward, keeping your point in line with his forearm while doing so. This will give you the distance he has lost and will place you quickly in a position to attack again.

Patience is very necessary in épée. Bide the best time for your attack. Many fencers have won championships using only one or two special attacks, but they all carefully chose the right time to launch those attacks.

If your arm gets tired, retreat out of reach of your opponent, bend it back and extend it several times, drop your arm or turn it, relax it-any movement which will allow the blood to flow back into the arm; and then resume your guard position.

It is a mistake to extend your arm excessively on a feint. Against a fencer who does so, execute a bind or double bind, or a flèche attack, with opposition.

The length of your lunge will depend upon the distance between your point and the portion of the target you wish to touch. Regardless of the distance and the length of the lunge taken, however, the left leg must be snapped open and stretched fully at every lunge to secure the maximum speed from the muscles of the foot and leg. The calibre of a fencer depends not so much on his strength or the complexity of his attacks as it does upon his guard position, his sense of timing and his ability to take immediate and effective advantage of any opening or weakness.

A fencer who continually provokes a corps-a-corps will never rise above mediocrity as a fencer.

An épée man often encounters difficulty against an opponent who fences épée like foil, with his arm bent. Against such an opponent, (1) do not engage blades, (2) keep your point just below the level of your épée guard, and (3) never answer his feint. Use the stop-thrust to the arm. Attack often in the low line. Make flèche attacks without taking the blade.

Against an adversary who keeps his arm extended: (1) Attack by taking his blade; for example, make an expulsion and straight thrust to his arm, or a beat, thrust to the arm. (2) Attack by taking his blade with quarte, sixte, counter-quarte, counter-sixte, or seconde opposition, followed by a simple attack. (3) Attack by taking his blade with a bind or double bind with quarte, sixte or seconde opposition. (4) Make a flèche attack, taking his blade with the hand in quinte, and touch to the body or leg.

To sum up the conduct of a bout in épée: fall on guard as indicated in this book, without contact of the blades and with the point slightly below the level of your hand. Keep out of reach of your opponent, closing only to attack. Your legs must be in as constant a state of motion as your arm. Keep varying the distance, advancing and retreating by short steps. Make short lunges. Although your point must be in line as much as possible, keep moving your hand slowly, describing close movements and varying the cadence, passing through sixte, counter-sixte, seconde, then, for example, two counter-sixte, seconde, sixte, or two counter-quarte, seconde, sixte and counter-sixte. If after taking several counter-parries your opponent attacks with a double, take a simple parry on his first feint. If after taking several simple parries, your opponent attacks with a 1-2, for example, take a counter-parry on his first feint. fake your movements precise; what is not simple and clean-cut is dangerous. A stop-thrust to the arm can upset the most careful and complicated preparation.

Never underestimate your opponent. A beginner is often more dangerous than an advanced fencer, simply by not knowing just what he is doing. Sometimes the movements he executes by chance happen to be the right answer for your attack. Overconfidence alone has lost many a bout.

In general, remember that the best movement in épée is the stop-thrust, which must be executed whenever the adversary leaves a line open, even momentarily, during his attack. In order to avoid a stop-thrust, never start the final movement of your attack until your point is in line and your arm protected behind your épée guard.

Left-Handed Fencers

The directions given throughout this book are of course predicated upon the use of the right arm in fencing. The left-handed fencer will have to substitute "counterclockwise" for "clockwise," "left" for "right," "inside" for "outside," and so on.

A left-hander should stay slightly more on guard in sixte than a right-hander. In this way he can oblige a right-hander to attack him in quarte, or low quarte. which are his strongest parries and from which he can launch his strongest ripostes. When the left-hander does take quarte parry, however, he should execute it narrowly; he should not go any farther to the right than the right-hander's sixte position. His hand then will come from the outside line and will stop directly in front of his left breast.

A left-handed fencer should be especially trained to execute the stop-thrust as he moves his body back or he moves his left leg back. The stop will usually be directed to the outside of the forearm.

When a right-hander fences a left-hander, his hand should take a guard position a little more to the right than usual. This closes his sixte line, his weakest line against a left-hander, and leaves his quarte line open. This is to be recommended, as against a left-hander the efficacy of the parries is completely reversed; here the quarte and counter-quarte parries are to be preferred to sixte and counter-sixte. The right-hander's chief strategy in fencing a left-hander should be to try to open up the latter's line of sixte. To

196

this encl, the right-hander should use the false attack. He should also make full use of the bind from quarte to the low line, as well as the double bind from the same line. Another effective attack is the beat in quarte and an immediate thrust to the outside line. The right-hander should by all means avoid ending his attack in the left-hander's inside line, for, as has been said before and as is here emphasized again, the left-hander's quarte is his strongest line. If the right-hander persists in letting the left-hander get on his outside line, he is pitting his weakest position against his opponent's strongest position; the consequences are dangerous. In this position, a sharp beat by the left-hander can easily disarm the right-hander, or temporarily dislocate the grip in his hand.

In a bout between two right-handed fencers, the flèche will usually be made passing to the left side of the strip, that is, in the outside line. Against a left-handed fencer, however, this will generally not succeed, as the left is the left-hander's strongest line. It is better to execute the flèche passing to the right, or to use the forward flèche to the body or leg, preceded by the quinte opposition. In this flèche the attacker runs straight forward, stopping just short of his opponent's body.

Book III: The Sabre

CHAPTER I
Preliminary Phases

The sabre consists of four parts: the blade, the first third of which is flat and the other two-thirds triangular; the guard, which protects the hand; the grip, which is held in the hand; and the pommel, which is the small, rounded nut that locks the parts together. The "forte" of the blade begins at the guard and ends slightly beyond the middle; the remainder of the blade to the tip is the "foible." The blade has two cutting edges: the front edge runs the entire length of the blade; the back edge runs from the tip along approximately the first third of the blade. Attacks may be made with either cutting edge or with the point.

For competitions, the rules prescribe that the overall length of the sabre must be less than 41.3 inches, and its weight (everything included and ready for use) must be more than 11.5 oz. and less than 17.6 oz. The prime requisite of a good sabre is fine balance. When holding the sabre in your hand in the guard position, the balance should be such that when the last three fingers are relaxed the point will drop slowly of its own weight. Too heavy a point will slow up your attack and will cause your wrist to tire quickly. Too light a point will cause your attack to be wide and miss; it will make both your attacks and parries insufficient. The blade should be made of medium weight, with or without grooves, and of the maximum length allowed by

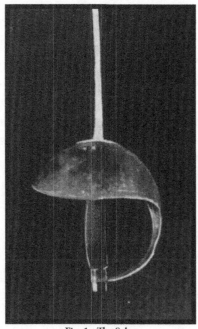

Fig. 1 - The Sabre

the rules. The guard should be of light steel, aluminum, or of a composite alloy. The guard may be center or off-center. The author prefers the center guard, for although the off-center guard will furnish more protection for your forearm, the center guard will yield better balance and greater precision in your movements.

The grip should be as simple as possible, light, slender and slightly curved so as to adapt itself to the hand. It should be made of wood with slightly raised wooden squares on it to facilitate gripping. The bigger the grip, the more fully it fills the hand and the less you can use your fingers. Do not use any trimmings on the grip, such as bulges for the fingers or palm, and the like. Standard grips are the result of painstaking research by experts for generations. Do not try to improve them.

A General Discussion Of Sabre Fencing

Sabre fencing today, unlike its historical prototype, is a sport bound by certain rules and conventions. A brief resume of these conventions follows.

Not all parts of the body are valid sabre targets. The sabre target includes only those parts of the body, including the head, arms and hands, above a horizontal line drawn around the body and passing through the highest points of the intersections of the thighs and trunk of the fencer when in the "on guard" position. Cuts or thrusts to all other parts of the body are called fouls, and stop the action with no awards and no penalties. Such normally invalid body surfaces may, however, be considered valid when the fencer-intentionally or as the result of an abnormal position-substitutes them for a valid body surface.

Sabre bouts are decided in five touches. The first contestant to score that number is the winner. Touches may be scored with the point (thrusts), with any part of the front cutting edge of the blade (cuts), or with the forward third of the back edge of the blade (counter-cuts). To be counted, point thrusts must arrive clearly and cleanly; those thrusts that just graze the target without making the blade bend, even slightly, should not be counted as touches but should be considered as having passed by.

Since the sabre blade is thin and flexible, it often occurs that even though a cut is cleanly parried the blade of the attacker will whip over the parrying blade or guard and touch. This is not considered a touch and should not nullify any subsequent action.

If such an attack touches through the parry because the parry was insufficient, the touch will count.

If a thrust or a cut directed at a valid surface is parried, and as a result of the parry strikes an invalid surface, there is no foul, and the action should continue.

When both contestants have been touched in a phrase, not simultaneously, the first touch counts. When the touches land simultaneously, the right of way must be determined. If a foul has the right of way, the whole action is thrown out. If no right of way can be determined for simultaneous touches, the action is considered a double touch and is thrown out, even if one of the touches is a foul. It can be seen, therefore, that the right of way in the sabre, like the foil and unlike the épée, is of extreme importance. This right of way passes back and forth quickly from one contestant to the other, according to the action each one takes. The original right of way lies with the fencer initiating the original attack. If that attack is parried, the right of way passes to the defender, who now has the right to return the attack (riposte). The original attacker does not have the right to counter-riposte until he has parried the defender's riposte; and so on.

If the defender has his point in line, that is, his arm extended and his point directed at a legitimate part of the target, the attacker must first deviate the defender's threatening point by an opposition, a beat, press, bind, or the like, so as to avoid falling on the defender's point. If this attempt to deviate a threatening point fails, then the right of way passes to the defender.

Sabre fencing is the most spectacular of the three weapons. The action is wide and easily followed by the eye. Sabre fencing requires fine muscular coordination and tone, and perhaps demands more strength and endurance than the other two weapons. Foot-work is more vigorous; the jump forward and backward is often used.

The sabre bout is fought on the same strip as the foil and the épée bouts. The jury is composed of a director or referee and four judges. The director stands midway between the two contestants, about four yards from the strip: the judges form a quadrangle about the contestants, one at each side of each contestant, at least a yard from him and behind him. The two judges flanking Fencer A will watch Fencer B, and the two flanking Fencer B will watch Fencer A.

The two contestants assume their places at the two ends of the strip. They are in the position preparatory to coming on guard. At the director's command to fall on guard, both execute the salute and fall on guard, a short distance from the center of the strip. The director, after asking the contestants if they are ready, gives the command, "Fence!" The two contestants are now free to conduct their combat in any manner consistent with the rules of fencing. (For a full exposition of these rules, see the book "Fencing Rules" published in New York by the Amateur Fencers' League of America.) After any decisive phase, the director will call "Halt!" and call for a note of the jury. Each of the four judges of the jury has one vote; he may vote only on the materiality of any action, that is, whether any attack actually arrived and whether on valid or foul territory. The director has 1 ½ votes; he is the only one who may vote on validity, that is, on time and the right of way. To the vote of the jury the director will add his own and render the decision. After the decision, the director will place the two contestants on guard again, and the play will continue in this manner until one of the two has scored three touches. At this point the contestants will change sides, and the play will continue until one of the two has scored five touches. Upon the announcement of the last decision, the two contestants salute each other, remove their masks and shake hands.

This in brief is an overall picture of the conventions of sabre fencing and the conduct of a bout. A detailed discussion of the technique of the sabre follows.

Holding The Sabre

Hold the sabre with the cutting edge down. Allow the grip to rest on the second phalanx of the index finger of the right hand. Press the thumb flat against the back of the grip. With the other fingers held close together, encircle the grip so that the fingers will rest on the left side. The pommel will fall slightly below the center of the base of the palm. Grip the sabre lightly but firmly; if you grip it too tightly, free finger-play will be impossible.

Finger-, Wrist-, Forearm- And Arm-Play

The fingers and wrist are used much more than the forearm in sabre play. The rest of the arm and the shoulder are little used.

Make the elbow your pivot. If the shoulder is used in this capacity, your forearm and elbow will be exposed, both in parrying and in launching an attack. In all your movements your forearm should be kept protected as much and as long as possible behind the sabre guard. When your forearm is in motion, use your arm to maintain the direction. If you use the shoulder as a pivot, you are likely to lose this direction, since the error from a slight deviation will increase with the distance of the pivot from the target.

In executing a feint above or below your opponent's blade, alternately contract and relax your fingers on the grip, with the help of the wrist. Contract your fingers slightly also in the parries and relax them slightly in the ripostes. If you do not relax your fingers during a bout, your arm will become unduly tightened and

203

tired. Practice, then, to contract your fingers only in the execution of parries, feints, beats, presses and expulsions.

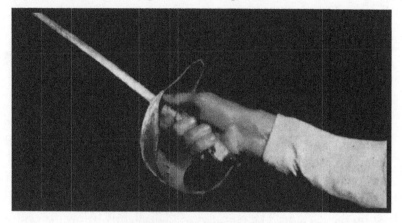

Fig. 2 - Holding the sabre: vertical cut

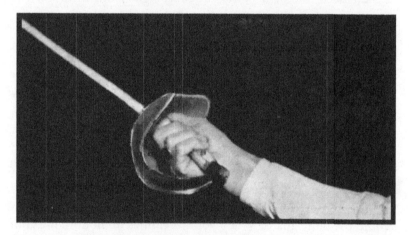

Fig. 3 - Holding the sabre: horizontal cut from right to left

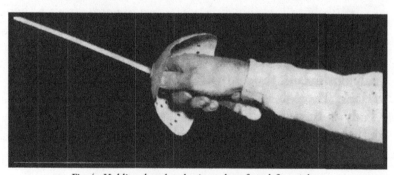

Fig. 4 - Holding the sabre: horizontal cut from left to right

204

The forearm is brought into use in the different positions of the parries, and in the extension of the arm in feints, attacks and ripostes.

The forearm, wrist and fingers are all brought into use in the execution of a cut and a moulinet.

Position Preparatory To Coming On Guard

Preparatory to coming on guard, place your feet at right angles, heels together with your right toe pointing toward your opponent. Keep the legs straight. Extend your right arm fully from the body, obliquely downward, the sabre in line with your arm. Your thumb is at 9 o'clock. The point of your blade is a few inches from the strip. Your body is turned well to the left, while your head faces front. Your left arm is extended fully and obliquely downward so that your hand is about fifteen inches from your side, the palm held up in a natural manner.

Fig. 5 - Position preparatory to coming on guard

Fig. 6 - The guard position

The Guard Position

The guard position is assumed in three counts, which are to be practiced until they flow into each other.

Count 1. Being in the preparatory position, raise the sabre, keeping your arm extended and stopping the hand at the height

205

of the right shoulder and slightly to the right. Your thumb is still at 8 o'clock. The sabre is still in a prolongation of your arm, its point level with your eyes and its cutting edge still to the right.

Count 2. Now bend back the right arm until it is almost three-fourths extended, turning the hand at the same time until the thumb is back at 9 o'clock, the cutting edge to the right. The hand is now at the height of the right breast. The right elbow is about six inches from the side of your body; it is turned in, that is, displaced slightly to the left across your body. The point of the sabre is at the height of your eyes. Simultaneously with the bending of the right arm, the left arm describes a short arc upward, turns and takes its place below the left hip at the point of articulation with the left leg.

Count 3. Immediately after these arm movements, bend the knees, simultaneously moving the right foot forward flatly, just above the strip, to a distance of approximately two feet. The right leg from the knee down is perpendicular to the strip and the right heel is in line with the left heel. The left leg is bent to the extent that a perpendicular dropped from the left knee will fall just slightly inside the arch of the foot. Keep the body erect on its haunches, with the left shoulder back, and present as narrow a target to your adversary's blade as your own physical make-up will allow.

This guard position is the basis, unless otherwise specified, for all the movements and positions described in this book. This tierce guard places your hand in the center of all the parry positions, enabling you to make a rapid displacement of your hand to any of the parries. You will also find the tierce guard favorable toward the execution of any attack.

While the tierce guard is the one generally advocated in this book, there are several basic guard positions for the sabre. The beginner is urged, however, not to experiment with other guards until he has mastered the tierce guard. The Italian guard position is usually tierce or a high tierce with the point slightly down. The arm is bent only slightly. The Hungarian guard is usually a low tierce with the point slightly down; no contact at all is made with the opponent's blade. The French guard is generally tierce and sometimes quarte.

Reassembling

Reassembling is the movement by which the fencer assumes, from the guard position, the position preparatory to coming on guard. It is executed by reversing the movements of coming on guard.

Reassemble whenever the instructor gives a brief rest period during a lesson; at the end of your lesson, followed by a salute; and at the end of a bout, followed by a salute. You may reassemble either forward or to the rear.

The Salute

From the preparatory position or Count 1 of coming on guard, to salute, bend the arm and move the hand (turning the thumb from 9 to 3 o'clock) until it is level with the chin and about five inches from it. Keep the sabre in a prolongation of the forearm. Then lower the blade forward in an arc, completely extending your arm and turning the thumb back to 9 o'clock, until it is again in the position preparatory to coming on guard.

From this position, to salute to the left, raise your right hand back to the level of the left breast, turning the thumb to 3 o'clock and keeping the arm only three-fourths extended. The tip of the blade will fall outside the left limit of the body. Turn your head to follow the blade.

From here, to salute to the right, move the hand horizontally across the body to a position in front of the right breast, turning the thumb back to 9 o'clock and keeping the arm still three-fourths bent. The tip of the blade should fall outside the right limit of the body. Turn your head to follow the blade.

The Advance

The advance is used to approach an adversary out of reach of your blade. To advance, move the right foot forward and follow up with the left to the correct guard distance, without otherwise disturbing the position. Take small, quick, light steps so that you maintain perfect balance at all times. Advance with caution. Watch your opponent's movements all the time, and be ready instantly to parry a surprise attack made against your advance. Coordinate your arm movements with your leg movements; the first movement of the arm must be made at the same time as the advance.

The Retreat

The retreat is used to get out of the reach of your adversary's blade. To retreat, move your left foot to the rear and follow immediately with the right until the proper guard distance is attained. Do not otherwise disturb the guard position. Maintain perfect balance at all times.

Ordinarily, a slightly longer step is used for the retreat than for the advance.

Jumping Forward

The jump forward is used as a quick, disconcerting means of shortening the distance, and, when used in conjunction with an attack, as a source of speed and power for the attack.

The jump forward should be very short, preferably less than fifteen inches. The shorter the distance covered, the faster the attack and the easier the maintenance of balance. At the end of the jump forward, both feet strike the strip lightly, simultaneously and flatly. The guard position is not otherwise disturbed.

Jumping Backward

The jump backward is used to regain the proper guard distance from the opponent. It is generally used, rather than the simple retreat, after a full lunge in which some distance was lost because of sliding, and in coping with a flèche attack. As in the jump forward, the feet strike the floor flatly and at the same time, and the guard position remains unchanged.

Foot-Signals

To execute the foot-signals, tap the strip lightly with the right heel and follow immediately with a heavier stamp of the entire right sole. The weight of your body will be shifted slightly to your left leg. Do not otherwise disturb the guard position.

Use foot-signals to check your balance while on guard, or in the midst of a bout to attract the attention of the judges to the fact that you have a request to make.

Distance

In sabre combat, the proper distance is such that with a full lunge you can touch your opponent on the middle of his forearm. Be careful that in the excitement of a bout you do not forget to maintain this distance.

Before a competition, test out your judgment of distance by taking a few full lunges against an opponent.

In practice, train yourself to maintain this distance at all times by following the advances and retreats of your partner with corresponding movements, until the maintenance of the proper distance becomes automatic to you.

Extension Of The Arm

Extend the arm horizon tally without jerking, without exaggeration and without moving the shoulder. Keep the sabre in a prolongation of the arm. The hand will be at such a height that the forearm and elbow are protected behind the sabre guard. The thumb can be in almost any position of the clock, depending on the direction of the cut, counter-cut or thrust: 12 o'clock for a cut to the head, 2 o'clock for a cut to the banderole, 3 o'clock for a cut to the left side, 4 to 5 o'clock for a cut under the cuff, 8 to 10 o'clock for a cut to the outside of the right arm, and so on.

Coming Back On Guard After Extension Of The Arm

To come back on guard after the extension of the arm, bend the arm without jerking and without moving the shoulder, and take up the correct guard position.

Fig. 7 - The lunge

The Lunge

The lunge is the extension given the guard position in an attempt to touch the opponent. To lunge, first extend your arm as indicated above. Then snap open your left leg until it is fully extended, keeping the sole of the left foot flat against the strip. At the same time, move your right foot forward, closely skimming the strip, such a distance that when the right sole is flat on the strip, the right leg from the knee down will be perpendicular to the floor. The right foot is in line with the left heel. The left hand remains in place. The body rests firmly on its haunches, inclined slightly forward in a natural manner. The left shoulder is maintained back as much as possible, and the hips are in a line coincidental with the line of the lunge.

Keep your chin in and your eyes fixed on your opponent's guard.

Recovery Of The Guard Position After The Lunge

The recovery of the guard position after the lunge is, like the lunge, a combination of distinct movements of arm, body and legs that must be mastered to split-second timing to be effective. In the lunge position, the weight of the body is slightly forward. The first movement of the recovery is the bending of the left leg; this movement starts the body weight backward s. Immediately after, the right foot pushes against the strip, thus completing the shifting of the weight to the rear, and the right foot skims backwards over the strip to its original guard position. At the same time as the movement of the right foot—and not before—the right arm bends back to the guard position.

It is also possible to recover the guard position forward after a lunge. Such a recovery will gain for you any distance lost by the opponent during his retreat. The occasional use of this movement will disconcert your opponent. In the forward recovery, the weight of the body is held forward on the right leg, which does not move, while the left leg is brought forward to the proper guard distance.

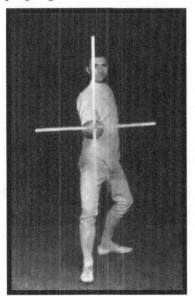

High Line

Low Line

Line

Line

Outside

Inside

Fig. 8 - The lines

The Lines

The lines are those parts of the body where definite parries are made and to which attacks and ripostes are directed. The lines are not the same for all three weapons, since they are relative to the position of the hand. In the sabre, the normal guard position is at the right limit of the body. To set the lines, therefore, the hand is arbitrarily placed at a point directly above the knee and level with the right breast. Every part of the target above the horizontal plane of the hand will be the high line; every part of the target below it will be the low line; the target to the right of the hand will be the outside line; the target to the left will be the inside line. Since the hand is set to the right of center, there will obviously be little of the target in the outside line.

It can be seen, therefore, that attacks to the right cheek and cuff (above) will fall in the outside high line; attacks to the right flank and cuff (below) will fall in the outside low line; attacks to the head, left cheek, banderole and cuff (above) will fall in the inside high line; and attacks to the left flank and cuff (below) will fall in the inside low line. In the next chapter it will be seen that each of these quadrangles-outside high, outside low, inside high and inside low has its appropriate parries.

The Point In Line

In the sabre, where the cutting edge and the point can both be used, the definition "point in line" is applicable only when the arm is extended and the point of the sabre is directed toward a valid part of the target. This expression would not be employed in an attack with the cutting edge, because in this case the sabre edge must be directed a little outside the intended target in such a way as to give a cut at the conclusion of the lunge.

The action "point in line" is a defensive threat which confers the right of way upon the fencer executing it. In order to obtain the right of way for an attack against a "point in line," the attacker must first divert the extended blade.

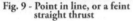

Fig. 9 - Point in line, or a feint straight thrust

Fig. 10 - The high guard

Engagement

Engagement is the contacting of the adversary's blade three or four inches below the point with the foible of your own blade, the body being in the guard position for the purpose of protecting yourself on that side. It may be executed in any of the guard positions. The most suitable engagement, however, is that of tierce, because from that position your hand may move easily to any of the parry positions or attacks.

The engagement of quarte may be used occasionally, but is inadvisable as a general practice because it exposes the cuff too much and does not favor the launching of attacks.

The Engagement Of Tierce

Being on guard, contact your adversary's blade in the outside line and move your sabre to the right limit of your body. Your thumb is at 9 o'clock. Your right elbow is directly in front of your right side and about six inches from it. Your hand is in front of your right breast and level with it; this position will protect your forearm and elbow behind your sabre guard. Your point is level with the top of your head, a little to the right of center.

213

The High Guard

Another effective engagement is the high guard. Being on guard, contact your adversary's blade in the outside line and move your sabre to the right limit of your body. Your thumb is at 7 o'clock. Your hand, elbow and shoulder are on the same level, with the elbow only slightly bent; to do this, your elbow will have to be outside. Your point is level with your belt-line, a little to the right of center. Protect your forearm and elbow as much as possible behind the guard.

Since in this guard the elbow is outside, you gain an advantage in the parries by being able to take them much closer to the body, if the need arises. An additional advantage is derived from having your arm in a position to attack.

Many fencers find, however, that this position is more tiring to the arm than tierce.

CHAPTER II
The Parries

The parry is the act of deflecting from the target an attack made by an adversary. Parries are direct or circular; when executed through the shortest possible distance, they are direct or simple parries; when executed in a circular fashion, they are counter-parries. All parries can be made by beat or opposition. In the parry by beat, the opponent's blade is deflected from the target by means of a sharp tap given by contraction of the fingers and wrist, which opens the opponent's line strongly and thus prepares the way for an immediate riposte. In the parry by opposition, the opponent's blade is contacted without shock and maintained by means of pressure outside the line in which his attack ends.

In either case, the parry is taken with the blade in such a position as to facilitate the riposte. Ordinarily, the parry will be taken cutting edge to cutting edge; but occasionally it will be more convenient for the ensuing riposte to take certain parries with the back of the blade, or even with the cutting edge against the back of the opponent's blade.

Whenever possible, the parry is executed with the forte of the blade against the foible of the adversary's blade.

The arm should never be extended in the parries. As far as possible, all the positions of the parries are taken with the elbow as the pivot.

A parry taken on the advance or during the retreat should he completed by the time the step is taken. It may be said that in general all movements in sabre, whether offensive or defensive, must, to be effective, coordinate the activity of arms and legs.

The chief parries to he encountered in this book are:

1. The head parry.

2. The prime parry (a left flank parry).

3. The right flank parry.

4. Tierce parry (a right check parry).

5. Quarte parry (a left cheek parry).

6. Low tierce parry (a right flank parry).

7. Low quarte parry (a left flank parry).

Fig. 11 - The head parry   Fig. 12 - The prime parry

The Head Parry

Raise your right hand above your right shoulder until it is at the height of your forehead, and move it forward until your arm is three-fourths extended. Turn your thumb down; your nails will be forward. Keep your forearm protected behind the guard. Your blade will slant diagonally across the body from right to left. The cutting edge of your blade will be up; the tip will be slightly below your hand and just inside the left limit of your body.

From this position you will have to neutralize the force of your opponent's attack by a beat or by taking opposition. You will better be able to control his blade if you take the parry with the forte of your blade.

From the head parry position, lo lake a counter head parry on a thrust under the blade, describe the smallest possible circle in a clockwise direction, using only the fingers and wrist.

The head parry with the point slightly up would give you the advantage of not having to lean backward slightly in taking the parry and thus enable you to riposte more rapidly; but this same parry would also give you the more serious disadvantage of being able to be deceived more successfully. The recommended head parry with the point slightly down docs force you to bend back your body slightly in taking the parry and thus makes your riposte a trifle slower, but this also forces your adversary to take a fuller lunge and thus makes his recovery correspondingly slower. Also, if you take the parry with the point slightly down and your parry is deceived, your point will have to cover only a small arc to deflect the real attack, since it is already pointing slightly downward.

The Left Flank Parry (Prime)

Move your right hand across your body, extending your arm until it is three-fourths extended, and at the same time raise your hand until it is just below your chin and at the left limit of your body. Your thumb is down and your nails arc forward. The cutting edge of your blade will be to your left. The tip of your blade will be down, directed to the lowest part of your adversary's groin line.

From the prime position, to take a counter-prime parry on a thrust under the blade, describe the smallest possible circle in a clockwise direction, using the fingers and wrist. Parry by beat or opposition.

The Right Flank Parry

From the tierce position, to execute a right flank parry, keep your thumb in the same position, but bend your wrist downward until the tip of your blade is directed to the lowest part of your opponent's groin line. Raise your hand until it is at the height of your right shoulder, and directly in front of it. Your arm will be three-fourths extended. The cutting edge of your blade will be to the right. Protect your elbow as much as possible behind your sabre guard. Neutralize the shock of your opponent's attack by a beat or by taking sufficient opposition.

From the right flank parry position, to take a counter right flank parry on a disengage over the blade to the inside line, describe the smallest possible circle in a counterclockwise direction, using the fingers and wrist. Deflect your adversary's blade by a beat or by opposition.

Tierce Parry

Tierce parry is used to deflect any attack ending in the outside high line.

You will find the position of tierce guard as previously described and the position of tierce parry practically the same, except that with the parry the point is farther to the right. Your thumb will be at 9 o'clock, your arm three-fourths extended. Raise your hand to the level of your right breast. Slant your blade upward so that the tip is level with the top of your mask. Keep your point slightly outside so that your opponent's blade will be directed to the forte of your blade or to your sabre guard. Protect your elbow as much as possible behind your sabre guard.

From tierce, to take a counter-tierce parry on a thrust to your inside line, describe as small a circle as possible in a clockwise direction, using your fingers and wrist. Deflect the attack by a beat or by opposition.

High tierce is the same as tierce except that here you raise your hand to the level of your right shoulder.

Quarte Parry

Quarte is used to deflect any attack ending in the inside high line. From tierce, to execute quarte parry, move your hand across your body, arm three-fourths extended, to a point in front of your left breast, at the same time turning your hand until your thumb is at 3 o'clock. The cutting edge of your blade will now be to the left. The tip of your blade will slant upward so that the point is level with the top of your mask, and slightly outside to the left. Keep your elbow inside as much as possible without cramping your muscles.

Incline your blade slightly outward also so that your adversary's blade will be directed downward to your sabre guard.

From quarte, to execute a counter-quarte parry on a cut or thrust to your outside line, describe the smallest possible circle in a counter-clockwise direction. Parry by beat or by opposition.

High quarte is the same as quarte, except that the hand is raised to the level of your left shoulder.

Fig. 15 - The quarte parry   Fig. 16 - The low tierce parry

Low Tierce Parry

From the tierce guard position, to take a low tierce parry on an attack to the outside low line, drop your hand to a point between your waist and your groin line and at the right limit of your body. Slant your blade slightly more vertically than for tierce. Keep the tip of the blade slightly outside to give you better control of your opponent's blade. Parry by beat or by opposition.

From low tierce, to take a counter low tierce parry on a cuff attack or a thrust to your inside line, describe a clockwise circle as in tierce and neutralize the attack with a beat or opposition.

Low Quarte Parry

From the tierce guard position, to take a low quarte parry on an attack to the inside low line, move your hand across your body diagonally downward to a point between your waist and your groin line and at the left limit of your body. At the same time, turn your thumb from 9 to 3 o'clock. Slant your blade slightly more vertically than in quarte, but keep the tip still slightly outside. Parry by beat or by opposition.

From low quarte, to take a counter-low quarte parry on a cut or a thrust to your outside line, describe a counterclockwise circle as in quarte and give a beat or take opposition.

Fig. 17 - The low quarte parry   Fig. 18 - The seconde parry

Seconde Parry

The seconde parry may be used to deflect any attack to the outside low line made in such a way that your opponent's blade moves upward from a very low position. For all other attacks to the outside low line, the low tierce and right flank parries are better.

From the tierce position, to take seconde parry on a low attack outside, drop the forearm, using the elbow as a pivot and stopping the hand level with the waistline. The thumb is still at 9 o'clock, but the point has dropped to a position several inches below the level of the hand and at the right limit of the body.

From seconde, to take a counter-seconde parry on a thrust to the inside low line, describe a counterclockwise circle with the blade and give a beat or opposition.

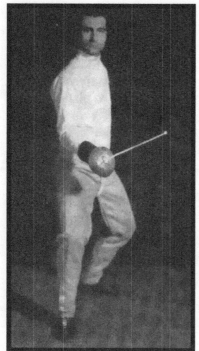

Fig. 19 - The quinte parry

Quinte Parry

The quinte parry may be used to deflect any attack to the inside low line made in such a way that your opponent's blade moves upward from a very low position. For all other attacks ending in the inside low line, the low quarte and left flank parries are better.

From tierce position, to take quinte parry on a low attack inside, move the hand to the waistline directly in front of the center of the body, at the same time turning the thumb from 9 o'clock to 12 o'clock. The blade will slant diagonally from the center of the

222

body to a few inches outside the left limit of the body. The edge is down, the point slightly higher than the hand.

From quinte, to take a counter-quinte parry on a thrust over the blade, describe a counterclockwise circle, returning to the original quinte position. Counter-quinte is not much used with the sabre.

The High Right Cheek Parry

Use this parry, the high right cheek parry, and the one next described, the high left cheek parry, only on the short distance during the time you are recovering your guard from an attack to the high line, and only when you have to protect your right or left cheek.

To take the high right cheek parry, raise your hand a few inches above your head, thumb at 8 o'clock. Since the distance will be short, keep your arm well bent; in fact, if the distance is very short, you may have to take the parry just few inches from your head. Bend your ·wrist down sharply so that the blade slants downward sharply also, at the right limit of your body. The point is slightly forward and level with your waist. Keep your elbow back. Neutralize the shock of the attack by taking opposition a few inches from your cheek rather than by giving a beat.

The High Left Cheek Parry

To execute a high left cheek parry on a riposte to the high line after an attack to the high line, raise your hand a few inches above and to the left of your head, thumb at 4 o'clock. Bend your wrist down sharply so that the blade slants downward sharply also at the extreme left of your body. The point is slightly forward and level with your waist. Keep your elbow back. Parry more by opposition than by beat.

The Use Of The Different Parries

Being on the defensive, at the guard distance, you have a choice of two styles of fencing sabre-taking your parries "point up"

223

or taking them "point down." At this distance, your guard can be tierce (point up) or the high guard (point down). Regardless of which guard you choose, however, make all your parries consistently in the same style.

If you assume the tierce guard, keep your parries within this group:

1. Tierce parry (or counter-tierce, as the case may be) against a straight thrust, a disengage, a head cut, a right cheek attack, or an attack to the outside of your cuff.

2. Quarte parry (or counter-quarte, as the case may be) against a straight thrust, a disengage, a head cut, a left cheek attack, or an attack to the inside of your cuff.

3. Low tierce parry against a right flank attack.

4. Low quarte parry against a left flank attack.

If you assume the high guard with the point down, keep your parries within this group:

1. Head parry against a head attack.

2. Prime parry against a chest attack, a banderole attack, a left flank attack, or an attack to the inside of your cuff.

3. Right flank parry, against a right flank attack or an attack to the outside of your cuff.

4. High tierce parry against a right cheek attack.

5. High quarte parry against a left cheek attack.

Of course, there are some exceptions. On the long distance, for example, even if you are using the high guard with the point down, you can still parry a cheek attack by tierce or quarte instead of taking a high right or high left cheek parry. The whole idea, in going from one parry to another, is to expose your forearm or arm for the shortest possible time. On a compound attack, head, right flank, for example, you would not shift a head parry (point down) to tierce, but would rather parry with a head

224

parry followed by a right flank parry, both with the point clown. On a compound attack, right flank, left flank, to take another case in point, you would not parry tierce and then prime, but rather tierce followed by quarte.

Of the two styles, the point-down system is preferable. This style will enable you to parry more with the forte of your blade, it will allow you to increase the distance by taking the parry closer to your body, and it will better protect your head.

The point-up style, however, is especially useful for the foil-man who wishes to learn something about sabre without changing his style. In this style of parrying, however, the parries for the upper part of your body are weaker than the corresponding parries with the point down. If you try to protect yourself from a riposte by taking low tierce or low quarte, you may often be touched through your parry.

On the short distance, there is no choice. During the time you are recovering your guard position after an attack to the high line, you will notice that most of the ripostes are directed to your head. Therefore, after making an attack, protect yourself during your recovery by taking a head parry, point down, in such a way that your hand will be in the center of all the necessary parries. There will be no time to shift styles on the short distance, so take all your parries with the point down. Accustom yourself to protect your cheek, on this short distance, by taking a high right or high left cheek parry close to your body, and not by taking tierce or quark.

The head parry, point down and with the hand in the center of all the necessary parries, will give you the maxim um protection against a riposte to the head, by enabling you to take your parry with utmost speed, and it will also place your hand in a position favorable for an immediate counter-riposte.

CHAPTER III
Simple and Compound Attacks

The Feint

The feint is the simulation of an attack made by extending the arm without lunging, in order to force the opponent to take a parry. (See Fig. No. 9.)

With the foil, only the feint with the palm up is recommended; with the sabre, since it is possible to cut as well as thrust, the palm can be up, down or sideways.

Make several feints at the beginning of a bout, especially against an unknown opponent, to "feel out" what kind of a fencer your opponent is, to see whether or not he will respond to a feint, and to help you decide where, against that particular opponent, you will find your best openings.

Keep in mind that on the short distance you can be touched by a feint.

Do not use your shoulder in the execution of your feint; moving it will cut down your speed and destroy perfect balance.

The Attacks

The attack is that movement or combination of movements by means of which it is attempted to touch the adversary. Attacks may be simple or compound. Executed as a single motion, the attack is simple; in all other cases, it is compound. Both kinds of attack may be executed in place or in motion, with or without any preparation. When an attack is made immediately after a parry, it is known as a riposte.

The attack may be made by point—by a straight thrust or by a disengage—,or the attack may be ended by a cut or a moulinet. The cut will always cover a comparatively short arc, whereas a moulinet, making greater use of the wrist, covers a much

226

wider arc-a semi-circle or a full ellipse. Any cut or moulinet given with the flat part of the blade, of course, does not count.

In executing your attack, whether by point or edge, raise your hand to the height of your chest, and keep your arm well protected behind the sabre guard. If you raise your arm too high or drop it too low in your attack, you are inviting a stop-cut.

In any case, never lunge until your point or cutting edge is already in its final line and your arm is fully extended.

Moulinets

In the moulinet, the point describes an almost complete ellipse, aided principally by the wrist and fingers and to a small degree by the forearm. The arm is almost fully extended and protected behind the guard as much as possible, so as not to invite a stop-thrust. The grip is held firmly only by the thumb and index finger; the other fingers are relaxed in describing the circle with the point.

It is good practice to use moulinets from time to time in your attack. Used sparingly, they will give your attack an element of surprise and additional force. Take care not to start the moulinet from the guard position, but only after your arm is almost fully extended and your point in line.

The moulinet is usually one of two kinds:

1.   Vertical: on your right side or on your left side.

2.   Horizontal: from right to left, and from left to right.

The Vertical Moulinet On The Left

Starting from the position of a feint to the head, rotate the wrist so that your sabre describes a clockwise circle downward to the left of your body, then up close to your side, and back to the original position, so that the cutting edge will strike the target. Use your wrist almost exclusively; relax your last three fingers during the completion of the circle. Keep your arm almost fully extended;

227

both your forearm and arm will remain practically in place during the entire movement. The target may be the head or the cuff.

If you reverse this moulinet by describing the circle in the opposite direction, counterclockwise, you may direct your attack to the right flank or below the cuff.

When the moulinet is executed with a lunge or a half-lunge, the blade should arrive at the same time the right foot strikes the floor.

The Vertical Moulinet On The Right

Execute the vertical moulinet on the right in the same fashion as above, except that here you must make your circle counterclockwise and as close to your right shoulder as possible. You will find moulinets in the inside line easier to execute than those in the outside line.

The vertical moulinet on the right is not very practical as an attack but is an excellent finger and wrist exercise.

This moulinet may be reversed by describing the circle clockwise.

The Horizontal Moulinet From Left To Right

To execute a horizontal moulinet from left to right from the feint position, describe a horizontal circle counter-clockwise, using your wrist and relaxing your last three fingers on the grip during the completion of the circle. When you end your moulin et, your nails will be up when the movement is over, turn your nails down again.

Use this horizontal moulinet as an attack to any part of the inside line.

The Horizontal Moulinet From Right To Left

From the feint position, tum the palm up and describe the moulinet in a clockwise direction. When you finish your moulinet here, your nails will be clown.

228

Use this moulinet as an attack to any part of the outside line.

If you do not use these moulinets as attacks, use them at least for finger and wrist exercises, since the alternate contraction and relaxation of your fingers and the use of your wrist as a pivot will develop suppleness and strength in them. When practiced thus, the moulinets may be combined, that is, they may follow one another in immediate succession.

While the moulinet is often clumsy as a direct attack, it may be very effective as a riposte after a parry, for the reason that your opponent is usually set to parry a direct riposte and is disconcerted by the whirling blade.

1. After a parry made with the point down—head parry, prime or right flank—riposte with the horizontal moulinet from left to right, ending in the inside line or the head.

2. After a tierce or counter-tierce parry, riposte with the horizontal moulinet from right to left, ending in the outside line.

3. After a quarte parry, riposte with the horizontal moulinet from right to left, ending in the outside line.

The Cut

Extending your arm and using your wrist and fingers, bring the cutting edge a few inches outside the limit of the target and the tip of the blade a few inches beyond the target. Then give the cut by sharply contracting your fingers. In this way, your cut will never be a slash. Hold the sabre guard in such a way as to protect your arm from a stop-thrust during the execution of your attack.

The Head Attack

Extend your arm, thumb at 12 o'clock, passing your blade either over or under your adversary's blade. Your cutting edge will

229

then be down. Lunge and cut on the head, using your fingers and wrist.

Fig. 20 - Right cheek attack

The Right Cheek Attack

Extend your arm, thumb at 9 o'clock, lunge and cut on the right cheek, using your fingers and wrist.

Fig. 21 - Left cheek attack

The Right Flank Attack

Extend your arm as for the right cheek attack, lunge and cut on the right flank.

The Left Cheek Attack

Extend your arm, thumb at 3 o'clock, passing your blade over or under your opponent's blade, lunge and cut on the left cheek.

The Left Flank Attack

Extend your arm as for the left cheek attack and cut on the left flank.

The Banderole Attack

Extend your arm, thumb at 1 o'clock, passing your blade over or under your adversary's blade, lunge and cut on the banderole (the space between the neck and left shoulder).

Cuff Attacks

To attack the outside of the cuff from below, turn your thumb from 9 to 7 o'clock, at the same time lowering your hand enough to cut diagonally upward under the forearm on the outside of the cuff. To attack the inside of the cuff, turn your thumb from 9 to 2 o'clock, at the same time lowering your hand slightly downward to cut diagonally on the inside of the cuff.

These cuff attacks are best executed on an opponent's feint to your high line.

To attack the outside of the cuff from above, turn your thumb to 11 o'clock, extend your arm on your opponent's guard position and lunge, cutting down on the outside of the cuff.

To attack the inside of the cuff from above, turn your thumb to 1 o'clock, extend your arm and lunge, cutting down on the inside of the cuff.

Fig. 22 - Cuff attack

These cuff attacks from above are best executed when your adversary drops his guard or when he makes a low feint.

To attack the outside of the cuff from the side, precede your arm extension with a beat in tierce or counter-tierce to expose your opponent's cuff; for an attack to the inside of the cuff from the side, give your beat with the back of your blade or give a beat in quarte.

Any of the cuff attacks can be delivered with the back edge of the third of the blade nearest the tip.

When you are using a cuff attack as a stop-cut on an advancing attack, accompany it with a short step or jump backward to avoid being touched yourself.

The Point Thrust

The thrust is the carrying of your point to your opponent's target. During its execution, your arm should be raised slightly to protect your arm behind your sabre guard against a possible stop-cut.

To execute a thrust, extend your arm at the height of your right shoulder and direct the point toward the target you have selected.

232

Your thumb is at 9 o'clock, cutting edge to the right, and your point slightly below the level of your hand. Lunge, if necessary, and touch with the point.

When the thrust ends in the same line as that of the engagement, it is known as a straight thrust.

Fig. 23 - Point thrust

The Disengage

The disengage is a thrust ending in a different line than that of the engagement.

All the attacks given in this chapter may be preceded by a preparation.

Compound Attacks

The two-movement attack consists of a feint followed by a direct attack; the three-movement attack consists of two feints followed by a direct attack.

Your feint will have served its purpose if it makes your opponent move his hand; if it does not, then abstain from compound attacks and depend entirely on single-movement attacks, with or without a preparation. In general, the simplest attacks arc the best.

It is dangerous to use compound attacks because you may be stopped during their execution by a cut to the cuff or by a thrust. This does not mean that compound attacks should be avoided, but rather that care should be used in their execution.

Use three-movement attacks only for training purposes, to enable you to execute the simpler movements better.

You make up your own compound attacks by combining the simple attacks in almost countless combinations. Combine them in such a way as to fulfill your own particular needs. You will find the best combinations listed later in the lessons.

CHAPTER IV
The Riposte and Counter-Riposte

The Riposte

The riposte is the attack which immediately follows a parry. A direct riposte is one executed immediately after a parry in the same line as that in which the parry was taken. A compound riposte is one executed with more than one movement.

If there is a hesitation between the parry and the riposte, the riposte becomes a delayed riposte. This type of riposte is used against an opponent who protects himself well from a direct riposte while coming back on guard.

The direct riposte is ordinarily the best, however, since it is the fastest.

All three types of riposte can be executed in place, or with the advance and retreat.

Against some opponents, especially those who use low tierce and low quarte parries, you might find it better to riposte to the right arm or shoulder rather than to the cuff. You may be able to touch such adversaries through their parries, whereas if you riposte to the cuff, your touch may not be counted because of "too much steel" (hitting the sabre guard at the same time as the target). The riposte or counter-riposte, aimed at the cuff, will of ten land on the arm anyway, because the distance has been shortened.

The Counter-Riposte And Second Counter-Riposte

The counter-riposte is the attack which follows the parry of the riposte. As with the riposte, the counter-riposte can be direct, compound or delayed. These can be executed from the guard position in place, advancing, retreating, and, whenever necessary, from the lunge position.

The second counter-riposte is the attack following the parry of the counter-riposte, and follows the same principles as the riposte and counter-riposte.

Redoubling Of The Riposte

Redoubling of the riposte consists of two immediately consecutive ripostes against an adversary who, after parrying your first riposte, foils to counter-riposte, or who has avoided the first riposte without parrying. Note that between the riposte and the redoubling of the riposte, there can be no break in time.

An example of redoubling of the riposte would be the following: your opponent cuts to your head, you parry and riposte to the right flank. Your adversary parries your riposte and then fails to counter-riposte. You immediately continue with a straight thrust.

If you made your riposte without a lunge or with a half-lunge, it may be necessary for you to lunge on your redouble, especially if your opponent returned to the guard position to parry your first riposte.

The Phrase (Phrase D' Armes)

A phrase is an entire succession of movements—the attacks, parries, ripostes and counter-ripostes—both given and received without interruption, ending either decisively or indecisively.

CHAPTER V
Preparations to the Attack

Preparations To The Attack

The preparation to an attack is the movement or movements made before the attack to assure its greater success.

Begin these preparations with your arm bent; in some cases, your arm will remain bent throughout the preparation; in other cases, your arm will be finally extended. Keep you r arm bent throughout the time you are executing a change of guard, a beat, a press, or an opposition in tierce or in quarte. Your arm will become extended finally in the execution of an expulsion, a glide or in the different feints executed for the purpose of preparation.

Preparations may also be executed on the advance or during a retreat.

Take care that during the execution of a preparation you are not surprised by a stop-thrust or cut to your arm.

Begin to use preparations as early as possible in your lessons.

Preparations Striking The Blade: The Beat; The Expulsion

Preparations striking the blade open up the line by means of a sudden shock delivered to your opponent's blade. Strong contact is suddenly made and abruptly broken off. The beat and the expulsion fall in this category.

The beat: the beat is a quick sharp blow executed with the middle of your blade against your opponent's foible. The beat may be given with the cutting edge or, in a change of line, with the back of the blade (a counter-beat).

From the tierce guard position, you can give a beat, palm down, on the outside of your opponent's blade, or, palm still down, you can pass your blade under his and deliver your beat with the back of your blade on the inside of his blade. Or, from

237

tierce, you can pass under his blade, then turn your palm up and give your beat with your cutting edge against the inside of his blade, and then attack with your palm still up or with your palm reversed to its original position. You can also give a beat i n quarte, nails up.

Occasionally, you can give a beat in quinte on a feint to your inside line. From tierce, turn your thumb to 12 o'clock with your blade held diagonally across your body, beat down sharply on your opponent's blade. Stop your forearm when it is parallel to the strip. The natural position and movement of the fingers, wrist and forearm, as well as the weigh t of the sabre itself, should give your beat a great deal of force. ·when the line is opened, cut to the forearm or to the head.

Do not "telegraph" your beat. If it is properly made, the forearm moves only a short distance and the contraction of the fingers does the rest. It is the movement of the forearm that warns the adversary; he cannot see your fingers.

Maintain your blade where the beat was given. Do not let your own force carry you outside the line. You will only have to regain that distance in the ensuing attack. Also, if your opponent deceives your beat, it will be easy for him to stop-cut you on the cuff if your arm has gone past the limit of your body. And in any case, your arm should be held during the execution of the beat in such a way that any attempt to stop-cut to your cuff will fall on your guard.

The expulsion (froissement): The expulsion is a sharp, continually increasing, slightly diagonal pressure exerted with the middle of the blade all the way down your opponent's blade from foible to forte, resulting in the expulsion of his blade from the line and opening a line of attack. At the end of the movement, the arm is extended; this extension is the source of most of the power of the expulsion. The expulsion is executed against an extended arm. It may be made in the line of engagement or with a change of line (counter-expulsion).

238

On a feint to the outside line, make your expulsion in tierce or low tierce, which will prepare your riposte to the high line, inside or outside.

On a feint to the inside line, make your expulsion in quarte, low quarte or quinte; from quarte or low quarte, make your attack to the high line, inside or outside; from quinte, attack with the point.

Do not over-emphasize this preparation, as it is wide and will prove dangerous to you if deceived. A beat or a press is a better preparation.

Preparations Maintaining The Blade: The Press; Opposition; The Glide

In preparations maintaining the blade, contact is established and maintained with the opponent's blade without shock.

The press: The press is a pressure exerted against the adversary's foible in order to open up a line. The arm is in the same position as after the beat. The press is executed smoothly, by sharply contracting the fingers, aided by the wrist.

Do not "telegraph" your press in advance to your opponent by excessive wrist play or by any other give-away motion.

Maintain your blade at the place where the press was given.

If your adversary fails to respond to your press, attack immediately in the same line; if he does respond, deceive that response by a disengage or a cut.

The press may be accompanied by an advance or a retreat. Coordinate both movements.

Opposition: Opposition is the maintenance of the adversary's blade outside the limits of the target by exerting continual and sufficient resistance to his blade. Contact is made without a beat.

Opposition is most effective against a feint from the adversary.

Tierce, quarte and counter-tierce opposition are taken in the same way that those parries are taken. In opposition, the hand and blade, however, may have to pass the limits of the body, but only slightly.

Since opposition opens the line laterally, the best attack to follow the taking of an opposition is a lateral attack or a thrust. For example, after taking opposition in tierce, reverse the position of your hand until your palm is up, and then cut to the left flank, the banderole, the left cheek or to the inside of the cuff. After taking opposition in quarte, reverse the position of your hand until your palm is down, and then cut to the right check or to the outside of the cuff.

Opposition is especially useful to maintain your opponent's blade outside the limits of your body during an advance or retreat.

Opposition may be taken against either a bent or extended arm.

The glide (coule): The glide is like the feint straight thrust, but is made with contact of the opponent's blade. Slide your cutting edge or the back of your blade along your adversary's blade from foible to forte by extending your arm. At the encl of the glide, your forte should be against his foible, so that you will be able to overcome his opposition. Follow immediately with a straight thrust, or, if your opponent responds strongly, with a disengage or a cut.

Do not use the glide much in sabre; it is a much better preparation for foil and épée, where only the point is used.

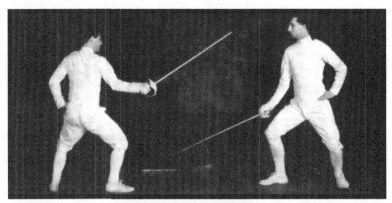

Fig. 24 - Invitation to the attack

The Invitation To The Attack (Absence D' Épée)

The invitation to the attack is a deliberate and exaggerated opening up of a line so as to encourage your adversary to attack in a line in which you wish him to attack. In sabre, the invitation to the attack is usually given by dropping the point close to the strip.

The invitation is useful against an opponent who does not wish to attack or one stronger on the defensive than the offensive.

Fine precision and an accurate sense of distance and timing are necessary to execute the invitation successfully. In effect, you are pitting your judgment against that of your opponent. He knows what you are doing. He will not attack until he believes that you have misjudged, that you have made the invitation too wide to be able to defend yourself in time. It is up to you to make him believe so, without actually passing the thin margin of safety.

Closing In On Your Opponent (Se Loger)

You close in on your opponent by any series of movements which drives the edge or point of your sabre closer and closer to your adversary's target, so as to make his parry of your final attack more difficult and to assure the ultimate success of your attack.

241

Deceiving The Preparation To The Attack: The Avoidance; The Attack On A Preparation

The preparation to an attack may be deceived by either of two methods: by removing your blade from your opponent's control, or by a surprise attack as he begins his.

The avoidance (dérobement): Avoidance is the deception of your opponent's blade by a feint-disengage or by a feint-cut just at the moment he starts to execute a preparation for his attack.

Your arm is extended after the avoidance, but you <lo not attack; you merely avoid.

The attack on a preparation: An attack on a preparation is one launched from a state of complete immobility in such a way as to surprise your opponent in the midst of preparation for his own attack.

Use this attack on an invitation, on a preparation, on a feint outside your body—on any movement your adversary makes with the idea of bringing his point or edge close to your target to assure the success of his final attack.

Use a simple movement. You will find it most effective against an opponent who uses too many movements in preparing his attack.

Deceive a beat, a press, an expulsion, opposition or a glide by disengaging and cutting to the cuff. Deceive a change of guard by a cut to the head.

CHAPTER VI
Special Attacks

The False Attack

The false attack is an attack in one or several movements made without any intention of touching the opponent, accompanied by a simulated lunge in which the right foot is brought forward a short distance.

At the end of the false attack, several moves are possible:

1.   If your opponent does not respond, either return on guard and try again, or make a direct cut or thrust.

2.   If he responds by taking a simple or counter-parry, deceive that parry by a cut or thrust, high or low.

3.   If he responds by taking a parry and then making a riposte, parry his riposte and counter-riposte yourself with a lunge.

The false attack may of course be preceded by a preparation.

You should begin a bout against a new opponent by using a false attack; it will enable you to "feel out" his strength and ability. In addition, it will enable you to close in on him.

The Stop-Cut And Stop-Thrust (Coup D'Arrêt)

The stop-cut and stop-thrust are quick simple movements executed with or without a lunge against the opponent's attack, with the intention of scoring a touch with edge or point cleanly before his attack arrives.

Launch your cut or thrust at the very instant your opponent begins his attack. Most of the time your target will be the cuff-under the cuff on your opponent's attack to your head, and above the cuff on the feint of any other attack.

Against an adversary who is lunging, make your stop-cut as you are retreating or jumping backward. The stop-thrust is made with a lunge, or a half-lunge, or a step forward.

Against an opponent who continually attempts a stop-cut or thrust, use a false attack. As he extends his arm for the stop, make some suitable preparation on his extended blade and follow with a simple attack. This really will be a counter time-attack.

Do not start practicing the stop too soon. If you stress it too much you will hinder the development of your own parries.

Fig. 25 - Stop-cut to cuff (under)

Fig. 26 - Stop-cut to cuff (above)

244

The Time-Attack

The time-attack is one which fulfills at the same time the functions of a parry and a riposte, by extending the arm as much as is necessary to touch and simultaneously closing the line in which the adversary's attack will terminate.

For example, on your adversary's feint to your head followed by an attack to your right flank, first take a head parry by opposition and then meet the Hank attack by making a straight thrust with a light opposition to the right.

Or, on your opponent's feint to your right flank followed by a disengage, parry his feint by taking a right flank parry with opposition and then meet his disengage by extending your arm and touching by point to his body, with a light opposition in prime.

Judge very carefully the instant to launch your time-attack, for to be successful your timing will have to be exceptionally well gauged.

The beginner should not concern himself with the time-attack until the end of his second year.

Fig. 27 - Time-attack(a.) Action starts with feint to head, met by head parry

245

Fig. 28 - Time-attack(b.) Action continues with disengage to right flank, met by time-thrust to right flank

The Counter Time-Attack

The counter time-attack is a time-attack executed against your adversary just as he is preparing to make a stop-thrust or a time-attack.

The opponent's blade is taken by beat or by an expulsion just as he begins to extend his arm for a stop, and this is followed immediately by a simple attack on the same side as that in which the beat or expulsion was given. Maintain the opposition and touch.

The best way to execute a counter time-attack is to provoke a stop-thrust or a time-attack by making a false attack.

Only the advanced student should attempt the counter time-attack

Redoubling

Redoubling is a second attack made from the lunge position immediately after the opponent fails to riposte after taking a parry.

1. If your opponent parries your head-cut and loses contact with the blade, maintain your lunge position and cut again to the head.

2. If your opponent parries your cut with counter-tierce and maintains his point in line without riposting, beat in tierce, cut to the arm.

3. If your opponent parries your head-cut and maintains his parry position, dislodge his blade with a downward beat and cut to the head.

4. If your opponent parries your flank attack by quarte or prime, beat on the same side, cut to left flank or banderole.

5. If your opponent parries your right flank attack and maintains the opposition, redouble by cut to the head or left flank.

6. If your opponent parries prime, redouble to the outside (arm, right flank, right cheek), or thrust to the body.

In any case, the redouble should go to an open line, or should be preceded by a beat opening up the line of the parry.

Occasionally, you will be able to redouble against an opponent who retreats or jumps backward but is still within your reach.

To protect yourself against redoubling, do not neglect to riposte yourself after your parry.

The Remise

The remise is the second attack made from the lunge position against an adversary who makes a riposte; it fulfills at the same time the functions of a parry by opposition and a counter-riposte. It is almost always made with the point. The remise will always be made in the same line as that in which the parry was taken.

The remise is best executed against ripostes ending in the outside line, because opposition is easily taken in that line. It is very difficult to remise against a riposte ending in the inside line, but it can be done by deviating the opponent's blade outside by a counter right flank or counter-tierce opposition, touching over the opponent's blade with the point in the opponent's outside line.

The remise is nothing but a special type of time-attack, with these two differences: the remise is executed against a riposte, whereas the time-attack is executed against an attack; and the remise is executed from the lunge position, whereas the time-attack is executed from the guard position.

Suppose you made a beat, right cheek attack, and your opponent parried tierce and riposted to your right flank. On his riposte, instead of taking a parry, riposte directly with a straight thrust or a cut to the body, maintaining the opposition to the right and raising your hand at the same time to the height of your right cheek to prevent being touched on your right cheek during the execution of the remise.

Or, suppose you try a head cut; your partner takes a head parry and ripostes with a thrust to the body. On his riposte, extend your arm, rotating your blade over his, and touch with the point to the body, maintaining the opposition to the right. Execute this opposition parry and counter-riposte as a single movement.

As a final example, suppose you try a right flank attack and your opponent takes a right flank parry and ripostes in two movements, right flank and right cheek. Parry his feint by opposition and then remise by a straight thrust to his right shoulder with opposition.

Do not attach much importance to the remise until the end of your second year. A counter-riposte gives the same result and is much easier and safer to execute.

The Bind (Liement)

Do not try the bind in sabre. The displacement of the blade is so much wider in sabre than in foil or épée that it is almost impossible for you to maintain contact with your adversary's blade during your attempt without being touched yourself. You will not find the double bind useful either.

The Cross (Croisé)

The cross is the act of transposing the adversary's blade from the high line to the low line during his attack, in order to riposte without a lunge in the latter line, fulfilling simultaneously the functions of a parry and riposte. This movement is very seldom used in the sabre.

The Envelopment

The envelopment is the act of transposing the adversary's blade from the low line to the high line during his attack, in order to riposte without a lunge in the latter line, fulfilling simultaneously the functions of a parry and riposte. It will be noted that the envelopment is the same movement as the cross, made in exactly the opposite direction. This movement is very seldom used in the sabre.

The Flèche

The flèche is a running attack executed in the following manner:

1.   The arm is extended, with the blade directed at the part of the target it is desired to touch.

2.   The weight is shifted from the left to the right leg, and the left leg is moved to a position slightly in front of the right leg.

3.   From this position, the distance is closed rapidly with a rush, bringing the edge or point within striking distance

and at the same time preventing the opponent from riposting.

The flèche can be made with opposition, the hand in tierce, quarte or occasionally in quinte, or by a direct attack at the exact moment a line is opened.

The placing of the left foot in front of the right foot will enable you to keep facing your opponent as you run forward. You may make your rush directly forward, in which case you limit it so as not to come in bodily contact with your adversary, or you may pass him either to the left or right. Passing him to the left is preferable. If possible, avoid running off the strip, for the moment you do so any subsequent action on your part during the phrase is nullified; whereas your opponent is allowed one immediate riposte, which is valid even if you are off the strip.

The flèche is most effectively executed just as your opponent is recovering his guard position from some action of his. If the flèche is executed after a parry as a riposte, maintain your final parry by opposition and run in as he recovers his guard position.

To protect yourself from the flèche attack, take a high guard position, point in line.

Do not use the flèche attack often in sabre; its occasional use, will secure the maximum surprise.

The Delayed Attack

If for any reason the attack is slowed down or interrupted by the attacker, thus causing a loss of time in its execution, it is called a delayed attack. Such an attack almost always results in the loss of the right of way.

It is therefore obvious that the attack should not be made too slowly and should be made without halting, so as to avoid giving your adversary the time to make a stop-thrust against you before the end of your attack.

Retaking The Attack (Reprise D' Attaque)

Retaking the attack is any attack, simple or compound, which follows any inconclusive phrase.

Fig. 29 - The flèche(a.) Counter-tierce opposition

Fig. 30 - The flèche(b.) Run outside, with cut to left cheek, hand in quarte

251

CHAPTER VII
Exercises

Some Alternative Exercises

The alternative exercises given here have for goal the preparation of the beginning fencer for the actual bout. The first exercise should be executed in this manner: two fencers should get on guard so that their blades cross just below the tips. One makes a feint disengage (no lunge) to the right flank; the other takes a right flank parry and ripostes with a feint disengage to the head. The first then parries this riposte with a head parry and counter-ripostes in turn to the right flank; and so on. As the movements proceed without interruption, the distance should be gradually shortened by very short steps forward and the speed increased until a touch is scored to end the exercise.

The movements must be clean-cut at all times. Correctness of execution must not be sacrificed to speed. In the long run, it will be seen that the correct way to execute any given movement in fencing is also the fastest way.

The two fencers executing these exercises are referred to as the "instructor" and the "pupil." They may be executed by any two fencers in any stage of advancement, however; an occasional check by the instructor would be sufficient to insure correctness of execution.

Instructor's Attack	Pupil's Parry	Pupil's Riposte	Instructor's Parry
Single-movement exercises			
1. Right flank	Right flank	Head	Head. Repeat exercise until touch is scored
2. Head	Head	Right flank	Right flank. Repeat
3. Left flank	Prime	Right flank	Right flank. Repeat
4. Right flank	Right flank	Left flank	Prime. Repeat
5. Right cheek	Tierce	Right flank	Right flank. Repeat
6. Right flank	Right flank	Right cheek	Tierce. Repeat
7. Left flank	Prime	Left flank	Prime. Repeat
8. Disengage	Counter-tierce	Disengage	Counter-tierce. Repeat
9. Head	Head	Head by inside moulinet	Head. Repeat
10. Right cheek	Tierce	Left cheek	Quarte. Repeat
11. Left cheek	Quarte	Right cheek	Tierce. Repeat
Two-movement exercises			
12. Feint right flank, left flank attack	Right flank opposition, prime	Feint to right flank, left flank attack	Right flank opposition, prime. Repeat
13. Feint left flank, right flank attack	Prime opposition, right flank parry	Feint left flank, right flank attack	Prime opposition, right flank. Repeat
14. Feint head, right flank	Head parry by opposition, right flank parry	Feint head, right flank attack	Head opposition, right flank. Repeat
15. Feint right flank, head cut	Right flank, opposition, head parry	Feint right flank, head attack	Right flank opposition, head. Repeat
16. Feint left cheek, right cheek attack	Quarte opposition, tierce parry	Feint to left cheek, right cheek attack	Quarte opposition, tierce. Repeat
17. Feint right flank, right cheek attack	Right flank opposition, tierce parry	Feint to right flank, right cheek attack	Right flank opposition, tierce. Repeat
18. Feint disengage, followed by disengage deceiving a counter-parry in the same line	Two counter-tierce parries	By double (Same as Instructor's attack)	Two counter-tierce parries. Repeat
19. Feint disengage, followed by disengage deceiving a lateral parry	Quarte, tierce	By 1-2 (Same as Instructor's attack)	Quarte, tierce. Repeat

Execute these exercises slowly at first at the short distance without a lunge. The speed can then be gradually increased until a touch is scored. When the exercises are familiar to you. repeat them with a lunge.

253

Some Counter-Riposte Exercises

Pupil's Attack	Instructor's		Pupil's	
	Parry	Riposte (no lunge)	Parry of Riposte	Counter-riposte (Lunge)
1. Feint to head	Head	Right flank	Right flank	Head
2. Feint to right flank	Right flank	Left flank	Prime	Left flank
3. Feint to left flank	Prime	Head	Head	Right flank
4. Feint to head	Head	Moulinet to left flank	Prime	Straight thrust to body
5. Feint right flank, feint left flank	Right flank, prime	Head	Head	Feint to right flank, head
6. Feint left cheek, feint right cheek	Quarte, tierce	Left cheek	Quarte	Head
7. Cuff, under	Low tierce	Disengage	Counter-tierce	Head
8. Banderole	Prime	Right flank	Right flank	Left flank by moulinet
9. Right cheek	Tierce	Left cheek	Prime	Cuff, under
10. Right flank	Right flank	Disengage	Counter right flank	Right cheek
11. Disengage	Counter-tierce	Head cut	Head	Inside of cuff
12. Left flank	Prime	Left flank	Prime	Straight thrust to body
13. Feint head, feint right flank	Head, right flank	Right cheek	Tierce	Feint to head, left flank
14. Feint head, feint left flank	Head, prime	Head moulinet (inside)	Head	Feint right flank, banderole
15. Feint head, banderole	Head, prime	Right cheek	Tierce	Cuff
16. Feint head, left cheek	Head, high left cheek	Straight thrust to body	Counter right flank	Head
17. Feint head, right cheek	Head, high right cheek	Right flank	Right flank	Straight thrust to body
18. Feint head, cuff	Head, high right cheek	Right flank	Right flank	Head
19. Feint head, disengage to body	Head, counter-head parry	Moulinet to left flank	Prime	Moulinet to left flank
20. Feint left flank, moulinet to right flank	Prime, right flank	Cuff	Right flank	Straight thrust to body
21. Head	Counter-tierce opposition	Feint to left cheek, right cheek	Quarte, tierce	Cut to left cheek
22. Feint left flank, moulinet to right flank	Low quarte, low tierce	Head	Head	Feint to left flank, moulinet right flank

These exercises are to be executed first in place, and then advancing and retreating.

254

Some Second Counter-Riposte Exercises

Instructor's Feint	Pupil's		Instructor's		Pupil's	
	Parry	Feint Riposte	Parry of Riposte	Feint Counter-riposte	Parry of Counter-riposte	Second counter-riposte
1. Right flank	Right flank	Head	Head	Right flank	Right flank	Head
2. Head	Head	Right flank	Right flank	Left flank	Prime	Left flank
3. Right cheek	Tierce	Left flank	Prime	Head	Head	Feint right flank, head
4. Left cheek	Quarte	Head	Head	Left flank	Prime	Straight thrust to body
5. Left flank	Prime	Right flank, left flank	Right flank, prime	Head moulinet	Head	Feint right flank, head
6. Disengage	Counter-tierce	Left cheek, right cheek	Quarte, tierce	Cut to left cheek	Quarte	Head
7. Right flank	Low tierce	Cuff	Tierce	Right cheek, right flank	Tierce, low tierce	Left flank
8. Banderole	Prime	Banderole	Prime	Straight thrust to body	Counter right flank	Head moulinet
9. Right flank	Right flank	Right cheek	Tierce	Left flank	Prime	Cuff
10. Disengage	Counter-tierce	Disengage	Counter-tierce	Right flank	Right flank	Head
11. Disengage	Prime	Head moulinet	Head	Right flank	Right flank	Right cheek
12. Head	Head	Left flank	Prime	Moulinet to left flank	Prime	Straight thrust to body
13. Left flank	Low quarte	Head, right flank	Head, right flank	Right cheek	Tierce	Left cheek
14. Head, left flank	Head, prime	Head, left flank	Head, prime	Left cheek	Quarte	Right cheek
15. Right cheek, left cheek	Tierce, quarte	Left flank, right flank	Low quarte, low tierce	Right cheek	Tierce	Right flank
16. Disengage	Prime	Head, left cheek	Head, high left cheek	Right flank	Right flank	Cuff
17. Right flank	Right flank	Left flank	Prime	Head, right flank	Head, right flank	Feint left flank, right flank
18. Left flank	Prime	Head*	Head	Left flank	Prime#	Straight thrust#
19. Head	Head	Head moulinet*	Head	Right flank	Right flank#	Feint right flank, left flank#
20. Disengage	Counter-tierce	Head	Quarte	Left cheek, right flank	Quarte, low tierce	Disengage point-thrust

255

21. Head, right flank	Head, right flank	Head, right flank	Head, right flank	Banderole	Prime	Banderole
22. Banderole, right flank	Prime, right flank	Head moulinet	Head	Straight thrust to body	Right flank	Right cheek

These exercises are to be executed first in place, and then advancing and retreating.

*Lunge, stay on lunge. #From the lunge position

256

CHAPTER VIII
Lessons

The Lesson

For the sabre lessons given below, take a tierce guard. At the beginning you may cross blades, but later you should accustom yourself to fence without taking an engagement.

Protect your arm as fully as possible behind your sabre guard as you extend your arm and as you lunge. When you make a cut, you should make the point describe only a small arc, using your fingers and wrist and moving your forearm as little as possible. When you extend your arm in the first feint of a compound attack, remember that your arm must still be protected during your execution of the remaining feints. You will accomplish this by using your fingers and wrist.

Practice the advance and retreat and the jump forward and backward with all your attacks. Practice attacks on your instructor's advance. Practice the jump backward with your stop-cut to the cuff against an advancing attack.

Accustom yourself to use the jump backward to recover the proper distance.

To make your lunge faster and more direct, have the weight of your body slightly forward at the start of your lunge. When you recover your guard and when you parry, shift the weight of your body slightly back. Hold your lunge from time to time and check on this fundamental position. From time to time during your lesson make a straight thrust or a disengage with a full lunge. Get into the habit of deciding for yourself, even from the start, whether or not you need to lunge to touch. When your instructor lunges or advances you will not need to lunge on your riposte or second counter-riposte; if your instructor remains in place, you should realize for yourself without being told that you

257

will have to lunge. Maintain the proper distance also without being told.

Get into the habit of taking the special head parry in the center of all the point-down parries immediately after completing your lunge, in order to protect yourself while you are recovering your guard. Once you recover your guard you can go-back to your original guard. Accustom yourself to take advantage of openings. If your instructor does not open a line widely for your attack, open it up yourself by a beat or by opposition. If he brings his elbow out and forward, make a cuff attack; if he moves his sabre to the left, attack the right flank or right cheek. If he makes an invitation to an attack, execute a straight thrust or a head attack. If he presses or is obviously going to give a beat, disengage. If he moves his sabre too far to the right, attack the left side or banderole. You may need some verbal prompting at first, but learn t0 be on your own as soon and as much as possible.

A parry exercise should consist of a phrase where you will parry and riposte repeatedly in place or with a lunge. When your instructor wishes to end the phrase, he will neglect to take a parry. He should occasionally neglect to take a parry just to see if your attack would have landed.

The Make-Up Of A Complete Lesson

The following order of progression has given the author the most satisfactory results in teaching the sabre. Each step will be taken up in more detail in the next paragraph. These steps are:

1.   On guard, advance, retreat, jumping forward and backward, lunge. Slow-motion at first.

2.   One-movement attacks.

3.   Simple parries, counter-parries, simple and compound ripostes.

4.   Compound attacks deceiving a simple or counter-parry.

258

5.   Compound parries for the above compound attacks. Repeat with simple or compound ripostes.

6.   A counter-riposte exercise, in place and then with a lunge.

7.   A second counter-riposte exercise.

8.   Speed exercise: one-movement or two-movement attacks.

9.   Speed exercise: parries of the above one-movement attacks, and ripostes.

10.   If suitable, the introduction of a new movement.

11.   Correction of fundamental positions by slow-motion execution.

12.   Reassemble and salute.

In the following, the author refers to himself as the "instructor" and to the student as "you."

1.   Take the guard position. The instructor will check that position, make you advance and retreat several times by advancing and retreating without any verbal warning. Make several one-movement attacks which your instructor will not parry. Stay on a full lunge while this position is checked and corrected.

2.   Execute some one-movement attacks preceded by some preparation.

3.   Parry the same attacks when executed by your instructor, by taking simple or counter-parries as required; riposte with a simple or compound movement.

4.   Make some compound attacks, deceiving a simple or a counter-parry. If you use more than one feint, wait until the instructor begins to parry that feint before you go on to the next feint. When you deceive the instructor's last parry, make the final movement of your attack with your lunge at your full speed. The cadence of your attack is set by the pace of the parries you have to deceive. If this

259

cadence is varied deliberately, it will help you develop judgment and timing. Remember that the feint is all-important in compound attacks; if it does not accomplish its purpose of opening up a line for the final attack, you will fall on a closed line and will risk being touched by a riposte.

5.   In a compound parry exercise, take the parries up to the final one by opposition; the final parry, however, may be given by opposition or by beat.

6.   In the counter-riposte exercise, you will attack after parrying the instructor's riposte. Come back to a parry position with your arm three-quarters extended before you launch your counter-riposte. Your attack, riposte and counter-riposte may be executed in place, with a lunge, or on the lunge.

7.   In the second counter-riposte exercise, the instructor will begin the exercise. There will be one more attack, parry and riposte than in the previous exercise.

8.   In the attack speed exercise, use your full speed.

9.   In the parry and riposte speed exercise, your instructor will gradually increase the speed and gradually close the distance to make the parry more difficult to execute.

10.   After the speed exercises, the explanation of a new movement will serve as a rest period. The instructor will first explain the movement to you, then demonstrate it; finally, you will attempt it yourself.

11.   The slow-motion movements for corrective purposes will taper off the lesson.

12.   Reassemble and salute at the end of every lesson.

If it is desired to spread the following lessons over a period of two years, they should be divided as follows:

1st year: Lessons 1-9

2nd year: Lessons 1-18.

No fencer is so far advanced that he can afford to stop practicing fundamentals.

Lesson 1

1. Explanation of the make-up of the sabre.
2. Holding the sabre.
3. Coming on guard (in three counts). The advance. The retreat.
4. Reassembling. The salute.
5. Explanation of finger- all wrist-play.
6. Extension of the arm and coming back in guard.
7. Extension of the arm, the lunge and recovery of the guard position.
8. The feint. Point in line. The engagement.
9. The tierce guard position.
10. The high guard. The thrust. The cut.
11. Explanation of the lines.
12. Explanation of the attack.
13. The straight thrust. Extension of the arm before lunging.
14. Distance.
15. The head attack.
16. Reassembling forward.
17. Reassemble. Salute.

To prevent stiffness, do some warming-up exercises before taking the lesson. Repeat the lesson until the movements can be made with facility. The importance of correct fundamental positions cannot be over-emphasized.

Lesson 2

1. The guard position. The advance. The retreat.
2. Explanation and execution, in two counts ("Feint!", and "Lunge!"), of the following simple attacks: head, right flank, right cheek, and cuff.
3. Explanation of the parries.
4. Parries of the above attacks by head parry, right flank parry, tierce for the right cheek attack, and quarte for the cuff attack.
5. Explanation and execution, in two counts, of the following simple attacks: left flank, left cheek, straight thrust and the disengage.
6. Parries of the attacks in #5 above by prime, quarte, tierce, and quarte respectively.
7. Explanation of the riposte.
8. Execution of the moulinets, inside, outside, horizontal from right to left, and from left to right.
9. Parry and riposte exercise:

Instructor's Attack (with advance)	Pupil's Parry	Pupil's Riposte (no lunge)
a. Head	Head	Right flank
b. Right flank	Right flank	Head
c. Right cheek	Tierce	Left cheek
d. Left flank	Prime	Left flank
e. Left cheek	Quarte	Right cheek
f. Cuff inside	Quarte	Head
g. Cuff outside	Tierce	Right flank
h. Straight thrust to body	Quarte	Cuff
i. Banderole	Quarte	Right cheek

10. Explanation and execution of low quarte and low tierce parries.
11. Reassemble and salute.

This is a very important lesson. It should be repeated several times during two or three weeks.

Lesson 3

1. The guard position. The advance. The retreat. Correction of the guard position.
2. Single-movement attacks accompanied by an advance: head, right flank, left flank, right cheek and left cheek.
3. Parry and riposte exercise:

Instructor's Attack (advance without lunge)	Pupil's Parry (while retreating)	Pupil's Riposte (no lunge)
a. Head	Head	Left flank
b. Right flank	Right flank	Right flank
c. Right cheek	Tierce	Head
d. Left flank	Prime	Straight thrust to body
e. Left cheek	Quarte	Straight thrust to body

4. Single-movement attacks: banderole, straight thrust, cuff (under), disengage and cuff (outside).
5. Parry and riposte exercise:

Instructor's Attack (advance without lunge)	Pupil's Parry	Pupil's Riposte (no lunge)
a. Banderole	Quarte	Head
b. Straight thrust	Tierce	Right flank
c. Cuff (under)	Low Quarte	Left cheek
d. Disengage	Quarte	Right cheek
e. Cuff (outside)	Low Tierce	Left flank

6. Explanation of the counter-riposte and the second counter-riposte.
7. Counter-riposte exercise.
8. Second counter-riposte exercise.
9. Explanation and execution of the following counter-parries: tierce, quarte, head, right flank, prime. From the tierce position, on a disengage to your inside line, take a counter-tierce parry. From the quarte position, on a disengage to your outside line, take a counter-quarte. From the head parry position, on a thrust to the body, take a counter-head parry. From the right flank parry position, on a disengage to your inside line, parry counter right flank. From prime, on a disengage to your outside line, parry counter-prime.
10. Reassemble and salute.

264

Lesson 4

1.   The guard position, the advance, the retreat, the lunge, for corrective purposes.
2.   Single-movement attacks: head, right flank, straight thrust, cuff (outside), disengage.
3.   Parry and riposte exercise:

Instructor's Attack (advance without lunge)	Pupil's Parry (while retreating)	Pupil's Riposte (no lunge)
a. Head	Head	Head
b. Right flank	Right flank	Cuff (half-lunge)
c. Straight thrust	Quarte	Left cheek
d. Cuff (Outside)	Right flank	Right flank
e. Disengage	Quarte	Straight thrust to body

4.   Single-movement attacks accompanied by an advance: left flank, banderole, cuff (under), right cheek, left cheek.
5.   Parry and riposte exercise:

Instructor's Attack (advance without lunge)	Pupil's Parry (while retreating)	Pupil's Riposte (no lunge)
a. Left flank	Low quarte	Right cheek
b. Banderole	Prime	Head moulinet
c. Cuff (under)	Low quarte	Head
d. Right cheek	Tierce	Left cheek by horizontal moulinet
e. Left cheek	Quarte	Right cheek

6.   Counter-riposte exercise.
7.   Second counter-riposte exercise.
8.   Speed exercise, attack: execute with full speed five disengages and then five head attacks.
9.   Speed exercise, parry and riposte: on the instructor's disengage, parry counter-tierce and riposte, without lunging to the head; 5 times. On the instructor's head attack, parry head and riposte to the right flank without lunging; 5 times.
10.   Explanation and execution of the high right cheek and high left cheek parries.
11.   Explanation of preparation s to the attack. The beat.
12.   Several slow-motion lunges.
13.   Reassemble and salute.

Each of these first four lessons will take about two weeks to master. Do not leave any lesson until it has been mastered.

Lesson 5

1. The guard position, the advance, the retreat, the lunge, for corrective purposes.
2. Single-movement attacks: head, banderole, left flank, right flank, right cheek, left cheek.
3. Parry and riposte exercise:

Instructor's Attack	Pupil's Parry	Pupil's Riposte (no lunge)
a. Head	Head	Right flank
b. Banderole	Quarte	Right cheek
c. Left flank	Prime	Left flank (moulinet)
d. Right flank	Right flank	Left cheek
e. Right cheek	Tierce	Straight thrust to body
f. Left cheek	Quarte	Head

4. Explanation of the compound attack.
5. Two-movement attacks: feint right flank, left flank; feint to head, right flank; feint to left flank, right flank; feint to left flank, head; feint to head, left flank.
6. Parry and riposte exercise:

Instructor's Attack	Pupil's Parry	Pupil's Riposte (no lunge)
a. Feint right flank, left flank	Right flank, prime	Head
b. Feint head, right flank	Head, right flank	Right cheek
c. Feint left flank, right flank	Prime, right flank	Head
d. Feint left flank, head	Prime, head	Right flank
e. Feint head, left flank	Head, prime	Left flank

7. Counter-riposte exercise.
8. Second counter-riposte exercise.
9. Speed exercise, attack: right flank attack; 5 times. Left flank attack; 5 times.
10. Speed exercise, parry and riposte: on instructor's right flank attack; parry right flank and riposte without lunge to the head; 5 times. On instructor's left flank attack, parry prime and riposte without lunge to the right cheek; 5 times.
11. Explanation and execution of the expulsion, the press, the glide, opposition.
12. Reassemble and salute.

Lesson 6

1. The guard position, the advance, the retreat, the jump forward and back ward.
2. Single-movement attacks accompanied by.an advance: head, right flank, left flank, cuff (outside), disengage, right cheek, left cheek.
3. Parry and riposte exercise:

Instructor's Attack	Pupil's Parry	Pupil's Riposte (no lunge)
a. Head	Head	Cuff
b. Right flank	Right flank	Head
c. Left flank	Prime	Left flank
d. Cuff (outside)	Tierce	Right flank
e. Disengage	Counter-tierce	Left flank
f. Right cheek	Tierce	Cuff (outside)
g. Left cheek	Quarte	Cuff (inside)

4. Two-movement attacks: feint right Hank, left cheek; feint left cheek, right flank; feint right flank, disengage; feint head, disengage; feint left flank, cuff; feint left flank, disengage.
5. Parry and riposte exercise for the above attacks:

Instructor's Attack	Pupil's Parry	Pupil's Riposte
a. Feint right flank, left cheek	Right flank, high quarte	Right cheek
b. Feint left cheek, right flank	High quarte, right flank	Straight thrust to body
c. Feint right flank, disengage with point	Right flank, counter right flank	Cuff
d. Head feint, disengage	Head, counter-head	Right flank
e. Feint left flank, cuff	Prime, tierce	Head
f. Feint left flank, disengage	Prime, counter-prime	Inside moulinet to head

6. Counter-riposte exercise.
7. Second counter-riposte exercise.
8. Speed exercise, attack: beat, head attack; 5 times. Beat, right flank attack; 5 times.
9. Speed exercise, parry and riposte: on instructor's beat, head attack, parry with head parry and riposte to right flank; 5 times. On instructor's beat, right flank attack, parry with right flank parry and riposte to head; 5 times
10. Explanation and execution of the stop-thrust.
11. Several slow-motion lunges for corrective purposes.
12. Reassemble and salute.

267

Lesson 7

1. The guard position, the advance, the retreat, several slow-motion lunges. Forward recovery of the guard position.
2. Some point attacks:
    a. Straight thrust (inside and outside lines).
    b. Disengage (high and low lines).
    c. Feint straight and disengage high or low.
    d. 1-2, high and low lines.
3. Parry and riposte exercise; the point.

Instructor's Attack	Pupil's Parry	Pupil's Riposte (no lunge)
a. Disengage	Quarte	Straight to the body
b. Disengage	Counter-tierce	Straight to the body
c. Beat, straight	Tierce	Disengage
d. 1-2	Quarte, tierce	Straight or disengage

4. Two-movement attacks: feint head, cuff (under); feint left cheek, disengage to body; feint right cheek, disengage to body; 1-2 (a feint disengage followed by a disengage deceiving a simple parry); feint banderole, right flank.
5. Parry and riposte exercise for the above attacks:

Instructor's Attack	Pupil's Parry	Pupil's Riposte (no lunge)
a. Feint to head, cuff (under)	Head, tierce	Head
b. Feint left cheek, disengage	Quarte, tierce	Left flank
c. Feint right cheek, disengage	Tierce, counter-tierce	Left cheek
d. 1-2	Quarte, counter-quarte	Head
e. Feint banderole, right flank	Prime, right flank	Cut to right arm

6. Counter-riposte exercise.
7. Second counter-riposte exercise.
8. Speed exercise, attack: feint right flank, head; 5 times. Then feint to head, disengage; 5 times.
9. Speed exercise, parry and riposte: on instructor's feint right flank, head, parry right flank, head, and riposte to the right flank; 5 times. On instructor's feint to head, disengage, parry head, counter-head, and riposte with a disengage to the body; 5 times.
10. Alternative exercise.
11. Explanation and execution of redoubling.
12. Reassemble and salute.

Lesson 8

1. The guard position, the advance, the retreat, the jump forward and backward.
2. Single-movement attacks accompanied by an advance: banderole, head, disengage, right flank, left flank, right cheek, left cheek.
3. Parry and riposte exercise for the above attacks:

Instructor's Attack	Pupil's Parry (while retreating)	Pupil's Riposte (lunge)
a. Banderole	Prime	Right flank
b. Head	Head	Straight thrust
c. Disengage	Counter-tierce	Head
d. Right flank	Right flank	Cuff
e. Left flank	Prime	Left flank (moulinet)
f. Right cheek	Tierce	Right flank
g. Left cheek	Quarte	Right flank

4. Two-movement attacks: feint head, disengage; feint banderole, cuff (outside); feint right flank, banderole; feint left flank, cuff (outside); feint right flank, left flank moulinet.
5. Parry and riposte exercise for above attacks:

Instructor's Attack	Pupil's Parry	Pupil's Riposte
a. Feint head, disengage	Head, counter head	Left flank moulinet
b. Feint banderole, cuff (outside)	Quarte, tierce	Head
c. Feint right flank, banderole	Right flank, prime	Straight thrust
d. Feint left flank, cuff outside	Low quarte, tierce	Left cheek
e. Feint right flank, left flank moulinet	Right flank, prime	Right flank

6. Counter-riposte exercise.
7. Second counter-riposte exercise.
8. Speed exercise, attack: disengage; 5 times. Feint to head, left flank; 5 times.
9. Speed exercise, parry and riposte: on instructor's disengage, parry counter-tierce and riposte with a cut to the head; 5 times. On the instructor's feint to head, left flank, parry head and prime and riposte to the right flank; 5 times.
10. Alternative exercise.
11. Execution of the stop-thrust.
12. Several lunges for corrective purposes.
13. Reassemble and salute.

269

Lesson 9

1. The guard position, the advance, the retreat, the lunge, the forward guard.
2. Single-movement attacks preceded by a beat: beat, cuff (outside); beat cuff (inside); beat, straight thrust; beat, head attack; beat, right cheek (with the back of the blade).
3. Parry and riposte exercise for the above attacks:

Instructor's Attack	Pupil's Parry	Pupil's Riposte
a. Beat in tierce, cuff (outside)	Tierce	Head
b. Beat in quarte, cuff (inside)	Quarte	Right cheek
c. Beat in quarte, straight thrust	Counter-tierce	Left cheek
d. Beat in tierce, head	Head	Straight thrust
e. Beat in tierce, right cheek	Counter-tierce	Disengage

4. Two-movement attacks: feint left cheek, cuff (outside); feint right cheek, left flank; feint right flank, right cheek; feint left flank, left cheek; feint left cheek, moulinet to right cheek.
5. Parry and riposte exercise for the above compound attacks:

Instructor's Attack	Pupil's Parry	Pupil's Riposte
a. Feint left cheek, cuff (outside)	Quarte, tierce	Banderole
b. Feint right cheek, left flank	Tierce, low quarte	Cuff (Outside)
c. Feint right flank, right cheek	Low tierce, tierce	Head
d. Feint left flank, left cheek	Low quarte, quarte	Right flank
e. Feint left cheek, moulinet to right cheek	Quarte, tierce	Left cheek

6. Counter-riposte exercise: #7.
7. Second counter-riposte exercise: #7.
8. Speed exercise, attack: feint right flank, moulinet to left flank; 5 times. Then feint left flank, moulinet to right flank; 5 times.
9. Speed exercise, parry and riposte: on instructor's feint right flank, moulinet to left flank, parry right flank and prime and riposte to head; 5 times. On his feint left flank, moulinet to right flank, parry prime, right flank, and riposte with a straight thrust; 5 times.
10. Alternative exercise:#4 and #5.
11. Several attacks in slow-motion for corrective purposes.
12. Reassemble and salute.

Note that the beat in quarte may also be given with the back of the blade.

270

Lesson 10

1. The guard position, the advance, the retreat, the lunge, as warm-up exercises.

2. Single-movement attacks preceded by a preparation: press, disengage; expulsion, straight thrust; press with a change of guard (palm up), right cheek (palm down); press, right flank; press with change guard (palm up), left flank (palm up).

3. Parry and riposte exercise for the above attacks:

Instructor's Attack	Pupil's Parry	Pupil's Riposte
a. Press, disengage	Counter-tierce	Straight thrust
b. Expulsion, straight thrust	Tierce opposition	Feint head, right flank
c. Press with change of guard, right cheek	Counter-tierce	Feint right flank, head attack
d. Press, right flank	Right flank	Right cheek
e. Press with change of guard, left flank	Low quarte	Left cheek

4. Two-movement attacks: feint right flank, disengage inside; feint left flank, head; feint to head, cuff; feint right cheek, left cheek; feint left cheek, right cheek.

5. Parry and riposte exercise for the above compound attacks:

Instructor's Attack	Pupil's Parry	Pupil's Riposte
a. Feint right flank, left flank	Right flank, prime	Right flank
b. Feint left flank, head	Prime, head	Right cheek
c. Feint head, cuff	Head, high tierce	Straight thrust
d. Feint right cheek, left cheek	Tierce, quarte	Right cheek
e. Feint left cheek, right cheek	Quarte, tierce	Left cheek

6. Counter-riposte exercise: #8.

7. Second counter-riposte exercise: #8.

8. Speed exercise, an attack accompanied by an advance: press, disengage; 5 times. Press with change of guard (palm up), right check (palm down); 5 times.

9. Speed exercise, parry and riposte: on the instructor's advancing attack with press, disengage, parry counter-tierce while retreating and riposte with a straight thrust; 5 times. On his advancing attack with press, right cheek as described in #8 above, parry counter-tierce accompanied by a jump backward and riposte to the head; 5 times.

10. Alternative exercise: #6 and #7.

11. Execution of an invitation to the attack.

12. Several slow-motion lunges for corrective purposes.

13. Reassemble and salute.

271

Lesson 11

1. The guard position. Some slow-motion movements as warm-up.
2. Single-movement attack preceded by a preparation: beat, head cut; beat, cuff (outside); beat with back of blade, cuff (inside); beat with change of guard (palm up), left flank; expulsion, head.
3. Parry and riposte exercise for the above attacks:

Instructor's Attack	Pupil's Parry	Pupil's Riposte (Feint without lunge, then lunge)
a. Beat, head	Head	Feint right flank, head
b. Beat, cuff (outside)	Right flank	Feint head, right flank
c. Beat with back of blade, cuff (inside)	Quarte	Right cheek
d. Beat with change of guard (palm up), left flank (low)	Low quarte	Right cheek
e. Expulsion, head	Head	Feint left flank, right flank

4. Two-movement attack exercise, retreating as instructor advances: feint head, right flank; feint left flank, right flank; feint right flank, head; feint right flank, left flank; feint head, left flank.
5. Parry and riposte exercise for above compound attacks. The pupil will parry while retreating. The instructor will advance so that the pupil's riposte will reach without a lunge.

Instructor's Attack	Pupil's Parry	Pupil's Riposte
a. Feint head, right flank	Head, right flank	Straight thrust
b. Feint left flank, right flank	Prime, right flank	Straight thrust
c. Feint right flank, head	Right flank, head	Straight thrust
d. Feint right flank, left flank	Right flank, prime	Straight thrust
e. Feint head, left flank	Head, prime	Straight thrust

6. Counter-riposte exercise: #9.
7. Second counter-riposte exercise: #9.
8. Speed exercise, attack: feint head, right flank, with an advance; 5 times. Feint left flank, right flank, with an advance; 5 times.
9. Speed exercise, parry and riposte: on the instructor's feint head, right flank, pupil will parry head, right flank, and riposte with a straight thrust; 5 times. On instructor's feint left flank, right flank, pupil will parry prime, right flank, and riposte with a straight thrust; 5 times.
10. Alternative exercise: #7 and #8.
11. On the instructor's right flank attack, the pupil will execute a cuff attack while retreating.
12. Some slow-motion movements for corrective purposes.
13. Reassemble and salute.

Lesson 12

1. The guard position, the lunge, the advance, the retreat, as warm-up.
2. Single-movement attacks preceded by an expulsion: expulsion, head; expulsion, right flank; expulsion, straight thrust; expulsion, cuff (outside); expulsion with the back of the blade, cuff (inside).
3. Parry and riposte for the above attacks:

Instructor's Attack	Pupil's Parry	Pupil's Riposte
a. Expulsion, head	Head	Straight thrust
a. Expulsion, head	Head	Straight thrust
b. Expulsion, right flank	Right flank	Left flank
c. Expulsion, straight thrust	Tierce opposition	Head
d. Expulsion, cuff (outside)	Tierce opposition	Left cheek
e. Expulsion with back of blade, cuff (inside)	Quarte opposition	Cuff (inside)

4. Explanation of the false attack. Two-movement false attack exercise (the pupil will take a half-lunge on his first movement, deceive the first parry, and take a full lunge): feint right flank, head; feint right flank, left flank; feint head, straight thrust; feint straight thrust, disengage; feint right cheek, right flank. The instructor will parry only the feint.
5. Parry and compound riposte exercise for the above attacks:

Instructor's Attack	Pupil's Parry	Pupil's Riposte
a. Feint right flank, head	Right flank, head	Right flank, banderole
b. Feint right flank, left flank (low)	Low tierce, low quarte	Feint right flank, left flank
c. Feint to head, disengage with point	Head, counter-head	Feint left flank, right flank
d. Feint straight thrust, disengage	Tierce opposition, quarte	Feint head, cuff (inside)
e. Feint right cheek, right flank	Tierce, low tierce	Feint right cheek, left flank

6. Counter-riposte exercise: #10 and #11.
7. Second counter-riposte exercise: #10 and #11.
8. Speed exercise, attack: expulsion, cuff (outside); 5 times. Feint right check, right flank; 5 times.
9. Speed exercise, parry and riposte: on instructor's expulsion, cuff (outside), pupil will parry tierce and riposte to the head; 5 times. On instructor's feint right check, right flank, pupil will parry tierce, low tierce and riposte to right cheek; 5 times.
10. Alternative exercise: #8 and #9.
11. Execution of redoubling.
12. Several slow-motion movements for corrective purposes.
13. Reassemble and salute.

273

Lesson 13

1. The guard position, the advance, the retreat, the lunge, as warm-up.
2. Single-movement attack exercise, using a glide as a preparation: glide, straight thrust; glide, disengage; glide, head; glide, left flank (low); glide, right flank.
3. Parry and riposte exercise for the above attacks:

Instructor's Attack	Pupil's Parry	Pupil's Riposte
a. Glide, straight thrust	Tierce opposition	Straight thrust
b. Glide, disengage	Counter-tierce	Disengage
c. Glide, head	Head	Right flank
d. Glide, left flank	Low quarte	Right cheek
e. Glide, right flank	Low tierce	Left cheek

4. Two-movement attack exercise, accompanied by an advance: feint head, right flank; feint head, left flank (abdomen); feint right flank, head; feint right cheek, banderole; feint left flank, right flank.
5. Parry and compound riposte exercise for the above attacks:

Instructor's Attack	Pupil's Parry	Pupil's Riposte
a. Feint head, right flank	Head, right flank	Feint right cheek, right flank
b. Feint head, left flank (abdomen)	Head, prime	Feint right flank, left cheek
c. Feint right flank, head	Right flank, head	Feint right flank, left flank
d. Feint right cheek, banderole	Tierce, quarte	Feint head, right flank
e. Feint left flank, right flank	Prime, right flank	Feint right cheek, left cheek

6. Counter-riposte exercise: #12 and #13.
7. Second counter-riposte exercise: #12 and #13.
8. Speed exercise, attack: Feint head, right flank, accompanied by advance; 5 times. Then feint head, left flank (abdomen), accompanied by advance; 5 times.
9. Speed exercise, parry and riposte: on instructor's feint head, right flank, pupil will parry head, right flank, and riposte with a feint to the right cheek and an attack to the right flank; 5 times. On instructor's feint head, left flank, pupil will parry head, prime, and riposte with a feint to the right flank and an attack to the left flank; 5 times.
10. Alternative exercise: #9 and #10.
11. Explanation and execution of the avoidance.
12. Several slow-motion movements for corrective purposes.
13. Reassemble and salute.

Lesson 14

1. The guard position, the advance, the retreat, the lunge, as warm-up.
2. Single-movement attack preceded by a counter-beat: counter-beat, left cheek; counter-beat, right cheek; counter-beat, cuff (outside); counter-beat, cuff (inside); counter-beat, banderole.
3. Parry and compound riposte exercise:

Instructor's Attack	Pupil's Parry	Pupil's Riposte
a. Counter-beat, left cheek	Quarte	Feint right cheek, left flank
b. Counter-beat, right cheek	Counter-tierce	Feint head, right flank
c. Counter-beat, cuff (outside, by disengage)	Tierce opposition	Feint straight thrust, disengage
d. Counter-beat, cuff (inside)	Quarte opposition	Feint head, right flank
e. Counter-beat, banderole	Quarte	Feint straight thrust, head

4. Two-movement attack exercise, accompanied by a retreat: feint left cheek, cuff (outside); feint right cheek, cuff (inside); feint straight thrust, disengage; feint left flank, right cheek; feint left flank, cuff (outside).
5. Parry and riposte exercise for the above attacks:

Instructor's Attack	Pupil's Parry	Pupil's Riposte (Lunge)
a. Feint left cheek, cuff (outside)	Quarte, tierce	Head
b. Feint right cheek, cuff (inside)	Tierce, quarte	Right flank
c. Feint straight thrust, disengage	Tierce opposition, counter-tierce	Left flank (abdomen)
d. Feint left flank, right cheek	Prime, high tierce	Right flank
e. Feint left flank, cuff (outside)	Prime, right flank	Left flank

6. Counter-riposte exercise: #14 and #15.
7. Second counter-riposte exercise: #14 and,#15.
8. Speed exercise, attack: Counter-beat, left cheek; 5 times. Then counter-beat, right cheek; 5 times.
9. Speed exercise, parry and riposte: on instructor's attack with the counter-beat, left cheek, pupil will parry quarte and riposte with a feint to the left flank and an attack to the head; 5 times. On instructor's counter-beat, right cheek, pupil will parry counter-tierce and riposte with a feint to the right flank and an attack to the head; 5 times.
10. Alternative exercise: #10 and #11.
11. Some slow-motion movements for corrective purposes.
12. Reassemble and salute.

1.   The guard position, the advance, the retreat, the lunge, as warm-up.
2.   Single-movement attack and redoubling exercise (pupil will redouble on the instructor's failure to riposte after parrying by opposition):

Instructor's Attack	Pupil's Parry	Pupil's Redouble
a. Head	Head	Right flank
b. Right flank	Right flank	Head
c. Left flank	Prime	Cuff (outside)
d. Disengage	Counter-tierce	Disengage
e. Banderole	Quarte	Right cheek

3.   Three-movement attack exercise (two feints):
   a.   Right flank, head, right flank.
   b.   Head, right flank, head.
   c.   Left flank (abdomen), right flank, left flank (abdomen).
   d.   Left flank (chest), head, left flank (abdomen).
   e.   Right cheek, right flank, left cheek.
4.   Parry and riposte exercise for the above attacks: when the instructor attacks as listed in #3 above, the pupil will execute the following parries and ripostes:

Parries	Ripostes
a. Right flank, head, right flank	Straight thrust
b. Head, right flank, head	Head moulinet
c. Low quarte, low tierce, low quarte	Right cheek
d. Quarte, tierce, low quarte	Right flank
e. Tierce, right flank, high quarte	Left flank

5.   Second counter-riposte exercise: #16 and #17.
6.   Speed exercise, attack: right flank, head, right flank; 5 times. Then head, right flank, head; 5 times.
7.   Speed exercise, parry and riposte: on the instructor's attack to right flank, head, right flank, pupil will make the appropriate parries and riposte with a straight thrust; 5 times. On the instructor's attack to head, right flank, head, pupil will make the appropriate parries and riposte with a moulinet to the head; 5 times.
8.   Alternative exercise: #11 and #12.
9.   Execution of the stop-thrust and stop-cut.
10.   Some slow-motion movements for corrective purposes.
11.   Reassemble and salute.

Lesson 16

1.   The guard position, the advance, the retreat, the lunge, as warm-up.

2.   Single-movement attack exercise, preceded by a beat and simultaneous advance: beat, head; beat, right flank; beat, straight thrust; beat, cuff; beat with back of blade, straight thrust.

3.   Parry and riposte exercise for above attacks (the instructor will execute the attacks in #2 above without lunging; the pupil will advance during his parry and will riposte without a lunge):

Instructor's Attack	Pupil's Parry	Pupil's Riposte
a. Beat, head	Head	Right flank
b. Beat, right flank	Right flank	Head
c. Beat, straight thrust	Tierce opposition	Left cheek
d. Beat, cuff	Tierce opposition	Right flank
e. Beat with back of blade, straight thrust	Tierce	Left flank

4.   Three-movement attack exercise (two feints):
    a.   Right cheek, left cheek, right cheek.
    b.   Right flank, left flank (low), right flank.
    c.   Right cheek, left flank (chest), right cheek.
    d.   Left flank, right flank, head.
    e.   Head, right flank, left flank (abdomen).

5.   Parry and riposte exercise for the above attacks: on the instructor's execution of the above attacks, pupil will parry and riposte as follows:

Pupil's Parries	Pupil's Ripostes
a. Tierce, quarte, tierce	Cuff (under)
b. Right flank, prime, right flank	Straight thrust
c. Tierce, quarte, tierce	Left flank
d. Prime, right flank, head	Right flank
e. Head, right flank, prime	Left cheek

6.   Counter-riposte exercise: #18 and #19.

7.   Second counter-riposte exercise: #18 and #19.

8.   Speed exercise, attack: right cheek, left cheek, right cheek; 5 times. Then left flank, right flank, head; 5 times.

9.   Speed exercise, parry and riposte: on instructor's attack to right cheek, left cheek, right cheek, pupil will parry tierce, quarte, tierce, and will riposte to the cuff (under). On instructor's attack to left flank, right flank, head, pupil will parry prime, right flank, head, and will riposte to the right flank; 5 times.

10.   Alternative exercise: #12 and #13.

11.   Execution of the false attack.

12.   Explanation and demonstration of the attack on a preparation.

13.   Some slow-motion movements for corrective purposes.

14.   Reassemble and salute.

Lesson 17

1. The guard position, the advance, the retreat, the lunge, as warm-up.
2. Single-movement attack exercise, preceded by an opposition: tierce opposition, straight thrust; tierce opposition, disengage; quarte opposition, head; tierce opposition, left cheek; quarte opposition, right cheek.
3. Parry and riposte exercise for the attacks in #2 above:

Instructor's Attack	Pupil's Parry	Pupil's Riposte
a. Tierce opposition, straight thrust	Tierce	Head, right flank
b. Tierce opposition, disengage	Counter-tierce	Head, left flank (abdomen)
c. Quarte opposition, head	Head	Left flank, cuff (outside)
d. Tierce opposition, left cheek	Quarte	Left cheek, right flank
e. Quarte opposition, right cheek	Counter-tierce	Head, cuff (outside)

4. Three-movement attack exercise, executed with an advance:
    a. Right flank, disengage, left flank.
    b. Head, disengage, right flank.
    c. Left flank, disengage, right flank.
    d. Banderole, disengage, right cheek.
    e. Right cheek, disengage, left cheek.
5. Parries and ripostes for the above attacks: pupil will parry while retreating.

Pupil's Parries	Pupil's Ripostes
a. Right flank, counter right flank, prime	Head
b. Head, counter-head, right flank	Right flank
c. Prime, counter-prime, right flank	Left flank
d. Quarte, counter-quarte, tierce	Left cheek
e. Tierce, counter-tierce, quarte	Right cheek

6. Counter-riposte exercise: #20 and #21.
7. Second counter-riposte exercise: #20 and #21.
8. Alternative exercise: #13, #14, and #15.
9. Speed exercise, attack: right flank, disengage, left flank; 5 times. Then head, disengage, right flank; 5 times.
10. Speed exercise, parry and riposte: on the instructor's attack to right flank, disengage, left flank, pupil will parry right flank, counter right flank, prime, and will riposte to the head; 5 times. On the instructor's attack to head, disengage, right flank, pupil will parry head, counter-head, right flank, and will riposte to the right flank; 5 times.
11. Explanation and execution of the time-attack and the counter-time-attack.
12. Some slow-motion movements for corrective purposes.
13. Reassemble and salute.

278

Lesson 18

1. The guard position, the advance, the retreat, the lunge, as warm-up.
2. Single-movement attack exercise, executed to surprise the instructor on his advance: head, cuff (outside); disengage, left cheek; left flank.
3. Parry and compound riposte exercise for the above attacks:

Instructor's Attack (Advance)	Pupil's Parry (With jump backward)	Pupil's Riposte (Lunge)
a. Head	Head	Head, disengage
b. Cuff (outside)	Tierce opposition	Straight thrust, disengage
c. Disengage	Counter-tierce	Feint disengage, disengage
d. Left cheek	Quarte	Straight thrust, cuff
e. Left flank	Prime	Straight thrust, head

4. Three-movement attacks by beat:
   a. Beat, straight thrust, left cheek, right cheek.
   b. Beat, right flank, head, disengage.
   c. Beat, disengage, right cheek, left cheek.
   d. Beat, right cheek, left cheek, cuff (outside).
   e. Beat, left flank, right flank, cuff (inside).
5. Parry and riposte exercise for the above attacks: on the advancing attack of the instructor, pupil will retreat and parry riposte as follows:

Pupil's Parries	Pupil's Ripostes
a. Tierce, quarte, tierce	Head, right flank
b. Right flank, head, counter-head	Right flank, head
c. Quarte, tierce, quarte	Left flank, right flank
d. Tierce, quarte, tierce	Head, cuff
e. Prime, right flank, head	Banderole, right flank

6. Counter-riposte exercise: #22.
7. Second counter-riposte exercise: #22.
8. Speed exercise, attack: beat, right flank, head, disengage; 5 times. Then beat, left flank, right flank, cuff (inside); 5 times.
9. Speed exercise, parry and riposte: pupil will parry the instructor's first attack in #8 above with right flank, head, counter-head, and will riposte right flank, head; 5 times. Pupil will parry the second attack with prime, right flank, head, and will riposte to banderole, right flank.
10. Alternative exercise: #17, 18, 19.
11. Explanation and execution of the remise and redoubling of the riposte.
12. Some slow-motion movements for corrective purposes.
13. Reassemble and salute.

279

CHAPTER IX
Practical Advice

General Advice On The Bout

Have someone point out the errors you actually make during a bout. You may take your lessons correctly enough but act entirely differently in a bout. You may forget what you have learned, or be unable to apply it in practice.

Until you are an experienced, strong fencer, stick to the book. That is, do not use unorthodox positions and movements until you have mastered the orthodox ones. The latter would not have become standard practice if they were not generally effective. From time to time, check your positions with the book. For example, if you are touched on the cheek through your tierce or quarte parry, you would be justified in assuming that the parry was not correctly executed; your hand may not have been far enough to the side, or your point was not sufficiently outside to make your opponent's blade slide down to your sabre guard.

If you are often touched by your adversary's compound attack, it may be that you are trying to follow and parry his feints too fully. Make a full parry only on his final attack.

If your attacks are arriving too low, you may be dropping your shoulders on your lunge. Remember that even on a full lunge, the line from shoulder to shoulder should stay horizontal, while your body is going forward and clown.

If you are continually touched on a riposte or counter-riposte, you have probably got into the habit of failing to return immediately to the correct guard position, or failed to protect yourself behind the sabre guard while doing so. Do not remain on the lunge unless to redouble or remise. When you do recover, do so rapidly and with your feet at the normal guard distance, so that you will be ready to lunge immediately if necessary. This correct position of your feet, often neglected or forgotten in the excitement of a bout, will make it possible for you to riposte whenever necessary.

Keep your eyes on your opponent's hand.

Remember that attacks can be delivered by passing above or below an opponent's blade. A tall fencer should pass above the blade, a short fencer below the blade. In general, the offensive in sabre is more effective than the defensive. However, more than in the foil and épée, the counter-offensive may give good results in the sabre.

Foot-work in the sabre is more energetic than in the other weapons. The jump forward and the jump backward are used a great deal, as is the flèche. There is very little static play in the sabre. Since sabre movements are wide and must cover a great deal of territory, special care must be exercised in this weapon to coordinate foot-work with arm-work.

More strength is needed for sabre than for the foil and épée. It follows, therefore, that the condition of the fencer during a tournament is of great importance.

During your parry, adjust the position of your arm to the distance from which your opponent makes his attack. If he attacks from a long distance, the arm may be three-quarters extended for the parry; the closer the distance, the more bent your arm.

The best times to launch an attack are during your opponent's advance and on his preparation; in both cases the element of surprise will be on your side.

While the advancing attack is effective, you must learn to vary your attacks so as to include some without an advance. If your opponent is sure you will advance with each attack, he will soon learn to stop-thrust or cut every time your right foot begins to move. If your opponent retreats upon your attack, recover your guard forward, so as to gain the distance he has lost. As your opponent nears his end of the strip, his freedom of movement becomes seriously hampered.

If your opponent uses the stop-thrust and stop-cut against you successfully, it is probably for one of the following reasons:

1. Your arm during your feint is not sufficiently protected behind your guard.

2. You complicate your attack with too many movements.

3. After you have extended your arm in line for a feint, you move your forearm instead of your fingers and wrist.

4. You have failed to coordinate your feint with your foot-work.

5. In a flèche you rebend your arm preparatory to making the final cut or thrust. Once the arm is extended in line for a flèche, it should remain extended; any change of direction should be executed by the fingers and wrist.

Against a flèche you have no time to make a point-down parry. Stick to tierce, counter-tierce, seconde and quarte. These will take care of any flèche. A jump backward at the same time will give you more time to cover yourself.

If you have made a feint or a series of feints without attacking, simply to feel out your opponent's reaction, do not proceed immediately afterward to go through exactly the same motions in a real attack, as your opponent will have had time to prepare himself for them.

In a wider application, never do the same thing twice in succession. If you have been successful in making a touch with a beat in quarte, cut to the right cheek, let us say, do not do it again until you have first made another movement; otherwise, your opponent will be waiting for you. On the other hand, if you will go one step further, you will generally be successful in an immediate repetition. That is, suppose you were to beat in quarte, feint to the right cheek and disengage to the right flank. Your opponent will probably parry the feint to the right cheek with a counter-tierce, or he will present quarte opposition to your beat; in either case, your disengage to the low line will be successful.

Some fencers who have been trained in foil or épée rely in the sabre almost exclusively on the point thrust. The best parries against such attacks are tierce, counter-tierce and quarte. Such fencers are also easily hit with a stop-cut to the cuff, accompanied by a jump backward.

Never answer your opponent's feint. Since the target you have to cover is so wide, your reaction will leave your opponent a large field of attack.

Many sabre fencers riposte constantly to the same line. After one or two exchanges you should learn how to come back to your best advantage after an attack.

Left-Handed Fencers

The directions given throughout this book are predicated on the use of the right arm for fencing. The left-handed fencer will have to substitute "counter-clockwise" for "clockwise," "left" for "right," "inside" for "outside," and so on.

The left-hander's strongest parries are his inside parries, quarte, prime and low quarte. His guard position should therefore be slightly more outside than that of the right-hander, to provoke inside attacks.

The left-hander will find it easy to stop-cut a right-hander on his cuff as the latter attacks.

The right-hander will obtain the best results by attacking a left-hander finally in the inside line. The preparations can of course be taken in the inside line, but care must be taken to avoid a stop-cut to the cuff.

The right-hander will find the following attacks very effective against a left-hander:

283

1. Beat in the outside line with the back of the blade (nails down) or with the edge (nails up), cut to cuff.

2. Same beat, cut to right cheek.

3. Expulsion in the outside line, cut to cuff or right cheek, or straight thrust.

4. Outside beat or expulsion, cut to left flank.

5. Flèche with quarte opposition, cut or thrust to outside line. The right-hander's guard position should be slightly more outside than usual when he is fencing a left-hander. This will minimize his opponent's opportunities to stop-cut to the cuff during an attack.

Appendix

Fig. 1 - Dummy foil for target practice   Fig. 2 - Group practice on dummy foil

A. Sportsmanship

Fencing is a sport with a rigid code of etiquette going back to the time when only gentlemen wore and used a sword. Today, when the accident of birth has lost its ancient importance, the observance of this code will still mark a fencer as a gentleman. For in fencing, more than in any other similar sport, it is difficult to be a good sportsman. The reason lies in the difficulties inherent in the system of judging. In tennis, golf, track, wrestling, football, or what you will, the results are perfectly obvious to the referees and audience alike; there is little likelihood that the winner will be declared the loser through a mistaken decision. In fencing, on the other hand, the action is so close, so fast and so simultaneous that it would indeed require superhuman judges to render perfect decisions at all times. When the score is 4-4, the fact that a judge blinked at the wrong time may be sufficient to throw the final touch the wrong way. At such a time a good sportsman, knowing he has in reality won the bout, will still be able to congratulate the winner with cordiality and will give no sign that he believes he has won. To be known among fencers as a good sportsman is high praise indeed.

285

1. First of all, be sure that your clothing and equipment are above criticism. Your clothing should be neat and properly buttoned; your equipment should conform to the rules regarding length, weight, curvature of the blade, and so on.

2. When you arrive on the strip, wait until your opponent is in position, then salute, first your opponent, then to the left and to the right. Do not put on your mask until after the salute. At the encl of the bout, first remove your mask, then step forward to shake hands. Remove your mask if you have occasion to speak to the jury. If a long discussion occurs, remove your mask while awaiting the decision, and during this time do not appear to follow the discussion with great concern.

3. Observe strictly the rule, "A contestant shall not make any gestures or communications which might influence the decision of the jury."

4. Whenever it becomes necessary to stop for any purpose, use foot-signals or step back and salute. Needless to say, never do this during a phrase.

5. You have the right to address the director in order to protect your own interests. This privilege should not be abused. To address the director, first say "Excuse me," and remove your mask. It would be proper, for

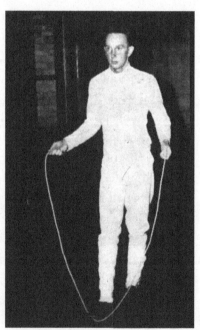

Fig. 3 - Warming-up exercise

example, to speak to the director in order to have him request you r opponent to straighten his blade, to ask which way a touch was awarded, or to ask the score. It would also be proper, when you believe that a fencing rule has been violated, to ask for an interpretation of the rule in question; this, however, is a very delicate matter and you must be very cautious in pursuing it, for even if you are right you have probably aroused some resentment in the erring judge.

6.   If you disarm your opponent, always hasten to pick up his weapon for him.

7.   Do not take unfair advantage of your opponent. The rule is, "A fencer shall not continue to fence after having noticed that his opponent is absolutely unable to defend himself as a consequence of anything which modified the normal condition of the combat, such as disarmament, an involuntary fall, a broken blade, a raised bib, a displaced mask, or the like." This does not, however, prevent you from grasping any opportunity that presents itself within the rules. If, for example, your opponent turns his back in the course of the bout, you have a perfect right to hit him. Also, a hit made after a disarmament is allowable if it follows immediately as a natural consequence of the preceding action; do not stop too soon and lose a chance to score.

8.   Never turn your back to your opponent at any time. During the action of a bout this would be dangerous, and is at all other times discourteous.

9.   You may acknowledge touches made against you, but you must do so immediately and before the judges' decision.

10.   Sometimes you may be so sure that your touch was clearly visible and in time that you may suspect the integrity of the judges. Try to understand the difficulties of the judges;

what is obvious to you as participant is far from being so obvious to them. It is a bad policy to lose your temper. The cool fencer is usually the winner.

Fig. 4 - Swinging ball for épée practice

11.   If you lose a bout, do not allow your manner to show either resentment or regret. Never permit yourself any display of temper or gesture of dissatisfaction, even after leaving the strip, such as throwing gear on the floor, or the like. Such gestures will not get you any sympathy, but will produce an unfavorable impression.

12.   While watching a bout, observe the rule, "Spectators shall do nothing which will tend to influence the fencers or the jury, and shall respect the decisions of the jury even when they do not approve of them." Applause and encouragement to your team-mates should be confined to the interval between the announcement of a touch and the subsequent coming on guard.

13.   If you are a member of a team, observe the rule, "Appeals may be made for interpretation of the rules to the Bout

Committee... Such appeals may be made only by the team captain."

14.   If you are a member of a team, cultivate a team spirit rather than too personal an attitude. If the coach sees fit to put a substitute in your place, yield gracefully and do all you can to encourage and advise the substitute.

Fig. 5 - Dummy épée for target practice   Fig. 6 - Group practice on dummy épées

B. The Importance Of A Correct Standard Interpretation Of Fencing Terms

There is much needless confusion regarding the exact meaning of various fencing terms. A remise is often called a redouble, a stop-thrust a time-attack, and so on. This confusion has a harmful effect on judging. Poor judging, probably more than any other single factor, has reacted unfavorably against fencing as a sport, not only through the spectators but through the contesting fencers themselves. Many a good fencer has been discouraged by poor judging in some local meet, and has finished his bouts with the feeling that he has been treated unfairly.

There is no excuse today for poor judging. The rules are clear and widely promulgated. Strict adherence to them will allow of only one interpretation of any situation on the fencing strip.

289

The fundamental sequence of attack, parry and riposte should be constantly kept in mind.

In modern times, there has been much progress in raising the quality of local judging, and recently a complete and authoritative set of rules has been compiled by the Amateur Fencers' League of America. Every local fencing unit, no matter how small, should have a copy on hand. Copies may be had by writing to the Secretary of the League.

C. Different Types Of Fencers

Each person, from birth, has a certain speed factor which, conditioned by his natural aptitude, the kind of work he does, and the kind of sport he practices, will place him in one of three classifications: 1. fast, 2. medium, or 3. slow.

1. The "fast" fencer: The fast fencer usually does not possess much coordination; while he is very fast in executing movements, he usually does not take the time or the patience to complete them. Often, his arm is still bent on the lunge, simply because in his impatience to go on the attack his feet have got ahead of his arm. Very often he loses his balance as he advances or retreats. He prefers to attack rather than to parry and riposte.

The best exercises for this type of fencer are complicated movements in the attack, so that he will be forced to extend his arm in the lunge. A four-movement attack, for example, will force the student to follow the cadence set by the instructor (which the instructor can vary at will, making one movement faster than another), and will force him to wait for the instructor's final parry before he lunges. In the bout, this type of fencer should be told, from time to time, to use simple movements. He is trained in form movements so that he can execute one or two movements perfectly. This type of fencer should also be taught to take several parries before he is allowed to make his riposte. In this way he can become accustomed to complete his parry before making his riposte.

Fig. 7 -Sabre dummy   Fig. 8 - Practic on sabre dummy

Such a fencer will give good results in a surprisingly short time, if trained properly. His principal deficiency is his small bag of tricks upon which he usually depends for his touches. His main drawback is his impatience.

2.   The "medium" fencer: The medium type of fencer is one who is inclined to be fast on some days and slow on other days without any special reason. The personality of this kind of fencer is also usually undetermined; he is usually indecisive.

This type of fencer should be trained progressively to maintain at all times the same speed of movement. He should be advanced as rapidly as possible to the alternative exercises, which were designed to promote regularity in the execution of movements.

This type of fencer usually yields good results after a year's work.

3. The "slow" fencer: The slow fencer of ten possesses perfect coordination in his movements but will execute them very slowly. This type of fencer should be given simple-movement attacks to execute but should be made to repeat these movements until he achieves some speed in them. The same applies for parries and ripostes. After, say, a year's time, this type of fencer should be made to attack with complicated movements; these generally give

291

good results, since he is always aware of what he is doing. This type of fencer can achieve a maximum understanding of fencing as well as maximum coordination. He will reach his true level at the end of his second or third year.

4. The tall fencer: The tall fencer should be trained especially to attack in place, to use the stop-thrust, and to attack the upper part of his opponent's body, since these attacks will protect him more than attacks to his adversary's low line.

5. The short fencer: The short fencer labors under a handicap which he must be trained to overcome by cleverness and generalship. When he fences a taller opponent there is a margin of reach favoring the latter. If the shorter fence!" allows his opponent to employ that margin to his advantage, he will lose the bout. The danger is that at a certain distance the shorter fencer may be reached by his opponent without being able to reach him in return.

The short fencer must be taught to stay out of reach, so that his adversary will be forced to take a step forward to begin his attack. He himself, of course, will also have to close the distance in attacking. By making the distance such that both fencers will have to close the distance in order to attack, the short fencer will have removed a great deal of his natural handicap.

The short fencer must be particularly strong on the defensive and must invite the attack; he must be taught to riposte with a lunge; particularly, he should learn how to make such a riposte during the time his taller opponent is recovering his own guard position after a lunge. He must be very wary in his advances, for at the start of his advance he may be reached by his opponent without himself being able to reach his adversary.

He should also be trained in the use of the stop-thrust with the lunge, the false attack, preparations striking the blade, and preparations taking and maintaining the blade, accompanied by a short step forward.

Fig. 9 - The Naval Academy fencing loft

In short, the fencer handicapped by lack of height and reach must overcome that handicap by the difficult process of perfecting himself in all phases of fencing, so as to out-general taller opponents and to make such opponents fight the kind of bout the shorter fencer wants.

D. Body Faults

1. The right arm: With many fencers, the right elbow is usually not sufficiently "inside." If the elbow is not maintained in its proper position, both sides of the blade (especially sixte) will display openings which the adversary's point will be able to find. If you cannot keep your elbow inside with the foil, take up sabre; you may do better with that weapon.

2. The left arm: The common fault here is the failure to drop the hand energetically enough on the lunge. Remember that the left arm acts like a lever, giving you more forward momentum, and at the same time enabling you to maintain better balance. The palm turned upwards on the lunge helps keep the left shoulder back and thus exposes less target for your opponent's point. The use of the left arm in conjunction with the right also aids the

physiological development of both sides of the body in a consistent, normal way.

3. The position of the body: The body should rest firmly on its haunches, perfectly balanced; the shoulders should be on the same level. Dropping the left arm energetically will help keep the left shoulder down. If the weight of the body is shifted even slightly back, the right foot will be raised too high on the lunge and the point will tend to shoot upward. If the weight of the body is placed too far forward, the high line is exposed and the point will fall too low, forcing you to take your parries weakly with the foible of the blade and causing the point to land too low at the end of an attack. A correct position, one which allows the heart and lungs to function properly and allows the body to develop harmoniously, will not only make fencing easier and more interesting, but will yield the maximum returns in health and efficiency.

Some fencers employing a faulty position have nevertheless managed to win championships. It should be realized that they win, nut because of their style, but in spite of it; they use several times the amount of effort which adherence to the simple fundamentals would have demanded. After such exertions; they are practically completely exhausted. Fencing is a sport which should develop the body harmoniously according to certain rules. A faulty position, from which the fencer may nevertheless win touches, will ultimately impair his health and may eventually reveal itself in bad circulation of the blood, in spinal trouble, or leading one shoulder to be carried higher than the other.

4. The legs: Often the distance between the feet is not correctly maintained in combat. To take your guard position with the feet not wide enough apart, or too wide apart, will disrupt your balance. If the knees are too much bent, the lunge will be slow in starting; if the knees are not bent enough, the lunge will have no spring to it. A lunge made from such positions cannot be normal,

with the result that you may misjudge distance on the attack, and so lose a point.

5. The lunge: The principal error committed on the lunge is the attempt to cover too much ground. The body should be kept perfectly in balance, with its weight resting solidly on both soles, to favor a quick return to the guard position. It is less tiring to take a slightly shorter lunge. If the right leg becomes tired from lunging, it is probably being raised too high off the strip; the sole of the right foot should just skim the strip. If the right heel becomes sore from lunging, the right foot is not striking the strip flatly on the lunge. A lunge that is too long will also cause the left foot to slip, with a loss of both the correct distance and balance. Carrying the body too far forward in the lunge will also cause the left foot to drag along the strip.

The lunge should be adapted to the physical make-up of each fencer. Gymnastic exercises, such as those suggested at the back of the book, will help develop suppleness in the thighs.

E. Muscular Contraction

In a bout, when the eyes perceive an opening for an attack or the correct time to parry, the brain must transmit, through the medium of the motor nerves, the message to the muscles. At this moment, if the muscles are too contracted, the start will be retarded. As a result, time will be lost and the possibility of failing to score the touch or to make the parry in time will be increased. Therefore, to cut down this time lag between perception and execution, the muscles should be slightly tensed, bu t not contracted or "frozen."

A fencer out of practice, for example, will require several weeks of practice to re-learn to keep his muscles partly relaxed in the bout. A fencer who is exhausted from over-training or from a hard bout will also find his muscles contracted. From this moment he begins to lose whatever superiority he possessed at the beginning of the bout.

Before beginning a bout, the fencer should limber-up with a few exercises on the order of those suggested at the end of the book. He should try a few deep lunges. He should never go into a bout cold.

F. Warming-Up Exercises

Before going into a bout or a lesson, the fencer should practice the exercises demonstrated in the following photographs until he feels warm and relaxed.

Figs. 10-11 - Some warming-up exercises

Figs. 12-16 - Some warming-up exercises

297

Made in the USA
Las Vegas, NV
03 December 2023

82061572R00184